Cannabis Banking
Legal Frameworks and Practical Solutions for Cultivating Compliance

ERIN O'DONNELL

J. MICHAEL BEIRD

MERIDITH BEIRD

WILEY

Copyright © 2025 by John Wiley & Sons, Inc. All rights reserved, including rights for text and data mining and training of artificial intelligence technologies or similar technologies.

Published by John Wiley & Sons, Inc., Hoboken, New Jersey.
Published simultaneously in Canada.

No part of this publication may be reproduced, stored in a retrieval system, or transmitted in any form or by any means, electronic, mechanical, photocopying, recording, scanning, or otherwise, except as permitted under Section 107 or 108 of the 1976 United States Copyright Act, without either the prior written permission of the Publisher, or authorization through payment of the appropriate per-copy fee to the Copyright Clearance Center, Inc., 222 Rosewood Drive, Danvers, MA 01923, (978) 750-8400, fax (978) 750-4470, or on the web at www.copyright.com. Requests to the Publisher for permission should be addressed to the Permissions Department, John Wiley & Sons, Inc., 111 River Street, Hoboken, NJ 07030, (201) 748-6011, fax (201) 748-6008, or online at http://www.wiley.com/go/permission.

Trademarks: Wiley and the Wiley logo are trademarks or registered trademarks of John Wiley & Sons, Inc. and/or its affiliates in the United States and other countries and may not be used without written permission. All other trademarks are the property of their respective owners. John Wiley & Sons, Inc. is not associated with any product or vendor mentioned in this book.

Limit of Liability/Disclaimer of Warranty: While the publisher and author have used their best efforts in preparing this book, they make no representations or warranties with respect to the accuracy or completeness of the contents of this book and specifically disclaim any implied warranties of merchantability or fitness for a particular purpose. No warranty may be created or extended by sales representatives or written sales materials. The advice and strategies contained herein may not be suitable for your situation. You should consult with a professional where appropriate. Further, readers should be aware that websites listed in this work may have changed or disappeared between when this work was written and when it is read. Neither the publisher nor authors shall be liable for any loss of profit or any other commercial damages, including but not limited to special, incidental, consequential, or other damages.

For general information on our other products and services or for technical support, please contact our Customer Care Department within the United States at (800) 762-2974, outside the United States at (317) 572-3993 or fax (317) 572-4002.

Wiley also publishes its books in a variety of electronic formats. Some content that appears in print may not be available in electronic formats. For more information about Wiley products, visit our website at www.wiley.com.

Library of Congress Cataloging-in-Publication Data is Available:

ISBN 9781394276264 (Cloth)
ISBN 9781394276288 (ePub)
ISBN 9781394276271 (ePDF)

Cover Design: Wiley
Cover Images: © Macrovector/Shutterstock, © diane555/Getty Images

SKY10093128_120624

This book is dedicated to all the cannabis bankers who have taught us that innovation and perseverance can transform even the most challenging situations. Your commitment to navigating complex regulations, advocating for fair practices, and ensuring financial inclusion for cannabis businesses has paved the way for a more equitable and sustainable industry. We also dedicate this to the minority and female-owned businesses across the cannabis industry. Thank you for your courage, resilience, and unwavering dedication to breaking new ground. The Association for Cannabis Banking (ACB) is dedicated to supporting these important businesses through educational programs and scholarships.

Meridith's Dedication

I'd like to dedicate this book first and foremost to my family: my parents, Mike and Daria, and to my sister, Allyssa. Their constant encouragement and guidance have led me to where I am today. I'd also like to dedicate this book to Jon Blome, whose love and support continue to inspire me.

Michael's Dedication

I dedicate this book to my mother, Joyce, who taught me how to face adversity, pain, and challenges with perseverance and determination, not pity or capitulation. I also dedicate it to my wife, Daria, and my daughters, co-author Meridith and Allyssa, my Ninja Warrior daughter, who have collectively tolerated my consulting life for decades. Finally, I could not dedicate this book without acknowledging my brothers, Kermit and David, along with my sister-in-law, Lovie Beird, who have always inspired me by just being themselves.

Erin's Dedication

This book is dedicated to my children — Madeline, Connor, and Aidan Handel — and to my parents, Cornelius and Patricia O'Donnell. To my family: Carolyn, Kathleen, Brian, Jeff, Melissa, Scott, and Liam, as well as the Colleano clan. Also, to Lisa Gilliard Bonn, who was taken from us way too early, as not a day passes that I do not think of you. Finally, for Tiger, our special kitty, and Ginger, our sweet 16 golden retriever, who will live in our hearts forever.

Contents

Foreword ix

Preface xiii

Acknowledgments xv

Chapter 1: Understanding the Cannabis Industry 1

A Brief History of Cannabis 1
Cannabis Basics 4
Economic Impact 6
The Cannabis Industry Overview 7
Conclusion 9

Chapter 2: Overview of Banking in the United States 13

Part 1: Banking Basics 13
Part 2: Banking Solutions for Cannabis-Related Businesses 24

Chapter 3: Compliance and Regulatory Frameworks 31

Regulations Overview 31
The Bank Secrecy Act (BSA) and Anti-Money Laundering (AML) Laws 34
PATRIOT Act and Know Your Customer (KYC) 37
PATRIOT Act Compliance 40
Challenges in KYC for Cannabis Businesses 42
The Role of the Federal Reserve and FDIC 43
Overview of State Legal Variations 44
Banking Guidelines for Cannabis-Related Businesses (CRBs) 46
Understanding the Cole Memo 47
Practical Challenges in Cannabis Banking 51
Future Outlook and Legislative Changes 52
Conclusion 55

Chapter 4: Understanding Cannabis Businesses — 59

Cannabis Business Overview — 59
The Cannabis Industry — 60
Key Market Segments — 64
Seed-to-Sale: The Cannabis Life Cycle — 66
Cultivation and Growing Techniques — 70
Processing and Extraction — 74
Manufacturing and Product Development — 77
Distribution and Supply Chain Management — 79
Retail and Dispensing — 82
Conclusion — 85

Chapter 5: Risk Management for Cannabis Bankers — 89

Introduction — 89
Internal Controls and Audits — 92
Compliance with Policies and Procedures — 94
Customer Due Diligence (CDD) and Enhanced Due Diligence (EDD) — 96
Transaction Monitoring — 97
Reporting and Filing — 99
Managing High-Risk Banking — 102
Reporting and Recordkeeping Obligations — 104
Conclusion — 106

Chapter 6: Understanding the Payments Landscape in Cannabis Banking — 111

Introduction to Cannabis Payments — 111
The Basics of Cannabis Transactions and Payments — 112
Payment Methods and Risk Considerations — 117
Business-to-Consumer Payments — 118
Business-to-Business Payments — 122
Conclusion — 123

Chapter 7: Cannabis Lending — 125

Describing the Current Lending Needs — 125
Types of Loans Available to Cannabis Businesses — 126
Overview of the Lending Landscape — 130
Conclusion — 134

Chapter 8: Marketing Strategies for Cannabis Bankers   137

Importance of Marketing in Cannabis Banking	137
Understanding Your Market	138
Digital Marketing Techniques	142
Networking and Partnerships	145
Educational Marketing	148
Event Marketing and Sponsorships	149
Compliance-Centric Marketing	152
Analyzing and Adapting to Market Trends	155
Conclusion	157

Chapter 9: Competition   161

Introduction	161
Competitive Strategies of Traditional Banks	163
The Rise of Fintech Companies	166
Competitive Challenges and Opportunities	168

Chapter 10: Indigenous Tribes – Challenges, Opportunities, and Financial Access   171

Regulatory Landscape for Tribal Nations	171
Financial Access and Banking Challenges	172
Legal Challenges	173
Tribal Cannabis Operations	174
Economic and Social Impacts	174
Current Environment and Banking Challenges	175
Conclusion	179

Chapter 11: Cannabis Insurance and Its Impact on Bankers   181

Insurance Overview	181
Understanding Cannabis Insurance	183
Regulatory Landscape	184
The Role of Insurance in Risk Management	186
Insurance Considerations for Bankers	189
Challenges Faced by Bankers	191
Conclusion	193

Chapter 12: Innovations and Future Trends — 195

Introduction — 195
CRB Technology Options — 196
Internet of Things (IOT) — 196
Cloud Computing — 196
Open Banking APIs — 197
Cryptocurrencies and Blockchain — 197
Artificial Intelligence — 199
Miscellaneous Solutions — 201
International Cannabis Banking Trends — 203
Potential Federal Legalization Efforts — 205
Predictions for the Future of Cannabis Banking — 206

About the Authors — 211

Index — 215

Foreword

THE IMPORTANCE AND VALUE of this book is not predicated on your stance on cannabis.

As you read this, the state in which you reside either allows medical or recreational marijuana (or both) or is likely to in the coming years. More than half the states have made the legislative decision to allow its denizens access to cannabis products. But perhaps you feel that cannabis products are a dangerous drug that deserves its Schedule I federal designation, no different than fentanyl. You may feel that cannabis is just a gateway drug to harder, more dangerous drugs like cocaine or heroin (which is ironic since those drugs are Schedule I narcotics, the same designation as marijuana, so they can hardly be deemed "more" dangerous ...). There are studies that support this view of cannabis, and it is not for me to opine on the veracity of those claims.

Perhaps your view is that cannabis, with proper oversight and regulation, can have beneficial recreational or therapeutic benefits. Parkinson's and glaucoma patients can certainly attest to their own results in using cannabis products to effectively manage the negative effects those diseases have on their bodies. For every study on the dangers of cannabis, there is one (or more) studies that highlight the medical and recreational benefits. Can cannabis be abused? Of course. But so can alcohol (or chocolate for that matter). The main issue is that certain states have deemed cannabis products to be legal in their state and yet, as of this writing, cannabis is still a Schedule I drug according to the Drug Enforcement Administration (DEA). It is a federal crime to grow, possess, sell, or distribute cannabis products with a tetrahydrocannabinol (THC) greater than 0.3%. This places everyone in the entire ecosystem of cannabis at risk of being completely legal in their state and yet completely illegal according to federal law. And there is no greater example of that than in how financial institutions are limited in their ability to provide basic banking services to anyone associated with the seed-to-sale process of growing, processing, and selling cannabis.

This book examines and provides valuable insight on this most important issue: how cannabis businesses and those that want to provide financial services to them navigate the current environment where state and federal laws run counter to each other. In those states where cannabis is legal, it is feasible that a cannabis business cannot have access to a bank account and perform legitimate transactions or have access to the same payment rails that convenience or liquor stores have. A farmer wishing to grow cannabis for hemp or THC products should have access to an ag production loan, no different than a tobacco farmer receives today. A dispensary selling THC products should not have to pay their employees in cash; especially since that cash is unlikely to be able to be deposited into a financial institution due to its obvious marijuana odor. Consider that a farmer that grows cannabis, a manufacturer that converts the plants into edibles, or the dispensary that sells the edibles to consumers cannot hire a plumber to come and fix the toilet. And why not? Because when the plumber accepts the cash paid for the service and deposits it in their bank account, they are written up as a possible criminal enterprise, as required by federal banking regulation, and subsequently finds their bank account closed. This is not hyperbole: there are many examples of this kind that occur in those states that have legalized cannabis.

Financial institutions are already well versed in how to properly bank high-risk businesses. They have robust controls to monitor high-cash businesses such as convenience or liquor stores. They have the expertise in managing agricultural loans where restrictions are placed on its cultivation, such as tobacco. They have expertise in payment processing for organizations that perform telemarketing and other high-risk enterprises. They are experts in understanding and managing government regulations and are regularly monitored to ensure that they are following all the rules. The financial institutions simply need to understand the cannabis business from seed-to-sale, the associated risks in providing banking services for cannabis organizations, and finally, what the state and federal regulations are governing their cannabis banking activities. This book provides a deep understanding of the cannabis business to bankers. And it provides cannabis businesses a look into the unique challenges that financial institutions face in delivering lending and deposit services to cannabis businesses.

Each financial institution can decide whether they will take on cannabis businesses as customers. Even if all state and federal laws were aligned, there are still some FIs that might choose to not bank any cannabis-related customers. And that is totally fine. It is no different than a bank who elects to not finance any hotels or offer checking accounts to grocery stores.

It's a business decision. But some banks are experts in servicing agribusinesses. And they would be well positioned to provide banking services to cannabis farmers. The same with banks that focus on manufacturing, or retail stores. Cannabis manufacturers and retailers should be a focus for them. Even still, there are banks operating that appear to be solely focused on cannabis, enabling the entire ecosystem from seed-to-sale. These are all business decisions, made with strategic plans and with the full oversight of their board of directors. The main issue is whether any financial institution that wants to bank cannabis businesses should be able to provide banking services and follow the associated regulations without fear of having federal regulators pulling the rug out from under them.

Until that day, it's a bit of a minefield of contradictory rules and regulations between states and the US government. That is why this book is so important: it illuminates the landscape enabling the successful negotiation of that minefield. Whether you are a banking regulator, a banker, a cannabis business, or just someone who has taken a gummy and wants to settle in for some educational reading, you will find the information complete, well sourced, and supremely beneficial.

—*David L. Peterson*

Entrepreneur, author, and speaker David Peterson has inspired leaders to rethink how innovation happens in their organization. He helps business leaders foster a culture of innovation that ignites enterprise-wide creativity driving measurable growth. As the founder and CEO of Goldleaf Technologies, he brought electronic payments to community banks to power their business customers. David is also the author of *Grounded: Anchor Management for Strategic Leadership and Effective Decision-Making*. David currently serves as Chief Innovation Officer of First National Bankers Bank, a correspondent bank serving community banks throughout the Southeastern US. He serves on the board of several industry-related companies and associations. He is a serial entrepreneur, powering start-ups in retail and professional services.

Preface

OVER THE PAST DECADE, the United States cannabis industry has experienced growth and change. As more states legalize cannabis, businesses related to cannabis have flourished, playing a role in the growth of economies around the globe. Despite this progress, navigating cannabis banking remains complex and misunderstood due to regulatory hurdles and financial uncertainties. This book addresses the pressing need for guidance on cannabis banking, offering insights for financial professionals operating in this dynamic field.

This book aims to provide insight into cannabis banking, helping institutions that are either already banking cannabis or curious about how to possibly begin. By delving into banking practices, compliance standards, risk management, and market strategies specific to the cannabis industry, this book seeks to empower financial professionals in making informed choices. It also seeks to simplify banking procedures for those in the cannabis industry by educating and assisting them in accessing services.

This book was written for students, teachers, financial institutions, and regulatory bodies overseeing the banking aspects of the cannabis industry, and cannabis entrepreneurs seeking guidance on banking choices and a greater understanding of the regulatory framework of the cannabis banking industry.

It's important to note that during the course of writing this book, cannabis was being considered for rescheduling by the US Drug Enforcement Agency; however, this decision has not yet been finalized. Therefore, throughout the book, we assume that cannabis is still a Schedule I drug. However, we do discuss implications in the cannabis industry should it become a Schedule III drug.

The text has been organized into 12 chapters. The first four chapters set up an introduction and baseline knowledge of the cannabis industry and the banking industry. The next seven chapters dive into more nuanced topics like risk management, payments, lending, marketing, competition, indigenous cannabis, and insurance for cannabis-related businesses, which will help financial professionals understand the issues beyond regulatory compliance and gain advanced insight into the industry. The final chapter discusses future trends in the industry and technologies that are currently being developed and our take on the innovations that are forthcoming and might create change in this industry.

Finally, the objective of this book is to share our practical knowledge, showcase areas that are currently changing, and create a framework for banking cannabis. This knowledge is not currently taught by formal education or training and that is why we thought this is an important book to write. However, practical knowledge on this subject doesn't end here; in fact, it's constantly evolving as the industry itself struggles to find the right balance between innovation and regulation, knowledge and curiosity. For consistency throughout the book, please note that we use the term "banking" to define transactional and operational processes including deposits, payments, lending, and other financial activities as a general, catch-all term, and apply these activities to all financial institutions, such as credit unions, thrifts, community banks, and fintechs, in addition to commercial banks.

Lastly, here are five websites that readers should bookmark in order to stay up to date on legislation and regulatory changes affecting the cannabis industry:

- Marijuana Policy Project (MPP) (https://mpp.org)
- Congressional Research Service (CRS) (https://www.loc.gov/crsinfo)
- Network for Public Health Law (https://www.networkforphl.org/?s=cannabis)
- Association for Cannabis Banking (ACB) (https://the-acb.org/industry-news)
- National Conference of State Legislatures (NCSL) (https://www.ncsl.org)

Acknowledgments

AFTER SO MANY YEARS devoted to serving the financial services industry in many different roles, naming individuals that have contributed to the content, thoughts, and opinions in this book would take another book altogether. Dedicating the last two decades to educating professionals who work for institutions, and those who support the industry peripherally, has been a true labor of love for us. We believe that the knowledge that we have gained through hosting thousands of webinars, live streaming dozens of events and conferences in the US and Europe, and consulting directly with thought leaders in the industry every day, has likely equaled or exceeded what our students have learned.

First and foremost, a special note of gratitude to Kirsten Trusko, Founder – Emerging Markets Coalition (EMC), a partner of the Association for Cannabis Banking (ACB) and co-resident in New Mexico. Kirsten and the EMC provided a wealth of knowledge, research, and contacts critical for this book. Thank you also to Alicia Greer, CPA and Partner at Berndt Associates, and Jeffrey Storch – Attorney at BoardmanClark in Madison, Wisconsin. Your unparalleled support and advice over the years have made the path to this book possible. Thanks to Christy Olsen and Kevin McLauchlin of Cadence SEO. We never understood the importance of having solid marketing and SEO technical support until we needed it from Cadence to help keep the lights on.

We are especially grateful to the Board of Directors at the ACB for their guidance, support, and involvement in this rapidly growing industry. These valuable people include: Danielle Boyle, Dart Bank; Amanda Carbajal, Minerva; Dana Chaves, FinResults; Scott Dance, Primo Payments; Justin Fisher, RiskScout; Jennifer Germano, ICS Consulting; Radhika Lipton, RADD; Melissa Maranda, Lighthouse Biz Solutions; David Peterson, First National Bankers Bank; Tony Repanich, Shield Compliance; Alex Rodriguez, Conduit GR; Jennifer Salazar, Dart Bank; and Yamil Santiago, BCB Bank.

Special thanks go out to Ethan Kratt and Kristin Parker of RiskScout, without whose help we couldn't have published our most recent research on what cannabis bankers are thinking. Thanks also to Lisa Ackerly, one of our many friends at Dart Bank. And a special thank you to our new friends in cannabis banking in New Mexico: Rep. Andrea Romero, a major force in advancing the legal cannabis industry in Santa Fe; Ben Lewinger, Executive Director – New Mexico Cannabis Chamber of Commerce; and David Swope, President/CEO – Better Business Bureau, New Mexico and Southwest Colorado. We can't forget our editor at Wiley, Judith Newlin, for approaching us with the idea for this book and for her constant support throughout the process. And to the team at Wiley, Stacey Rivera, Delainey Henson, and Deborah Williams – for walking these authors through our first book. It's been a pleasure working with all of you.

Thank you to my long-time friend, Dr. Caitlin Courtney, who allowed me the chance to learn about holistic medicine and see the medicinal effects of cannabidiol (CBD) and tetrahydrocannabinol (THC) firsthand. The opportunities you afforded me gave me the confidence and knowledge needed to step into the cannabis industry.

Special note of appreciation to Tom Brown, CEO – SecondCurve Capital and BankStocks.com, who has stood as a special mentor and friend over the decades. Your ongoing support and insights have always been a cornerstone of our careers, and for that, we thank you. Thank you also to Sue Harnett, leading executive advisor in financial services and former consulting client while CEO of Citibank, Germany. Your constant support has been a source of strength when we needed it most. To the Fuchsia House Honeys, friends and family in Allentown, Pennsylvania, and to the women of CannaChix, an ACB gathering of women interested in the cannabis industry, whose discussions gave us inspiration to dig deeper into all aspects of the business.

To our special speakers, family and friends, Jo Chern, Christina Dumlao, Marla Ellerman, Tammy Nagarajan, Cindy Orozco, Elizabeth Robillard, Reagan Sands, Terri Sands, Lisa Beck Schuck, Chris Van Dyck, and so many others. Your professionalism with personal flair has always been a major driver behind great customer feedback year-over-year, but more importantly it's the friendships we share.

CHAPTER ONE

Understanding the Cannabis Industry

 A BRIEF HISTORY OF CANNABIS

Before we jump into the rules and regulations surrounding cannabis banking, it is important to look at the basics. What is cannabis exactly, how have the political and social relationships with cannabis changed over the years, and where does cannabis currently stand in the eyes of the government? Let us get started!

The cultivation and use of the cannabis plant is not a new phenomenon. In fact, evidence of cannabis use dates back to around 2700 BCE in China by Emperor Shen Nung, whose teachings and medical practices with the plant were passed down for generations by word of mouth before being recorded in a book on herbal remedies, written around the second century CE.[1] Over time, the plant spread throughout Asia, into Europe, and by the sixteenth century, Spanish and English settlers were bringing it across to the Americas.

Within the United States, the cannabis plant has a long and complex history, with the first hemp law enacted in 1619. However, instead of a law banning the plant, which is more in line with what we see in the country today, this law actually required every farm in the colonies to plant hemp. At the time, hemp was a critical crop for the colonists, used for things like clothing, rope, paper, and even as a legal currency for some time in the colonies of Virginia, Pennsylvania, and Maryland.[2] Hemp production eventually lost out in popularity to cotton, which provided a softer clothing option; but by that time, marijuana, as an extract of the hemp plant, was already commonly used in medicines and tinctures. It wasn't until around the 1920s that a more recreational use for marijuana began to develop, the practice of which was primarily introduced by Mexican immigrants. With the initial rise in price of alcohol, followed shortly thereafter by prohibition, marijuana became a cheaper and more readily available alternative to drinking. Throughout the next decade or so, marijuana use became increasingly associated with Mexican immigrants – who the public resented due to the lack of jobs available during the depression – and the lower class, who were often seen as perpetrators of crime and violence. With the social stigma of marijuana now tainted, it wasn't long until the government stepped in.[3]

History of the Regulation of Hemp and Marijuana

Hemp, and by extension marijuana, was largely regulated as any other plant for many years in the US. And while the social stigma had taken a hit, it wasn't until the end of prohibition that it came back into the legal and political spotlight. With alcohol no longer being banned, the focus shifted to marijuana. By the early 1930s, the drug was being outlawed in cities all over the country, and states quickly started following suit – by 1931 it had been banned in 29 states. Federally, the US was hesitant to outlaw marijuana partly due to the medicinal uses of the drug being used and researched, and also partly due to the lucrative business coming from the hemp plant at large. However, there was no denying the shifting political focus and so the Marihuana Tax Act was passed in 1937. This act criminalized marijuana and created a tax on hemp, requiring official Marihuana Tax Act stamps for the importation and exportation of the plant. The aim of this act was to lessen or stop the use of marijuana for recreational purposes, but it resulted in some unintended consequences for the rest of the industry: the growth and exportation of hemp became much more difficult and expensive, leading to a decrease in production. Additionally, this all but stopped scientific studies on both the plant and the drug.[4]

Much like with prohibition, this did not stop the spread and use of marijuana, it simply got pushed underground and into fringe cultural groups. In the 1950s, marijuana became popular with the Beat generation, who favored a more Bohemian lifestyle; it also became connected with jazz enthusiasts following the song "Reefer Man" by Cab Calloway. In the 1960s and 1970s, marijuana was a common drug of choice for the hippy subculture as they saw it as a way to push back against the mainstream lifestyles.

Introducing the Controlled Substance Act (CSA)

In 1969, the Marihuana Tax Act was deemed unconstitutional after the court case of *Leary v. United States*.[5] Leary argued that his registration to purchase tax stamps would be self-incriminating (and therefore a violation of the fifth amendment) due to the fact that the sale and transfer of the drug was illegal, so having to register for intent to possess or use the drug would be an immediate red flag for authorities. For a short time, that meant there was technically no federal regulation for marijuana. However, the US shortly thereafter passed the Controlled Substance Act of 1970, which once again made marijuana illegal nation wide, and it classified marijuana as a drug that is considered as hazardous and addictive as others such as heroin, peyote, and LSD (Lysergic Acid Diethylamide).[6] Alongside promotions such as Nancy Reagan's "Just Say No" campaign, marijuana was deemed a dangerous drug and one we needed to keep away from the public at all costs. However, in the 1990s, that ideology began to shift.

In 1996, California became the first state to adopt a medical marijuana program. Set up under the Compassionate Use Act, this new legislation allowed people with certain medical ailments to obtain and use marijuana as a treatment with medical supervision.[7] Colorado followed suit just a couple of years later in 2000, and since then there has been a snowball effect of states opening their doors to the cannabis market. In 2013, marijuana again found itself in the headlines when the Deputy Attorney General at the time, James Cole, issued a memorandum (hereafter known as the Cole Memo) that essentially allowed for states to make their own decisions about the sale and distribution of marijuana and cannabis. The essence of the Cole Memo was this: the federal government has an interest in the bigger picture of marijuana, and as long as their main focus and goals are not impeded, states were henceforth allowed to implement programs for legal marijuana sales and distribution, if they so choose to.[8] (We will be talking about the Cole Memo in depth in Chapter 3.)

Since 2013, individual states have regularly been voting to adopt cannabis programs, whether for medical or recreational use. 2013 was also the first year that public support for cannabis legalization surpassed 50%, according to Gallup poll findings. And their research has shown that support has only continued to grow – as of October 2023, the nationwide support for cannabis legalization was up to a whopping 70%. More importantly, these numbers are reflected in the population regardless of demographics or current state legality. While self-identified conservatives and Republicans are the groups with the lowest percentages in favor, even these groups now show majority support for the cause (with 52% and 55%, respectively).[9]

Health Benefits of Marijuana

Additionally, more health studies are being conducted and are educating on how marijuana can be used for certain health ailments, such as epilepsy, Alzheimer's, Amyotrophic Lateral Sclerosis (ALS), chronic pain, and more. These are critical for marijuana's path to legislation for one simple reason: marijuana is still classified as a Schedule I drug by the Drug Enforcement Agency (DEA). This means that under federal law, marijuana is found to be a substance with a high probability of addiction and containing no medicinal benefits. While we know that the hemp plant has been used for medical treatments for centuries, it is crucial for the drug to be studied and measured against today's health standards and best practices. In early 2024, the Department of Health and Human Services sent a letter to the DEA recommending that they consider rescheduling marijuana to Schedule III. By definition, this category of drugs has a much lower potential for dependence and abuse, with examples such as Tylenol with Codeine, Anabolic Steroids, and Testosterone.[10] While this would be a critical step for the eventual legalization of marijuana on a federal level, it is just that – a step. This is not meant to magically open doors for dispensaries around the country but is instead a way to change the way that marijuana as a drug is viewed in the eyes of the law.

CANNABIS BASICS

What do we mean when we talk about "cannabis"? The term is colloquially used as a more acceptable substitution for the word "marijuana," which still has a slightly negative connotation in today's society. However, there is a scientific difference between these terms, and it is vital to understand how they differ. Dissecting the cannabis plant into its individual components may seem like a tedious task, but it is crucial when discussing federal and state legalities.

Components of Cannabis

Cannabis, while often used as a catchall term, is also the name of a plant genus under the Cannabaceae family. The species of *Hemp* and *Marijuana* are found within the *Cannabis* genus. Cannabis plants are made up of around 80–100

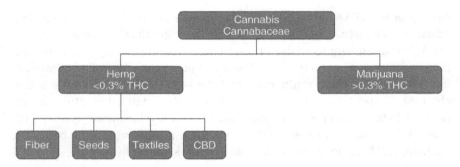

FIGURE 1.1 Flowchart of the cannabis plant and its primary components.
Source: Association for Cannabis Banking, 2024

cannabinoids, or chemical compounds, with the two main ones being cannabidiols (CBD) and delta-9 tetrahydrocannabinols (THC). While both CBD and THC have calming effects on the body, THC is the cannabinoid strain that produces a psychoactive effect. This is why CBD is less regulated as a product – because there is no "high" associated with it. The biggest difference between the hemp and marijuana plant is the amount of THC produced – hemp contains less than 0.3% THC by weight, whereas marijuana contains more than 0.3% THC[11] (Figure 1.1).

The plant production does not stop there, though. Other strains of cannabinoids have started to hit the market as well: delta-8 THC, CBG (Cannabigerol), CBN (Cannabinol), and CBC (Cannabichromene), just to name a few (to learn more about cannabinoids and their specific effects on the body, we suggest talking with your local budtender or with a certified herbalist). With all these acronyms flying around, it's easy to see how this space can seem confusing and convoluted. While hemp-based CBD is legal at the federal level, it is important to note that states still have the final say over what they sell and the restrictions imposed. For example, as of 2024, Idaho only allows hemp-derived CBD products containing 0% THC.[12] This is in contrast to most other states that allow CBD products as long as they contain less than 0.3% THC, as dictated by federal allowance.

Hemp has historically been used for many products, including textiles, fabrics, paper, ropes, seeds, etc. However, its production and sale were greatly limited by the Marihuana Tax Act of 1937 and eventually it became federally outlawed under the Controlled Substance Act of 1970 as a Schedule I substance. It wasn't until the Farm Bill passed in 2014 that hemp was allowed to be grown, as long as it was for research purposes by a higher education institution or the state department of agriculture.[13] Four years later, the passing of the 2018 Farm Bill saw hemp removed from the list of controlled substances altogether, legalizing hemp growth within the US once again.[14]

When discussing cannabis in legal terms, it is important to understand these key differences and the laws that are in place, both federally and within individual states. These distinctions and the laws that are constantly being changed or updated are one reason why so many financial institutions are hesitant to bring on customers from cannabis-related businesses (CRBs). For those that do bank CRBs, it is critical for them to understand the basics of cannabis and keep up to date with their state laws and allowances.

ECONOMIC IMPACT

Cannabis legalization poses many questions of risk vs. reward for states. One of the biggest selling points for states is that recreational cannabis industries open up job opportunities, and job opportunities create taxable enterprises. A congressional report published in November 2023 listed four categories for job potential within recreational cannabis businesses: cultivators and producers, manufacturers and processors, testers, and retailers. The impact that these jobs create in local communities is not insignificant. Additionally, they argue that industries such as commercial real estate could also benefit from recreational cannabis as these businesses could rent spaces that were previously sitting empty – a phenomenon enhanced by the pandemic.[15] While we do not know all the ways that this new industry can or will impact auxiliary industries, it is crucial to note that the creation of a recreational cannabis market does not happen in a vacuum. It is important to keep this in mind when discussing what a federal legalization of cannabis might look like, as it could have effects – positive or negative – on other industries that we have not yet seen or anticipated.

Taxation of Recreational Cannabis

Even though taxation of recreational cannabis has brought in substantial money for each state, it is not an easy, one-size-fits-all solution for fundraising. Since there is no federal oversight for cannabis sales, it is up to every state individually to decide on a taxation scheme to use. This will likely be upended if and when cannabis becomes legal at the federal level. While states would still be able to impose their own sales tax, a level of uniformity will be needed to ensure fair distribution and limit the cannabis sales across state lines. This has also been a difficult amount to establish for states. The taxation and economic benefits have been primary driving factors for states introducing a recreational cannabis program. But if the taxes are too high, they run the risk of customers turning to illegal black-market marijuana that has no sales tax, or they risk turning away canna-curious customers who are intimidated by the lofty price tags. The novelty of this industry poses many challenges for those involved, and for some states these unknown factors are too much of a risk. For those who have taken on that risk, the reward seems to have proven its worth, at least so far, as the industry continues to grow year over year.

The legalization of marijuana has been a lucrative business for the states that have taken this step. In 2014, Colorado's first year selling marijuana recreationally, the state brought in more than $70 million just from taxation alone.[16] Since then, the revenue brought in from recreational cannabis sales has continued to grow, and each state that has entered the market has also seen how beneficial these sales can be. From the onset of recreational sales in 2014 through the end of 2022, the total tax revenue brought in nation wide surpassed $15 billion.[16] And money alone is not the only positive outcome. Between 2017 and 2023, marijuana-related jobs within the US more than tripled, according to a 2023 Congressional report. They also suggest, however, that these numbers are largely due to new markets being opened in states around the country. In contrast, older markets, such as those in Colorado or Oregon, have recently seen a slight decline in job production and income.[15] Additionally, it is important to note that federal economic data does not include federally illegal jobs, so the job growth reports being researched and created are likely understated.

 THE CANNABIS INDUSTRY OVERVIEW

Every cannabis business falls into one of three categories: Tier 1, Tier 2, or Tier 3, as created by Steven Kemmerling. There are no hard lines distinguishing these tiers, and there is some debate around which tier certain types of businesses would fall under. But generally speaking, the tiers are defined as such:

Tier 1: Direct

Tier 1 CRBs are the businesses that are plant-touching and tend to be licensed operators. Some examples of Tier 1 businesses could include:

- Cultivators (plant growers)
- Processors (those who take the raw plants and turn them into marketable products)

- Dispensaries (the brick-and-mortar stores that sell cannabis products)
- Testing laboratories (ensuring the safety of cannabis products and adhering to quality standards)

Tier 2: Indirect

Tier 2 CRBs are indirectly associated with cannabis, though they still tend to receive substantial income from the cannabis industry and other Tier 1 businesses. However, it is not typically necessary for Tier 2 businesses to be licensed, as is common for Tier 1. Some of the examples within this tier include:

- Hydroponic suppliers (those who produce the products necessary for plant growth)
- Packaging manufacturers (those who produce tamper-proof packaging in accordance with regulations in the market or in the individual state)
- Security services (those who sell security systems to Tier 1 businesses or provide security officers to be on location)
- Marketing consultants (who work with Tier 1 businesses to help build their marketing strategy while maintaining compliance with both state and advisory regulations)

Tier 3: Auxiliary

The most indirect of the CRB tiers is Tier 3. These businesses may have some ties to the cannabis industry, but they do not make the majority of their income from Tier 1 businesses, as those in Tier 2 might. Some Tier 3 businesses might include:

- Lawyers/accountants/educators (these companies may take on CRB clients, either Tier 1 or Tier 2, but their practices likely contain clients from a plethora of industries, and therefore any income made from cannabis is minimal)
- Property management companies (those who rent space to dispensaries or factories for production and sale of cannabis products)
- Utility companies – water, electricity, waste removal, etc. (similar to product management companies, utility companies are also connected to the growth and sale of cannabis, though they do not represent the bulk of income for said utility companies)

As previously stated, these tier distinctions can be pretty blurry, especially between Tiers 2 and 3, and there can be a fair number of businesses that could fall into either category. For example, until cannabis becomes federally legal, financial services could fall into Tier 2 or Tier 3. Their designation would depend on the services the individual company offers. For example, some smaller banks and credit unions are taking on CRBs as customers as they see the potential within this space and are willing to do the due diligence required to take on the risk associated with CRBs. These financial institutions could then be categorized as Tier 2, depending on how involved they are, what products and services they are offering Tier 1 businesses, and how much income they are subsequently earning from the dispensaries, growers, etc. However, larger banks are not as keen to jump into this space and do not want to be associated with cannabis at this point in time. While they may bank customers indirectly related to the cannabis industry, such as law firms who may have a dispensary as one of their clients, they do not work with the CRBs directly and will not take them on as customers. These banks would then fall under the Tier 3 distinction.

While these tiers tend to be defined by the amount of income earned from working with plant-touching (Tier 1) businesses, another way to distinguish them is based on their perceived risk. For Tier 1 businesses that work with plants or products that are illegal at the federal level, there is a high risk associated with these businesses. As you move further away from the cannabis plant itself, the perceived risk diminishes. This is a primary reason why many financial institutions refuse to work with Tier 1 CRBs, but they may work with Tier 2 or 3 CRBs. There is much less risk associated with a marketing firm than there is for a dispensary.

CONCLUSION

The captivating history of cannabis spans across thousands of years, various cultures, and different parts of the world. It started with Emperor Shen Nung's use in China around 2700 BCE and traveled through Asia, Europe, and eventually made its way to the Americas by the sixteenth century. Cannabis has held a place in shaping the history of the United States; its story is intricate and ever-changing. Initially an essential crop for the newly founded colonies, hemp served purposes from clothing to currency. However, over time there was a shift toward focusing on the recreational aspects of cannabis rather than industrial hemp. This change led to a series of adjustments and social adaptations.

The legal environment surrounding cannabis in the United States has been turbulent, to say the least. While early colonial laws mandated hemp cultivation, attitudes shifted drastically by the mid-twentieth century due to marijuana being associated with immigrant communities and lower socioeconomic classes – resulting in its prohibition. The Marihuana Tax Act of 1937 marked a turning point as it introduced regulations that significantly impacted both industrial hemp production and cannabis research. Despite these challenges, cannabis continued to be used, gaining importance within various subcultures over time.

Today, it seems as though the landscape of marijuana legality is constantly changing. The Cole Memo of 2013 granted states control over regulating marijuana, resulting in legalization efforts. Public backing for legalizing cannabis has grown significantly, with more people recognizing its medicinal benefits. The potential reclassification of marijuana to Schedule III, proposed by the Department of Health and Human Services in 2024, marks a step toward broader acceptance and integration into existing laws.

Looking ahead, it's evident that there's more to come in the story of cannabis in the United States. Ongoing research into its medical uses, shifting opinions of the public, and evolving legal structures will shape what lies ahead for cannabis. Knowing its history gives us context for future developments in the industry, highlighting both the challenges and opportunities on the horizon.

NOTES

1. Pain, Stephanie. A potted history. *Nature*, 525, 7570, 2015, S10–S11. http://www.nature.com/articles/525S10a#:~:text=The%20earliest%20use%20of%20cannabis,Chinese%20book%20of%20herbal%20remedies. https://doi.org/10.1038/525s10a.
2. McNearney, Allison. "The Complicated History of Cannabis in the US." HISTORY, August 23, 2018, http://www.history.com/news/marijuana-criminalization-reefer-madness-history-flashback.
3. PBS. "Marijuana Timeline | Busted – America's War on Marijuana | FRONTLINE | PBS." *Pbs.org*, 2012, http://www.pbs.org/wgbh/pages/frontline/shows/dope/etc/cron.html.
4. PBS. "The Buyers – a Social History of America's Most Popular Drugs | Drug Wars | FRONTLINE | PBS." *Pbs.org*, 2014, http://www.pbs.org/wgbh/pages/frontline/shows/drugs/buyers/socialhistory.html.
5. *Leary v. United States*. May 19, 1969, http://supreme.justia.com/cases/federal/us/395/6/#top.
6. Drug Enforcement Administration. "Drug Scheduling." www.dea.gov, United States Drug Enforcement Administration, July 10, 2018, http://www.dea.gov/drug-information/drug-scheduling.
7. Bonta, Rob. "Medicinal Cannabis Guidelines." State of California - Department of Justice - Office of the Attorney General, December 30, 2022, http://oag.ca.gov/medicinal-cannabis#:~:text=In%201996%2C%20California%20voters%20approved.

8. Cole, James. Memorandum for All United States Attorneys, August 29, 2013, http://www.justice.gov/iso/opa/resources/3052013829132756857467.pdf.
9. Gallup Inc. "Grassroots Support for Legalizing Marijuana Hits Record 70%." *Gallup.com*, November 8, 2023, http://news.gallup.com/poll/514007/grassroots-support-legalizing-marijuana-hits-record.aspx.
10. "Federal Register:: Request Access." *Unblock.federalregister.gov*, May 21, 2024, http://www.federalregister.gov/documents/2024/05/21/2024-11137/schedules-of-controlled-substances-rescheduling-of-marijuana.
11. The Editors of Encyclopedia Britannica. "Hemp | Description & Uses." Encyclopædia Britannica, December 6, 2018, http://www.britannica.com/plant/hemp. Accessed February 10, 2024.
12. "Is CBD Oil Legal in Idaho? | IdahoCannabis.org." Idaho Cannabis Information Portal, http://idahocannabis.org/cbd.
13. "H.R.2642 – 113th Congress (2013–2014): Agricultural Act of 2014." *Congress.gov*, Library of Congress, February 7, 2014, https://www.congress.gov/bill/113th-congress/house-bill/2642
14. "H.R.2 – 115th Congress (2017–2018): An act to provide for the reform and continuation of agricultural and other programs of the Department of Agriculture through fiscal year 2023, and for other purposes." *Congress.gov*, Library of Congress, December 20, 2018, https://www.congress.gov/bill/115th-congress/house-bill/2.
15. Levin, Adam G. "Recreational Marijuana and Economic Development." November 7, 2023.
16. Marijuana Policy Project. "Cannabis Tax Revenue in States That Regulate Cannabis for Adult Use." *MPP*, April 5, 2022, http://www.mpp.org/issues/legalization/cannabis-tax-revenue-states-regulate-cannabis-adult-use.

CHAPTER TWO

Overview of Banking in the United States

 PART 1: BANKING BASICS

Introduction to the United States Banking System

It's crucial for individuals involved in handling transactions for businesses to have a grasp of how the United States banking system functions and the mutual expectations between customers and bankers regardless of their role in the company. This knowledge becomes more vital for businesses with risks when it comes to navigating the complexities of cannabis banking. Establishing this knowledge builds a bridge between two industries that may naturally distrust each other, but also rely on each other to an extent. While it's clear that the cannabis sector relies heavily on banking services, financial institutions also recognize the business opportunities in serving this industry. Understanding the background of banking history, operations, and regulatory framework enables bankers to better serve the public with consistency and mutual cooperation.

A Brief History of Banking

The historical background of banking paints a picture of how financial institutions have transformed into the foundation of present-day economies.

13

Understanding this progression is crucial for bankers who are spearheading the integration of a legalized industry into existing financial frameworks. Banking traces its roots back to civilizations where merchants extended loans to farmers and traders engaged in the exchange of goods between cities. These early banking practices formed the basis for the systems we have today.

The Roots of Modern-Day Banking

The emergence of banks occurred during the Renaissance era in Italy. Institutions like the Medici Bank established in the fifteenth century represented some of the examples of banks offering a wide range of services, such as deposits, loans, and foreign exchange. The success of the Medici Bank stemmed from its approaches to recordkeeping and its extensive network of branches. These advancements played a role in transitioning from barter systems to economies on currency and credit.[1]

The Bank of England established in 1694 stands as one of the banks that was set up to oversee government finances and stabilize currency values. During this time there was a rise in fractional reserve banking with banks starting to lend out more money than they actually had in deposits. This strategy helped boost the money supply and stimulate growth, shaping the foundation of banking practices. For those involved in banking it is essential to grasp the role of banks as they have a significant influence on monetary policies and financial rules that impact the entire banking industry.[2]

Colonial Times – Exchange Through Barter and Goods

During this period in America there was no banking system in place. Instead, settlers relied on bartering and using commodities like tobacco, beaver pelts, and wampum for trade. As the colonies expanded and commerce flourished there arose a need for methods of conducting transactions. Early colonial banks focused primarily on working with merchants, rather than individuals, but banking in colonial America came with risks. Businesses did not have assurances that money left with the bank would still be there the next month, as banks were not regulated and sometimes disappeared with no notification given.[3]

The Birth of Banks – A Revolutionary Venture

The era of the American Revolution brought a change in practices. In 1781, the Bank of North America (BNA) was chartered by the Continental Congress as the first bank in the newly formed nation. This marked a new chapter in financial history as banks took on crucial roles in facilitating trade, extending credit services, and overseeing national finances.[4]

Chartered May 26, 1781, by the Continental Congress under the Articles of Confederation, the Bank of North America was the first national and truly commercial bank in the United States. Officially titled The President, Directors, and Company of the Bank of North America (BNA) until 1825, the bank was the first created by the national government to do business with and for the government. Though Pennsylvania Bank was founded in 1780, it did little business apart from subscribers who in 1782 sold their shares to BNA, which expanded its financial connections.[5]

The absence of a connected, regulated banking system was further complicated by the absence of a national currency. Instead, individual banks issued their own currency with only the backing of the bank that issued them. Depositors, however, often found that other banks or merchants outside the immediate vicinity refused to accept them, with many of the notes proving to be counterfeit as well.

The Establishment and Dissolution of Initial Banks in America

In 1791, Alexander Hamilton, serving as the Secretary of Treasury at that time, advocated for creating the First Bank of the United States. This financial institution acted as a bank by issuing currency, managing government funds, and overseeing state banks. "Money is the very hinge on which commerce turns. And this does not merely mean gold and silver; many other things have served the purpose, with different degrees of utility. Paper has been extensively employed."[6]

However, its charter expired in 1811, and Congress, buckling to pressure from other banks, refused to renew the charter. This collapse resulted in the recurrence of the same problems from before. As Thomas Jefferson said, "and I sincerely believe, with you, that banking establishments are more dangerous than standing armies; and that the principle of spending money to be paid by posterity, under the name of funding, is but swindling futurity on a large scale."[7]

In 1816, the Second Bank of the United States was established to address these challenges. Similar to its predecessor it faced opposition from those concerned about its authority and impact. President Andrew Jackson, who strongly opposed banking, vetoed the renewal of the Second Bank in 1832, resulting in its downfall and another period of turmoil. Following the decline of the Second Bank came the Free Banking Era, characterized by an increase in state-chartered banks. These banks issued their money contributing to an unstable financial environment. The Civil War worsened these problems as both the Union and Confederacy introduced their paper currency.[8]

Overview of Banking in the United States

The National Banking Act of 1863 – Moving in the Right Direction
The passage of the National Banking Act in 1863 was a milestone that established a system of chartered banks and a consistent national currency. This represented a transformation in banking by bringing more stability and consistency to the financial system.

> Through the National Bank Act, Congress sought to achieve both short- and long-term goals. One crucial objective was to generate cash desperately needed to finance and fight the Civil War. After prospective national bank organizers submitted a business plan and had it approved by the OCC, they were required to purchase interest-bearing U.S. government bonds in an amount equal to one-third of their paid-in capital. Millions of much-needed dollars flowed into the Treasury in this manner. But the national banking system was also designed to achieve longer term economic goals. Under the new system, the purchased bonds were to be deposited with the Treasury, where they were held as security for a new kind of paper money: national currency.[9]

During the 1800s and early 1900s there was a time of economic growth and industrialization along with a significant increase in the banking industry. Despite this progress there were panics and instability as banks struggled to adapt to the changing situation.

The Federal Reserve Act of 1913 – The Foundation of Today
The creation of the Federal Reserve System through the Federal Reserve Act of 1913 aimed to establish an adaptable financial system.

> The Federal Reserve System is the central bank of the United States. It performs five general functions to promote the effective operation of the U.S. economy and, more generally, the public interest. The Federal Reserve:
>
> 1. Conducts the nation's monetary policy to promote maximum employment, stable prices, and moderate long-term interest rates in the U.S. economy.
> 2. Promotes the stability of the financial system and seeks to minimize and contain systemic risks through active monitoring and engagement in the U.S. and abroad.

3. Promotes the safety and soundness of individual financial institutions and monitors their impact on the financial system as a whole.
4. Fosters payment and settlement system safety and efficiency through services to the banking industry and the U.S. government that facilitate U.S.-dollar transactions and payments.
5. Promotes consumer protection and community development through consumer-focused supervision and examination, research and analysis of emerging consumer issues and trends, community economic development activities, and the administration of consumer laws and regulations.[10]

Additionally, the establishment of the Federal Deposit Insurance Corporation (FDIC) in 1933 helped protect depositors from bank failures during the Great Depression, importantly restoring faith in the banking sector.

Following World War II, there was an era of growth and prosperity coupled with significant expansion in banking services. Globalization and technological advancements led to offerings and global markets emerging. However, the financial crisis of 2008 shed light on the continuing vulnerabilities within finance systems. This resulted in an influx of regulations and reforms focused on fortifying banks and averting future financial crises.

The Role of Banking and Financial Services

In today's economy, banks play a role by acting as the central point for financial transactions and services. A bank is an institution that takes deposits from the public, provides credit, and offers loans to individuals, businesses, and governments. Of course, this basic description does not fully capture the complexity and significance of banks in ensuring the operation of economies.

At their most basic level, banks have always served as intermediaries between those who save money and those who borrow it. They gather deposits from individuals and organizations seeking places to keep their funds safe, while also paying interest on these deposits. For banks, deposits in the form of checks, cash, and other monetary instruments taken on behalf of customers are "liabilities" on the bank's balance sheet, since this is money the bank owes back to them.

Subsequently banks utilize these funds to extend loans to those in need of funding, charging interest on these loans to generate income. Loans made by a financial institution are "assets," since the money lent to customers still belongs to the institution. This intermediary function is critical as it ensures that money circulates efficiently throughout the economy enabling investments in businesses, homes, education, and more.

Money Creation Explained

While the Federal Reserve is responsible for printing currency and managing the money supply, the actual creation of money in the economy takes place, in large part, through the everyday activities of average citizens and businesses. People may still believe that the money they deposit one day is still in the bank and available days later, but the actual truth is what fuels our economy without impacting inflation directly. This is explained in a scene from "It's a Wonderful Life" when the bank manager (famously played by Jimmy Stewart) explains that the money from one customer is actually in the mortgage held by another customer.

Consider a simple example, starting with a customer depositing $1,000 cash into their local bank. Banks are required to maintain a certain level of deposits in reserves to ensure there is a cushion sufficient to handle increased consumer demand for withdrawals. For purposes of this illustration and simplicity, let us assume the reserve requirement is 10%. This means the bank can lend 90% of its deposits to other customers.

Here's how the process works:

1. Initial Deposit: A customer deposits $1,000 into their bank account.
2. Required Reserves: The bank must hold 10% of the deposit ($100) in reserve.
3. Excess Reserves: The remaining 90% ($900) is considered excess reserves, which the bank can lend out.
4. Loan Creation: The bank lends out the $900 to another customer, who deposits it into their own bank account.
5. More Reserves and Loans: This new deposit creates another $90 in required reserves and $810 in excess reserves that can be loaned out again.
6. Chain Reaction: This process continues, with each new loan creating more deposits and more potential for lending.

If the process were to play out to the maximum amount each bank can loan out, then the initial $1,000 cash deposit has actually "created" $10,000 in total money on the books of banks supporting the economy. In times when the economy is tight, banks can impact the overall money being created by holding onto more deposits and therefore lending less to businesses and consumers.

Implications for Cannabis Businesses
When banks finally accept the deposits of cannabis-related businesses (CRBs), the impact to money creation can be significant. Putting billions of dollars back into the economy legally and through the banking system feeds the money creation cycle. As more institutions bring in deposits from CRBs, they have greater capacity to make loans to businesses. The reality, however, is that as of the printing of this book, almost none of the institutions that accept CRB deposits will accept the risks associated with lending that money back to those same businesses. While that has little impact on the overall economy and the money creation process, it does have implications for the cannabis industry.

Bank Governance and Oversight
Banking institutions are important players in building trust within the system. They offer a place for people to deposit their money with the assurance that government insurance protects their funds, at least up to a limit. This trust is critical to financial system stability.

The agencies assigned with oversight associated with the cannabis industry, and banking functions specifically, include the following:

- Financial Crimes Enforcement Network (FinCEN)[11]:
    - Role: Issues guidance on Bank Secrecy Act (BSA) requirements for financial institutions serving cannabis-related businesses (CRBs). This includes guidelines for conducting due diligence, monitoring transactions, and reporting suspicious activity.
    - Implications: FinCEN's guidance provides a framework for banks to safely bank CRBs, but the compliance burden is high due to the strict reporting and monitoring requirements. For CRBs, access to banking services can be challenging due to the limited number of banks willing to take on the regulatory risk.
- Federal Reserve System (Fed)[12]:
    - Role: Oversees bank holding companies and state-chartered member banks. The Fed provides guidance on risk management and supervision for banks engaging in cannabis-related banking.
    - Implications: The Fed's guidance helps ensure the safety and soundness of banks involved in cannabis banking. However, the Fed's conservative approach can deter some banks from entering this market.
- Office of the Comptroller of the Currency (OCC)[13]:

- Role: Supervises national banks and federal savings associations. The OCC has issued guidance on providing banking services to hemp-related businesses, but not directly to CRBs involved in marijuana.
- Implications: The OCC's guidance for hemp businesses is more lenient than FinCEN's for marijuana businesses, reflecting the legal distinction between the two. This could create a regulatory gap for banks serving businesses operating in both areas.
- National Credit Union Administration (NCUA)[14]:
  - Role: Regulates and supervises federally insured credit unions. The NCUA has issued guidance similar to FinCEN's, outlining BSA and anti-money laundering (AML) compliance expectations for credit unions serving CRBs.
  - Implications: The NCUA's guidance provides credit unions with a pathway to serve CRBs, potentially increasing access to banking services for these businesses. However, the compliance burden remains high for credit unions.
- Department of Justice (DOJ)[15]:
  - Role: Enforces federal laws, including those related to controlled substances.
  - Implications: While the DOJ has generally taken a hands-off approach to enforcing federal marijuana laws in states where it is legal, the lack of clear guidance from the DOJ creates uncertainty for banks. The DOJ's stance on marijuana enforcement can influence banks' willingness to serve CRBs. A more lenient approach could encourage more banks to enter the market, while stricter enforcement could have the opposite effect.

It's crucial for individuals involved in handling transactions for businesses to have a grasp of how the United States banking system functions and the mutual expectations between customers and bankers. This knowledge becomes more vital for businesses with higher risks when it comes to navigating the complexities of cannabis banking. Establishing this knowledge builds a bridge between two industries that may naturally distrust each other, but also rely on each other to an extent. While it's clear that the cannabis sector relies heavily on banking services, financial institutions also recognize the business opportunities in serving this industry. Understanding the background of banking history, operations, and regulatory framework enables bankers to better serve the public with consistency and mutual cooperation.

Modern Banking Functions

Today's banking services are complex and crucial for the functioning of the United States economy. For those in the cannabis banking sector, having a grasp of these services is vital for offering a range of financial solutions to cannabis companies while adhering to intricate regulations.

- Deposits: Taking deposits stands out as a major function of modern banks. Banks serve as safe havens for individuals and businesses to safeguard their finances while ensuring access and convenience. This service holds increased significance for enterprises that often encounter obstacles in accessing traditional banking facilities. By accepting deposits, banks can help these businesses move away from cash transactions, thus enhancing security and operational efficiency. Deposits also serve as the foundation for banks to extend credit through lending products, which drives expansion of the economy as a whole.
- Lending: Providing loans represents another role in banking operations. Banks offer loan options such as personal loans, business loans, and mortgages that empower individuals and businesses to invest and expand their ventures. Access to loans can be transformative for cannabis firms, by enabling them to grow their operations, invest in technologies, and better manage their cash flow. Banks evaluate borrowers' creditworthiness, determine terms, and set interest rates based on a balance between supporting growth and managing risks.
- Payments: Banks and credit unions play a role in supporting payments by offering services like electronic funds transfers (EFT), payment processing, and online banking. These services help businesses carry out transactions securely and effectively in today's fast-paced digital economy.

Types of Banks and Financial Institutions

Over the last several decades there have been changes in the financial sector of the United States, especially concerning consumer and business banking. Commercial banks and credit unions have adjusted to evolving economic conditions, regulations, consumer preferences, and technological progress, resulting in a financial landscape unrecognizable in many ways to banking 60 or 70 years ago. This transformation has led to shifts in products and services offered, customer/membership criteria, and approaches to engaging with customers. It's essential for individuals and businesses navigating today's landscape to understand these developments.

Commercial Banks

Commercial banks have traditionally played a role in the system by offering various services like checking and savings accounts, loans, and investment options. Over time these institutions have expanded their services to include banking, mobile apps, as well as complex financial products such as derivatives and mortgage-backed securities. The deregulation trends of the 1980s and 1990s along with advancements have allowed banks to operate globally while providing financial solutions to both individuals and businesses.

Credit Unions

Credit unions initially started as organizations focusing on members by providing basic financial services to individuals sharing a common connection, like employees of a specific company or residents of a particular neighborhood. Over the years, credit unions have expanded eligibility criteria and range of service, placing emphasis on more customized services and perks such as attractive interest rates on savings accounts and lower loan rates compared to traditional banks (Figure 2.1).

Regulatory frameworks have also played a role in shaping the operations and structures of both banks and credit unions. In response to the financial crises of the twentieth and early twenty-first centuries, regulatory agencies have enforced stricter oversight and capital requirements to ensure stability and safeguard consumers. For example, the Dodd-Frank Wall Street Reform and Consumer Protection Act of 2010 brought about adjustments aimed at averting risky behaviors that precipitated the 2008 financial crisis. These regulations have compelled both banks and credit unions to adjust their approaches and strengthen their risk management practices.

Investment Banks

In the finance world, investment banks play an important role in connecting investors with companies seeking funding. They provide services such as supporting debt and equity transactions, facilitating mergers and acquisitions, offering financial guidance, and participating in securities trading. These functions are essential for keeping the markets functional by enabling businesses to access the capital for expansion and market fluctuations.

One important function of investment banks in finance is underwriting. This process involves investment banks buying stocks or bonds from companies that want to raise funds through issuing these securities and then selling them

Aspect	Commercial Banks	Credit Unions
Corporate Structure		
Corporate Structure	Corporation	Cooperative
Governance	Board of Directors	Volunteer Board
Ownership	Shareholders	Members
Financial Elements		
Capital Sources	Investors, Depositors	Member deposits
Credit Risk Exposure	Higher	Lower
Investment Opportunities	Higher risk	Lower risk
Profit Orientation	For-Profit	Non-Profit
Reserve Requirements	Higher	Lower
Revenue Generation	Interest, Fees	Member deposits, Fees
Risk Management	Formal policies	Member-centric
Tax Status	Taxable	Tax-Exempt
Marketing Focus		
Community Involvement	Lower	Higher
Customer Focus	Transactional	Relational
Customer Service	Transactional	Relational
Decision-Making Process	Hierarchical	Democratic
Market Competition	High	Moderate
Membership	Open to public	Members Only
Primary Purpose	Profit Maximization	Member Service
Transparency	Moderate	High
Products, Services, and Regulations		
Branch Accessibility	Widespread	Local
Deposit Interest Rates	Lower	Higher
Fees	Higher	Lower
Financial Literacy Programs	Variable	Frequent
Insurance	FDIC	NCUA
Interest Rates on Loans	Higher	Lower
Loan Approval Criteria	Stricter	Flexible
Regulation	Federal/State Agencies	Federal/State Agencies
Services Offered	Focus on personal & business products	Focus on personal accounts and loans
Size and Reach	Larger	Smaller
Technological Integration	Advanced	Moderate

FIGURE 2.1 Top-line comparison of banking institutions and credit unions across different key characteristics.

to investors. Investment banks assess the value of these securities, set prices, and take on the risk of selling them. Investment banks assist in mergers and acquisitions (M&A), aiding companies in acquiring or merging with other businesses by providing advice, conducting evaluations, and negotiating terms. Finally, investment banks engage in trading activities by executing buy and sell orders for clients to maintain market liquidity.

Summary of Part 1
The current banking landscape is intricate and diverse, encompassing types of entities like banks, credit unions, and investment banks. Each entity plays a role in facilitating transactions, providing credit facilities, managing finances, and promoting growth for both individuals and businesses.

For businesses operating in the cannabis industry, navigating within the established banking framework poses hurdles due to regulatory challenges. However, with financial institutions beginning to acknowledge the business prospects within this sector, having an understanding of banking operations, regulatory frameworks, and financial services becomes indispensable.

By getting a grasp of banking fundamentals and knowing its history, individuals in the cannabis banking field can navigate obstacles and make the most of the opportunities that come their way in this growing industry.

PART 2: BANKING SOLUTIONS FOR CANNABIS-RELATED BUSINESSES

Common Retail Banking Products and Services

As noted previously, banking services play an important role in the stability and growth of any business, offering a foundation for helping businesses reduce risks associated with handling cash. These services enable businesses to accurately track revenue and expenses, streamline operations, and manage payroll efficiently to maintain a workforce. In addition, access to banking establishes credit for business expansion by providing capital for infrastructure investment, inventory management, and future growth plans. For cannabis businesses, however, the true value of banking lies in their ability to initiate and receive payments in noncash form, a service facilitated by banks or third-party service providers.

CRBs and Standard Banking Services

For financial institutions that do service the cannabis vertical, recognizing the significance of these services is paramount and pivotal to establishing strong relationships with those businesses. Access to even the most basic banking products and services empowers cannabis businesses to pursue opportunities that may otherwise be unobtainable. Without these products and services, these companies struggle to attract investors, secure loans, and facilitate transactions critical for expanding operations and entering new growth markets. Processing payments and managing transactions securely through banking channels not only gives CRBs a sense of legitimacy, but also equips them with valuable financial insights to govern their strategic decisions.

Here are some key points for cannabis bankers that emphasize the significance of banking for businesses:

- Banking services provide infrastructure for financial transactions, reducing the risks associated with cash management.
- Access to banking is vital for maintaining records, budgeting effectively, and complying with tax regulations, thereby upholding business credibility and compliance.
- Establishing banking relationships facilitates the building of credit, ultimately enabling CRBs to access traditional sources of funding to grow the business.
- Leveraging electronic payment processing by accessing the ability to make and acquire payments through banks empowers cannabis enterprises to compete successfully.
- Offering banking services to cannabis establishments promotes development and stability within the industry, benefiting both the community and financial institutions themselves.

Limitations in the Context of the Cannabis Industry

In the cannabis industry at the present time, securing traditional financial services poses challenges due to the federal status of legality in the United States. Despite numerous states having already legalized cannabis for recreational purposes, most financial institutions still view cannabis businesses as too risky to bring on as customers due to the high-risk nature of cannabis businesses. Without access to bank accounts, credit lines, or loan programs, these businesses are forced to operate with cash, impeding efficiency and growth. The challenges of being able to only transact business with cash also complicates everyday accounting such as handling vendor payments, tax payments, or payroll.

The repercussions of being unbanked or underbanked extend beyond vendor services to impact aspects like property leasing (requiring bank references) and hindering research and development due to funding constraints. To overcome these hurdles, cannabis enterprises must innovate and forge strategic partnerships, but it is imperative that business owners understand the challenges bankers face:

- The federal legal classification of cannabis hinders access to banking services as most institutions want to avoid even the perception of any impropriety from directors, shareholders, employees, customers, or the community at large.

- Financial institutions that provide services for CRBs operate under increased scrutiny and must follow strict reporting and regulatory requirements, or risk penalties, fines, etc.
- Many cannabis businesses operate on a cash basis because of these barriers, which further raises concerns about theft, fraud, and regulatory challenges.

Preparing for an Initial Bank Meeting
Regardless of how often business owners may have opened new accounts with local financial institutions, the requirements they may encounter when approaching a bank or credit union to open a cannabis business checking account will likely seem almost punitive. Banks that are willing to open CRB accounts will likely require a plethora of documentation and information about the business, the owners, the investors, and the products provided before even finalizing the account setup. Preparation by the CRB before approaching the banker will help ease the due diligence and reduce some of the inevitable frustration they will likely face.

There are many different types of documentation required by most institutions during the vetting process and due diligence (Figure 2.2).

Treasury Services for Cannabis Bankers

In the cannabis industry, dealing with the challenges posed by regulatory constraints highlights the vital role of treasury services in effective financial management. For professionals in cannabis banking, offering treasury services involves creating a range of options that adhere to current regulations and cater to the specific needs of CRBs. Services like cash management, fraud protection, and access to moving money via domestic wires must be customized for the complexities of an industry on cash transactions and subject to rigorous oversight.

Essential Treasury Services for Managing Cash
Managing cash effectively is crucial in the cannabis sector due to its volume of cash transactions. Reliable cash management solutions equip CRBs with tools for handling, storing, and moving cash while optimizing liquidity and operational efficiency. These services should encompass aspects such as transport for cash deposits and withdrawals, currency counting machines, cash recyclers, dual-pouch transparent tamper-evident bags for moving securely between individuals, and secure vaulting facilities. Additionally, managing cash for CRBs often involves precise recordkeeping and reporting to meet regulatory

Documents Checklist for New Accounts

☐ **Proof of Identification**
Government-issued photo ID, (eg. driver's license or passport), for each account holder or authorized signer..

☐ **Social Security (SSN) or Taxpayer Identification (ITIN)**
SSN and/or ITIN is required for each account holder or signer

☐ **Business Formation Documents**
Copies of business formation documents, e.g. Articles of Incorporation, Organization, or Partnership.

☐ **Employer Identification Number (EIN)**
EIN letter issued by the IRS (CP-575) for your cannabis business.

☐ **Business License(s)**
Copy of state-issued business license, verifying the authority to operate a cannabis business in the jurisdiction.

☐ **Cannabis-Specific Licenses and Permits**
Applicable cannabis licenses and permits, including cultivation, manufacturing, distribution, and retail licenses.

☐ **Operating Agreement or Bylaws**
Copy of operating agreement or corporate bylaws, with rules and regulations governing your business operations.

☐ **Business plan**
Detailed business plan, with executive summary, market analysis, financial projections, and operations.

☐ **Financial statements**
Recent financial statements, including balance sheets, income statements, and cash flow statements.

☐ **Bank Account History**
Up to three-year history of any bank accounts (if available), with institutions and account information.

☐ **Industry certifications**
Any relevant certifications, such as a Good Manufacturing Practices (GMP) or ISO 9001 certification.

☐ **Community engagement and support**
Letters, testimonials, press, etc. detailing community involvement through charity initiatives, partnerships, sponsorships, or events.

☐ **Awards and recognitions**
Awards or recognitions, with documentation of achievements detailing commitment to excellence and leadership.

☐ **Media coverage**
Positive media coverage or press releases related to the cannabis business.

☐ **Employee training and development programs**
Provide information on your employee training and development programs, such as Certificates of Completion for programs, such as the Cannabis Banking Professional (CBP®) from the ACBA.

☐ **Security measures**
Detailed description of security measures and protocols, including physical security, cybersecurity, and cash handling procedures.

☐ **Professional advisors**
List of professional advisors, such as attorneys, accountants, or consultants that you access for advice.

© 2024 Association for Cannabis Banking, All Rights Reserved

FIGURE 2.2 New account opening for higher risk cannabis-related businesses requires a plethora of documents for due diligence.

standards and maintain transparent financial operations. It should be stated that when a financial institution refers to "cash management" it generally encompasses all of the options a business would have for managing the inflows and outflows of cash. When CRBs gain access to the full range of banking services and payment options, the cash management services from a financial institution would expand beyond cash to encompass all income and expense related-activities.

Preventing fraud stands as another component of treasury services provided by bankers. Dealing with large amounts of cash and navigating the complexities of operating at the state level while facing federal illegality, cannabis businesses are at a higher risk of being targeted by both internal and external fraud. It is crucial for treasury services to have fraud detection and prevention measures in place when monitoring transactions, in addition to establishing clear procedures for handling fraud incidents.

Conclusion

The future of cannabis banking relies on innovation coupled with regulatory reforms. Fintech solutions such as blockchain and cryptocurrency are already paving the way for more efficient cashless transactions and we'll discuss that in more detail later in the book. As these technologies advance and as the regulatory requirements change, the expectation is that CRBs will be able to take full advantage of accessible financial resources. Financial institutions that embrace these innovations may gain an edge by shaping the standards and direction of cannabis banking.

The journey ahead for those in the cannabis banking sector is filled with challenges and opportunities. Successfully navigating this path requires an approach to complying with regulations, a mindset to embrace and implement new financial technologies, and a strategic outlook to anticipate and adapt to future changes in the industry. The banks that will excel are those that not just meet the needs of the cannabis sector but also foresee upcoming trends and adjust their strategies accordingly and with agility. Any bank that is already steeped in providing agribusinesses of all types is in the best position to capitalize if their state approves recreational or medical cannabis and they plan in advance to capitalize with services tailored to the CRB industry.

NOTES

1. Medici Bank. Wikipedia. Last modified July 20, 2024. https://en.wikipedia.org/wiki/Medici_Bank.
2. Bank of England. "Home." Accessed July 23, 2024. www.bankofengland.co.uk.
3. Bank of North America. Encyclopedia of Greater Philadelphia. Accessed July 23, 2024. https://philadelphiaencyclopedia.org/archive/bank-of-north-america.
4. Ibid.
5. Ibid.
6. Hamilton, Alexander. "Excerpts from Alexander Hamilton's Report on Manufactures (1791)." Hanover College History Department. Accessed July 23, 2024. https://history.hanover.edu/courses/excerpts/111hamilton.html.
7. Jefferson, Thomas. "Letter to John Taylor." Teaching American History. Accessed July 23, 2024. https://teachingamericanhistory.org/document/letter-to-john-taylor.
8. American Bankers Association. *Principles of Banking*. Washington, D.C.: American Bankers Association, 2014.
9. Office of the Comptroller of the Currency. "Founding of the OCC & the National Banking System." Accessed July 23, 2024. https://www.occ.treas.gov/about/who-we-are/history/founding-occ-national-bank-system/index-founding-occ-national-banking-system.html.
10. Office of the Comptroller of the Currency. "Founding of the OCC & the National Banking System." Accessed July 3, 2024. https://www.occ.treas.gov/about/who-we-are/history/founding-occ-national-bank-system/index-founding-occ-national-banking-system.html.
11. Financial Crimes Enforcement Network. "BSA Expectations Regarding Marijuana-Related Businesses." Accessed July 3, 2024. https://www.fincen.gov/news/news-releases/fincen-issues-guidance-financial-institutions-marijuana-businesses.
12. Board of Governors of the Federal Reserve System. "The Fed Explained: What the Central Bank Does." Accessed July 3, 2024. https://www.federalreserve.gov/aboutthefed/files/the-fed-explained.pdf.
13. Office of the Comptroller of the Currency. "Founding of the OCC & the National Banking System." Accessed July 3, 2024. https://www.occ.treas.gov/about/who-we-are/history/founding-occ-national-bank-system/index-founding-occ-national-banking-system.html.
14. National Credit Union Administration. "Credit Union Regulations." Last modified February 6, 2024. Accessed July 23, 2024. https://www.ncua.gov/regulation-supervision/rules-regulations.
15. U.S. Department of Justice. "Justice Department Submits Proposed Regulation to Reschedule Marijuana." Accessed July 23, 2024. https://www.justice.gov/opa/pr/justice-department-submits-proposed-regulation-reschedule-marijuana.

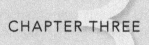

CHAPTER THREE

Compliance and Regulatory Frameworks

 REGULATIONS OVERVIEW

To navigate the rules and regulations in cannabis banking, an understanding of laws is crucial, especially with the ongoing conflict between federal and state regulations in the cannabis industry. There are multiple regulatory requirements that cannabis bankers must adhere to and in this very important chapter, we will delve into the compliance and regulatory frameworks that surround this unique industry.

Controlled Substances Act (CSA)

The CSA, enacted in 1970, forms the basis of United States drug policy by categorizing substances based on their abuse potential and addiction likelihood into five schedules. Cannabis currently falls under Schedule I, indicating high abuse potential and no recognized health benefits. This creates challenges for banks engaging with state cannabis businesses that operate within a gray area – compliant at state levels but violating federal laws.

Banks face the risk of being prosecuted under law when dealing with funds from cannabis transactions as it could be seen as money laundering due to the cash-intensive nature of the cannabis industry. This risk is heightened by the

Bank Secrecy Act (BSA) which requires banks to help the government detect and prevent money laundering. Handling transactions involving cannabis businesses involves monitoring, reporting, and the possibility of submitting Suspicious Activity Reports (SARs).

In light of these difficulties, there have been federal-level guidelines released to clarify how banks can engage with cannabis businesses. Particularly significant are the directives provided by the Financial Crimes Enforcement Network (FinCEN) in 2014. These guidelines outline how financial institutions can serve cannabis-related businesses (CRBs) while adhering to the BSA regulatory obligations. They stress thorough due diligence, continuous monitoring, and prompt SARs reporting when warranted.[1]

Bankers must stay well informed about any changes in federal policies. Changes in enforcement priorities under different presidential administrations can greatly influence regulatory scrutiny and prosecutorial focus on cannabis banking activities. Furthermore, proposed laws like the SAFER Banking Act (SAFER) could bring about changes to how the government deals with banking services for CRBs in states where such activities are permitted.

The interaction between the CSA and state cannabis laws presents an ever-changing issue for banking in this industry. Successfully navigating this landscape requires an understanding of drug regulations, a proactive stance on compliance, and ongoing monitoring of the political and legal environment surrounding cannabis. With the industry's growth and evolution, banks will need to adjust their strategies and policies to effectively balance regulatory requirements with business opportunities.

Overview of the 2018 Farm Bill

The 2018 Farm Bill, which was officially signed into law on 20 December 2018, stands as a moment in the history of agriculture and cannabis policy within the United States. Its impact on businesses centered on hemp has been profoundly reshaping the landscape for farmers, manufacturers, and financial entities alike.

A key highlight of the 2018 Farm Bill was its reclassification of hemp. Previously considered a controlled substance under the CSA, at a level and grouped with marijuana under Schedule I, the Farm Bill brought about a change by removing hemp from this category. This new distinction legally separated hemp – defined as cannabis containing less than 0.3% THC (tetrahydrocannabinol – a cannabinoid linked to the psychoactive effect of marijuana use) – from its relative, marijuana. This shift opened avenues for cultivation, transportation, and sale of products across state borders providing a significant boost to growers and businesses involved in producing items like CBD (cannabidiol – an extract of the hemp plant that contains <0.3% THC), oil, textiles, and food.[2]

For businesses working with hemp products, the passing of the Farm Bill meant a relaxation of regulations that had previously hindered their operations. Before this legislation came into effect, these businesses encountered obstacles such as access to banking services, federal support funds, and crop insurance. After hemp was reclassified, banks and other financial institutions began welcoming hemp entrepreneurs by providing services that were previously unavailable due to the plant's legal status at the federal level. This shift made banking operations run smoother and encouraged investments and other advancements within the industry.

The legalization under the 2018 Farm Bill also allowed hemp businesses to access grants, legal agricultural protections, and, importantly, federally supported crop insurance. The latter was especially crucial as it reduced risks and offered a safety cushion for farmers without worrying about losses from crop failures.

The regulatory structure introduced by the Farm Bill mandated states to submit cultivation plans to the United States Department of Agriculture (USDA), ensuring that state-level regulations were in line with standards. This move standardized cultivation methods and guaranteed quality and safety in production nationwide. Nevertheless, certain complexities arose from the 2018 Farm Bill. While it permitted hemp cultivation, the production and sale of CBD – a derivative of hemp – remained ambiguous, particularly regarding its inclusion in food items or dietary supplements. The Food and Drug Administration (FDA) continues to oversee commerce involving these products, at times causing confusion among producers and consumers.

In the banking industry, even though hemp has a federally legal status, many financial institutions continue to be cautious about working with businesses related to hemp due to the FDA's ongoing adjustments regarding CBD products. Banks and credit unions must carefully check that their clients follow all state laws and USDA regulations concerning production and sales.

The passing of the 2018 Farm Bill marked a turning point for businesses centered on hemp, sparking growth and regulatory modifications that continue to influence the industry. Establishing a financial structure is vital for maximizing the advantages of this versatile plant. Looking ahead, the effects of the 2018 Farm Bill on the hemp sector indicate growth and progress to changing regulations and increasing acceptance by financial institutions. As rules become more defined and the hemp market expands, it is expected that hemp will become an economically significant crop in the United States.

Implications of Cannabis' Schedule I Status on Banking

The classification of cannabis as a Schedule I drug according to the CSA has an impact on the banking sector for institutions considering providing financial services to businesses involved in cannabis. As per the CSA, substances categorized as Schedule I are deemed to have a high potential for abuse and no recognized medical use in treatment. This categorization groups cannabis together with heroin and LSD, subjecting it to regulations governing its sale, distribution, and production.

To address these obstacles, the FinCEN issued guidelines back in 2014 to clarify how financial institutions can serve CRBs while adhering to the BSA. According to FinCEN, banks are required to conduct diligence on clients involved in cannabis activities, which includes verifying their licensing and registration status with state authorities. As we discussed in Chapter 2, FinCEN recommends ongoing monitoring of these businesses and reporting any suspicious activities through SARs if the business engages in illegal actions or provides misleading information.

Despite the guidance provided by FinCEN, the banking sector remains cautious. This approach greatly limits the abilities of cannabis companies and impacts aspects such as managing payroll and expanding business operations. Proposed laws like the SAFER Banking Act aim to safeguard institutions offering services to CRBs in states where they are legal. If approved, this Act would be a move toward addressing the banking obstacles caused by cannabis being classified as a Schedule I substance by preventing banks from facing penalties for collaborating with CRBs.

In essence, the Schedule I classification of cannabis poses hurdles for the industry in terms of banking. Even after cannabis is potentially rescheduled, banks will continue to encounter substantial risks and operational hurdles when dealing with the cannabis sector until the SAFER Banking Act is passed or until cannabis is legalized federally.

THE BANK SECRECY ACT (BSA) AND ANTI-MONEY LAUNDERING (AML) LAWS

Requirements Under the BSA for Financial Institutions

The BSA, passed in 1970, outlines rules and guidelines for institutions in the United States to assist the government in identifying and preventing money laundering. For those working in the cannabis banking sector, understanding the complexities of the BSA is crucial due to the position of the cannabis industry straddling state legality and federal prohibition.

According to the BSA, financial institutions must uphold an AML program that aims to prevent their services from being used for illegal financial activities.

A financial institution's BSA program should involve:

- Creating policies, procedures, and controls
- Appointing a compliance officer
- Conducting staff training
- Arranging for independent audits to assess its effectiveness

A key aspect of the BSA is that financial institutions are required to report transactions to FinCEN, an arm of the US Department of Treasury. This reporting includes submitting Currency Transaction Reports (CTRs) for transactions exceeding $10,000 within a day. Besides CTRs, financial institutions must also submit SARs whenever they have suspicions or reasons to believe that unusual activities are taking place. This could include transactions carried out or attempted by, at, or through the bank involving $5,000 or more that the bank is aware of, suspects, or has reason to suspect involve funds obtained from illegal activities, or are meant to conceal funds obtained from illegal activities. For CRBs which are lawful under state regulations but unlawful under federal law, meeting the SAR filing requirement poses a significant hurdle. FinCEN has issued guidance on submitting SARs for businesses involved in cannabis-related operations that are covered in detail in Chapter 1. Apart from SARs and CTRs, the BSA also requires institutions to maintain records of all transactions exceeding $10,000 as well as gather and validate identification details from individuals opening accounts.[3]

The Customer Identification Program (CIP) is crucial for meeting the BSA's standards of ensuring that financial institutions understand their customers' true identities. The CIP involves verifying each customer's identity, checking if they are listed as known or suspected terrorists by any government agency, and keeping records of the verification process. Meeting these BSA requirements can be challenging and expensive for institutions dealing with cannabis businesses because they must maintain compliance through robust systems, ongoing vigilance, continuous training, and oversight commitments.

Implementing Effective Anti-Money Laundering (AML) Programs

For those banking CRBs, setting up an AML program is not just a regulatory necessity but also a crucial measure in minimizing financial crime risks linked to an industry under intense scrutiny. Dealing with the intricacies of cannabis banking, where lawful business activities intersect with significant limitations, demands a robust AML approach. This involves having a clear grasp of the AML framework outlined in guidelines, especially the BSA, and applying these principles to address the unique challenges faced in the cannabis industry.

A successful AML program begins with establishing a policy that clearly states the financial institution's dedication to preventing, detecting, and reporting potential money laundering activities. This policy should be well-documented and easily accessible to all staff members to ensure that AML practices are seamlessly integrated into the bank's operations. It should explicitly outline what constitutes suspicious activity and understand the ways in which money laundering can occur in transactions involving significant amounts of cash – a common occurrence within the cannabis sector.[4]

At the core of an AML program lies the appointment of an AML compliance officer. This position is crucial and demands an understanding of both the legal context surrounding cannabis banking and the operational functions of the bank. The AML officer has the role of overseeing the enforcement of AML policies and procedures within the bank, ensuring compliance with standards and serving as the primary liaison with regulatory authorities. It is also their responsibility to stay informed about changes and adjust the financial institution's AML strategies accordingly.

Training plays an important role in any AML program. It is essential that all bank employees, not only those directly involved in transactions, receive comprehensive training sessions.

These AML training sessions should cover:

- Details about BSA requirements
- Cannabis regulations at both state and federal levels
- The bank's monitoring and reporting procedures for suspicious activities
- Procedures for filling out SARs

Training programs need to be updated regularly to reflect changes or operational practices while emphasizing the importance of AML measures.

Transaction monitoring systems are critical to operating an AML program. These systems need to be advanced enough to detect any behaviors that could point to money laundering like large cash deposits or frequent transfers to offshore accounts. It's important for these systems to be customized to fit the transaction patterns of cannabis businesses, which can vary significantly from those types of clients.[5]

The effectiveness of an AML program also relies on how the institution communicates and collaborates with law enforcement and regulators. This involves submitting SARs and CTRs as mandated by the BSA. The accuracy and timeliness of these reports play an important role in enabling law enforcement to investigate and prosecute financial crime cases effectively.

For professionals working in cannabis banking, adhering to these AML laws and regulations is essential and involves several crucial steps:

- Establishing and upholding an effective AML compliance program in line with BSA requirements, which entails creating internal policies, procedures, and controls.
- Performing Customer Due Diligence (CDD) and Enhanced Due Diligence (EDD) to grasp the nature of the business, its proprietors, and financial transactions.
- Submitting SARs and CTRs as mandated by the FinCEN's guidelines for CRBs.
- Training staff members to ensure everyone comprehends their responsibilities in maintaining AML compliance and can recognize warning signs of money laundering activities and react quickly and appropriately.
- Staying informed about changes since AML obligations may change over time within the dynamic realm of cannabis banking.

In the bigger scheme of things, ensuring compliance with AML regulations in cannabis banking calls for a proactive stance. Those in the banking sector need to be vigilant in following AML laws and rules, adapting swiftly to industry changes, and prioritizing integrity and adherence to the law.[6]

PATRIOT ACT AND KNOW YOUR CUSTOMER (KYC)

The PATRIOT Act, a law created in response to the September 11, 2001 attacks, made critical changes to how financial institutions operate – in ways that especially affect the growing cannabis industry. This law focused on improving the country's security by emphasizing transparency, monitoring, and reporting. For banks involved with cannabis businesses, complying with this law means dealing with rules that interact with the complexities of operating in a market that is legal at the state level but restricted at the federal level.

Understanding the PATRIOT Act

Understanding the PATRIOT Act involves looking at its history and how it expanded law enforcement powers. The Act brought in measures that broadened oversight, significantly helping to track and stop money flows that could be linked to illicit and illegal activities. These measures increased the obligations of institutions by requiring stricter customer identification processes, thorough recordkeeping practices, and reporting standards. For the cannabis industry that often deals in cash due to restrictions on banking services, these compliance requirements have become even more important.

The overall goals of the PATRIOT Act in regulating finances are diverse, as they aim to strengthen America's system against misuse. Financial institutions are required to put in place measures to prevent money laundering and perform diligence to ensure they are not unknowingly aiding illegal activities. In the realm of cannabis banking, this means stepping up surveillance and establishing compliance programs to oversee, and report, transactions with the challenges posed by dealing with a federally prohibited product.

For CRBs, the impact of the PATRIOT Act is keenly felt. The Act's strict reporting and compliance standards necessitate that banks exercise caution when interacting with CRBs. They must implement KYC procedures to confirm the identity and authenticity of the CRBs they serve, while navigating regulatory requirements where errors can have significant repercussions. This effort is not just about meeting PATRIOT Act obligations, but additionally shielding the bank from reputational risks tied to servicing an industry like cannabis that operates in a legal gray area.

When it comes to addressing the PATRIOT Act and KYC requirements, those in banking should:

- Ensure Compliance: Rigorously follow the measures outlined by the PATRIOT Act, conducting thorough KYC verifications.
- Improve Customer Identification: Establish a detailed customer identification system that aligns with the elevated risks associated with the cannabis sector.
- Keep an Eye on Transactions: Establish systems for monitoring transactions that can identify and report any suspicious activities that may indicate money laundering or other illicit behaviors.

- Stay Informed about Legislation Changes: Stay vigilant in tracking any updates in laws and state regulations that might affect how the PATRIOT Act impacts the cannabis industry.
- Provide Education and Training for Staff: Regularly educate banking employees on the intricacies of the PATRIOT Act and KYC to ensure they are prepared to identify and respond to risks.

Successfully understanding the requirements of the PATRIOT Act demonstrates a financial institution's dedication to compliance and its ability to maneuver the relationship between regulation and state level legalization. This knowledge and expertise positions cannabis bankers as important players in upholding financial integrity and transparency in an industry under significant scrutiny due to its high-risk nature.

Understanding Know Your Customer (KYC)

The PATRIOT Act is a law that affects parts of the financial sector, significantly impacting those involved in banking cannabis businesses. It was put into effect after the 9/11 attacks to give power to US law enforcement to prevent terrorism. This act strengthened the rules around preventing money laundering and financing terrorism, and as a result banks now have requirements they must meet, which influence how they handle accounts and transactions linked to higher risk clients, such as those in the cannabis field.

The primary regulatory goals of the PATRIOT Act are to improve oversight and control measures to stop illegal activities within financial systems. Financial institutions must now have AML programs conduct proper due diligence checks and keep detailed records of all financial transactions. This includes setting up CIPs and EDD procedures for accounts that pose risks. These steps are intended to increase transparency in activities and make it easier to identify and report suspicious behavior.

The Impact of the PATRIOT Act on CRBs

The impact of the PATRIOT Act on the cannabis industry is substantial and cannot be underestimated. Cannabis bankers face the challenge of navigating the balance between state legalization and federal prohibition. The federal classification of cannabis as an illegal substance adds a significant responsibility on financial institutions to carefully assess CRBs under the PATRIOT Act. This legislation requires banks that serve these businesses to conduct evaluations of both financial risks and to establish robust KYC protocols to ensure compliance and prevent money laundering activities linked to cannabis profits.

Key points for bankers concerning the PATRIOT Act and KYC procedures include:

- Compliance Awareness: It is crucial for bankers to have a grasp of the PATRIOT Act to maintain compliance when engaging in financial transactions with cannabis enterprises.
- Risk Mitigation: Implementing KYC processes and EDD for CRBs helps in identifying and managing risks associated with these monitored accounts.
- Continuous Learning: Staying updated on changes in state regulations related to cannabis banking is essential for adapting KYC procedures and compliance measures.

For bankers, these actions go beyond adherence; they play a vital role in fostering a legitimate, reliable financial situation for an industry poised for widespread acceptance.

PATRIOT ACT COMPLIANCE

Compliance with the PATRIOT Act presents a challenge for bankers involved in the cannabis industry given the legal status of cannabis. Specific regulations outlined in the Act, such as the need to establish AML programs and carry out diligence procedures, directly influence how financial institutions engage with CRBs. The PATRIOT Act requires banks to have mechanisms in place to identify and report any activities that could be linked to money laundering or terrorist financing.[7]

Customer Due Diligence (CDD) and Enhanced Due Diligence (EDD) Basics

CDD processes hold importance in banking. Financial institutions must conduct background checks on all clients to ensure they follow state cannabis regulations and do not engage in illicit activities. EDD should be applied to higher risk customers such as those operating in jurisdictions with strict cannabis regulations. Effective CDD and EDD processes play a role in identifying risks and fostering transparent business relationships with customers.

Conducting EDD is particularly crucial. This process goes beyond due diligence practices for customers. When dealing with CRBs, EDD entails delving into the operations of the business, including verifying its legality through state licensing records, understanding its objectives and operations, and continuously monitoring its activities to ensure alignment with its stated purpose. The aim is to detect any transactions that deviate from the expected risk profile of the business. This rigorous scrutiny plays a role in safeguarding against crimes and preventing banks from unwittingly facilitating illicit activities.[8]

Creating a compliance strategy that aligns with the requirements of the PATRIOT Act involves several essential steps:

- A defined policy must be established by the bank to outline its approach to banking. This policy should detail the steps for onboarding clients, monitoring their activities, and reporting in accordance with the PATRIOT Act requirements.
- A risk assessment should be conducted to determine the level of risk associated with cannabis banking and to establish controls to manage these risks effectively. Training programs should also be put in place for staff members to ensure they understand and implement the bank's compliance procedures correctly.
- A review process is essential to have in place to keep the compliance plan up to date with any changes or shifts in business practices.

For those involved in banking elements of the PATRIOT Act, compliance encompasses:

- Formulating specific policies and procedures that address the unique risks associated with cannabis banking and implementing EDD measures for all customers classified as CRBs aimed at preventing crimes.
- Providing training and development opportunities for employees on compliance matters and updates in regulations.

Navigating through the PATRIOT Act compliance can be intricate, but it is also crucial. Adhering strictly to these requirements showcases an institution's dedication toward regulatory adherence and effective risk management.[9]

Implementing KYC Procedures

Implementing KYC protocols in cannabis banking presents several challenges unique to this industry. Cannabis companies are often at the crossroads of state compliance and federal legislation, which can complicate the KYC process. Financial institutions must maneuver this duality to ensure compliance without violating customer privacy. Protecting sensitive customer data while adhering to stringent regulatory requirements demands a delicate balance, especially given the detailed personal and financial information required by KYC procedures. Banks must implement robust data protection measures to safeguard against breaches that could erode customer trust and result in regulatory penalties.

Another significant challenge is addressing the needs of the unbanked and underbanked within the cannabis sector. These groups may not have the typical forms of identification or financial history that standard KYC processes require. For cannabis bankers, this necessitates the development of alternative verification methods that meet regulatory standards while enabling access to financial services. This could involve adopting non-traditional forms of identification or the utilization of advanced biometric verification technologies. By expanding the scope of acceptable KYC documentation, banks can open doors for legitimate cannabis businesses that might otherwise be excluded from the banking system.

For cannabis bankers, addressing the challenges in KYC involves:

- Developing KYC protocols that respect privacy while ensuring regulatory compliance, integrating advanced cybersecurity measures.
- Creating inclusive strategies that cater to the unbanked and underbanked CRBs, broadening access to banking services.
- Adapting risk assessment frameworks to thoroughly evaluate and monitor the unique risks presented by the cannabis industry.

Identifying these challenges successfully is critical for cannabis bankers to provide secure, compliant, and inclusive financial services to CRBs.[10]

CHALLENGES IN KYC FOR CANNABIS BUSINESSES

In the realm of cannabis banking, there exists a balance between meeting requirements and addressing privacy concerns. Cannabis companies, though operating legally at the state level, must adhere to KYC protocols when dealing with banks. These financial institutions face the challenge of complying with regulations while also safeguarding customer data and maintaining confidentiality.

Addressing the Unbanked and Underbanked

Furthermore, a key issue for bankers is how to serve those in the industry who are unbanked or underbanked. Traditional KYC processes often rely on a history that these groups may lack, posing obstacles to accessing banking services. For businesses and employees in the cannabis sector who have historically dealt mostly in cash due to banking hurdles, finding a bank that can cater to their needs is essential. Banks need approaches that meet KYC standards while accommodating these circumstances and integrating them into the regulated banking system. This may involve considering types of identification using technology to verify identities or establishing and acknowledging methods for credit and financial background checks.[11]

THE ROLE OF THE FEDERAL RESERVE AND FDIC

The Federal Reserve and the Federal Deposit Insurance Corporation (FDIC) play roles in influencing the operations of banks in the United States, including those that work with the cannabis industry. Understanding how these federal bodies impact banking activities can offer insights for cannabis bankers navigating the complex world of cannabis banking.

In the United States the Federal Reserve Bank oversees institutions and shapes monetary policy, thereby affecting banks' ability to serve the cannabis sector. The Federal Reserve has typically adopted a cautious approach due to regulatory and legal risks associated with providing services to businesses involved in activities deemed illegal under federal law.

On the other hand, the FDIC provides deposit insurance for banks in the United States, and operates as an independent agency established by Congress to uphold stability and public trust in the country's financial system. FDIC insurance typically safeguards depositors by covering their deposits balance (up to a limit) if a bank fails. However, the FDIC has made clear its position on cannabis-related funds. Since cannabis remains illegal at the federal level, engaging with cannabis businesses is seen as carrying higher risk, leading banks to face more scrutiny.[12]

This increased scrutiny includes expectations for compliance and monitoring. Banks must have systems in place to follow laws, especially AML regulations and the BSA. Noncompliance could cause sanctions, fines, or even loss of banking licenses, potentially putting the institution's FDIC insurance at risk. While the FDIC doesn't explicitly deny insurance for deposits from operating cannabis businesses in states where some form of cannabis use is legal, the complex compliance requirements can make serving these businesses less appealing for FDIC insured institutions. In addition, banks with FDIC insurance must report any activities, including those possibly linked to earnings from illegal activities, like cannabis sales.

Despite the opportunities in cannabis banking, the involvement of the Federal Reserve and the FDIC presents significant challenges and factors that need careful handling. Keeping aware of developments and being proactive in compliance will be crucial for operating within the boundaries established by these influential federal bodies.

How the Federal Reserve Influences Cannabis Banking

The Federal Reserve holds sway over the entire banking system through its monetary and regulatory policies. The Federal Reserve's monetary policies primarily affect banking by managing money supply and interest rates, which ultimately influence lending capacities and business expansion. For example, during periods of lower interest rates, there tends to be increased borrowing and growth opportunities advantageous for businesses seeking loans for development. However, the Fed's regulatory stance has an impact on cannabis banking. While there are no guidelines from the Federal Reserve regarding cannabis banking exclusively, its overall regulatory structure and enforcement of laws like the BSA and AML regulations indirectly determine how banks must manage relationships with cannabis ventures.

Additionally, the Federal Reserve's interpretation and enforcement of banking regulations can have an impact on the cannabis industry. For instance, if the Federal Reserve opts to enforce rules regarding money laundering or handling proceeds from activities deemed illegal under federal law, it could pose further challenges for banks serving cannabis businesses. On the other hand, adopting a more supportive approach – such as providing guidance indicating acceptance of banking services for cannabis businesses under stringent regulatory compliance – could encourage more banks to engage in this sector.[13]

OVERVIEW OF STATE LEGAL VARIATIONS

The cannabis industry in the United States is known for its various state laws governing recreational and medical cannabis use. These laws vary greatly in terms of legality, regulation, and taxation, posing both challenges and opportunities for bankers serving the industry.

Comparison of States with Recreational and Medical Cannabis Laws

In states where recreational cannabis is legal, like Colorado, California, and Washington, individuals aged 21 and older can purchase cannabis from retailers. This open approach typically leads to a bigger market size, increased sales activity, and more banking involvement compared to states with medical-only cannabis regulations, such as Oklahoma. Recreational laws often come with rules overseeing the production, distribution, and sale of cannabis including tracking systems to monitor product flow from cultivation to purchase (seed-to-sale), packaging requirements, labeling guidelines, and significant taxes.[14]

On the other hand, states like Florida, Oklahoma, and Pennsylvania that permit medical cannabis use limit access to individuals with specific qualifying medical conditions and who possess a prescription or medical card from an authorized healthcare provider. States with cannabis regulations often have rules on who can grow, sell, and distribute cannabis, resulting in a more tightly controlled market. These states typically require patient registries and closely monitor dispensaries. Banks in these areas face challenges such as increased requirements and the need for ongoing and thorough monitoring, to ensure their clients follow state laws on medical cannabis.

Regulatory Frameworks for Cannabis Businesses at the State Level

State level regulations for cannabis businesses are intricate and vary significantly across states, posing distinct challenges and demands for bankers in the cannabis industry. These frameworks not only determine the legality of cannabis operations but also outline specific rules that companies must adhere to in order to keep their licenses valid. Understanding these intricacies is crucial for banks and financial institutions looking to work with or provide services to cannabis enterprises.

At the state level, regulations mainly cover licensing, product safety, monitoring, and taxation. States like Colorado and California are well-known for their cannabis markets and have established regulatory structures that encompass specific requirements for cultivation, product testing, packaging, and sales. For instance, both states mandate that cannabis businesses track their products from seed-to-sale through designated systems like Marijuana Enforcement Tracking Reporting & Compliance (METRC) to prevent diversion and ensure product authenticity. These systems require reporting that can be reviewed by state authorities to ensure compliance.[15]

Furthermore, states impose guidelines on licensing procedures. Licenses are often categorized based on the nature of the business activities within the seed-to-sale framework, such as cultivation, processing, wholesale distribution, and retail sales. Each license type has its own rules and compliance standards. For example, growers may encounter rules regarding the use of pesticides and water consumption, while sellers are subject to regulations concerning the placement of their facilities and the security protocols they need to implement. The process of acquiring and upholding these licenses can have an impact on the aspects of cannabis enterprises, affecting their financial needs and banking practices.[16]

Adherence to state regulations also encompasses procedures and transparency. Most states mandate that cannabis companies maintain operations often requiring regular financial reporting and audits.[17] This is where experienced cannabis bankers can play a role by offering services that not only ensure regulatory compliance but also provide strategic guidance on financial management in line with state laws. Banking services focused on compliance are essential as they help cannabis businesses comprehend the complexities of various activities ranging from managing payroll to making investments.

Taxation is another area where state regulations have an influence on cannabis enterprises. States typically levy taxes on cannabis sales with rates varying. For instance, Washington imposes tax rates on cannabis sales at around 37%, whereas Colorado applies a 15% sales tax on cannabis products.[18] This disparity impacts the profitability and cash flow management of cannabis businesses, shaping how bankers tailor their financial service offerings and advice for these clients.

Bankers dealing with cannabis need to have a grasp of the state's frameworks to effectively support their clients in the cannabis industry. These regulations impact the day-to-day operations of cannabis companies and also influence the financial and banking services that can be offered. Therefore, keeping up with changes and understanding their consequences is crucial for banks involved in or considering entry into the cannabis banking sector. This understanding ensures adherence to rules and minimizes risks, and boosts the bank's capacity to deliver services catering to the distinct needs of cannabis enterprises.

BANKING GUIDELINES FOR CANNABIS-RELATED BUSINESSES (CRBs)

Before any bank decides to work with CRBs, it's essential to understand the nuances of the industry. While cannabis remains a Schedule I controlled substance at the federal level under the CSA, states that have legalized recreational marijuana often have their own specific rules and regulations in place.

Ensuring Communication and Accountability

Maintaining lines of communication between banks and cannabis businesses is crucial for adhering to regulations. Banks need details regarding the types of products, market sectors, and legal compliance status of their clientele. Consistent and thorough reporting is key to fostering the transparency needed to address financial risks and protect both the financial institutions and the CRB.

Continuous Learning and Skill Development

Given the nature of laws governing cannabis and their ongoing changes, it is essential for bank employees to undergo education and training. Training initiatives should encompass state cannabis regulations, guidelines outlined by FinCEN, and any updates in the regulatory environment that could impact the institution's policies.

Establishing Partnerships with Authorities

Engaging proactively with regulators can assist banks in navigating the uncertainties surrounding cannabis banking operations, involving dialogue with state and federal entities to ensure strict adherence to existing laws and directives.

Embracing Advancements

Utilizing technologies can streamline the complexities associated with cannabis banking. Solutions such as blockchain for tracking capabilities and robust compliance software that aligns with state and federal mandates are instrumental in simplifying compliance procedures while enhancing operational efficiency.

UNDERSTANDING THE COLE MEMO

The Cole Memo, released by former US Deputy Attorney General James M. Cole in 2013, offered guidance to prosecutors on how to handle laws in states where cannabis had been legalized for medical or recreational purposes. The memo aimed to address the conflict arising from differing state and federal cannabis laws with states opting to legalize cannabis, despite its federal ban. Its main goal was to focus enforcement efforts on areas concerning cannabis, such as preventing underage distribution, ensuring that sales revenue doesn't fund criminal activities, stopping the transportation of cannabis across state lines where it's illegal, and preventing legal cannabis operations from being a front organization for illicit actions.[19]

Detailed Background on the Cole Memo and Its Objectives

A significant principle highlighted in the Cole Memo was the concept of "respecting state regulations." This essentially meant that federal prosecutors were encouraged not to prioritize cases against individuals or businesses following state marijuana laws unless they violated enforcement priorities related to crime, violence, or criminal behavior associated with cannabis activities.

Another key aspect of the Cole Memo was its acknowledgment of the importance of state regulations in addressing issues related to cannabis use. It recognized that states had the authority to establish frameworks that could help mitigate these issues, such as by enforcing rules on how cannabis products are packaged and labeled, limiting advertising aimed at minors, and setting up comprehensive licensing and monitoring systems to prevent the illegal distribution of cannabis.[20]

While the Cole Memo held significance, it faced criticism. Critics argued that it did not provide protection for states with cannabis against federal interference as it still allowed federal prosecutors to target individuals and businesses complying with state laws. Others found fault with its lack of clarity, contending that it failed to offer instructions to prosecutors on how they should prioritize enforcement actions.

In January 2018, then Attorney General Jeff Sessions revoked the Cole Memo, marking a change in policy on cannabis. This decision led to uncertainty within the cannabis industry, raising concerns among states that had legalized marijuana. Even after the Cole Memo was removed, its core ideas, like respecting state laws and focusing on enforcement priorities, still play a role in shaping current cannabis policies.[21]

While no longer in effect, the Cole Memo had an impact on the US cannabis policy over several years and created the framework under which the cannabis industry was built and is operating today. Despite its rescission, its principles continue to influence cannabis policy and hold historical importance in the US cannabis legalization efforts.

The Impact of the Cole Memo on Law Enforcement and Banking

The Cole Memo had an impact on both law enforcement and the banking sector regarding cannabis. From a law enforcement perspective, the memo provided guidance to prosecutors on how to prioritize their actions in states where cannabis was legalized. By outlining enforcement priorities, such as preventing minors' access to cannabis and curbing its distribution across state lines, the memo aimed to focus resources on the critical activities.

One significant result of the Cole Memo on law enforcement was a decrease in prosecutions for cannabis-related offenses in states where cannabis was legal. This change occurred because federal prosecutors were instructed to concentrate on cases that went against the memo's priorities, like selling cannabis to minors or using state-sanctioned cannabis businesses for illegal activities.

The Cole Memo's impact on banking was also notable. The cannabis industry has faced challenges accessing banking services due to restrictions on cannabis. While banks are generally able to provide banking services to CRBs in states where marijuana is legal, it requires EDD and risk management techniques to stay in compliance with banking regulations.

Despite this limitation, the Cole Memo provided some reassurance to banks considering serving the cannabis industry. The memo suggested that federal prosecutors should not focus on charging individuals or businesses following state cannabis laws, providing some assurance to banks in entering the cannabis banking sector.

The Cole Memo had an impact on law enforcement and banking cannabis. While it provided some guidance for prosecutors and reassurance for banks, it did not fully resolve conflicts between state and federal cannabis laws, and those conflicts have yet to resolve to date. Consequently, the industry encounters challenges in accessing banking services while anticipating what might change surrounding cannabis legalization that would enable banks to safely offer services to this growing industry.

Changes and Revocations from the Cole Memo to the Sessions Memo and Their Implications

The transition from the Cole Memo to the Sessions Memo brought about a shift in cannabis policy with notable impacts on the cannabis industry, particularly in banking. Issued in 2013, the Cole Memo offered guidance to prosecutors on how to prioritize their enforcement efforts in states that had legalized cannabis.

In contrast, the Sessions Memo, released in 2018 under Attorney General Jeff Sessions, revoked the Cole Memo and signaled a potentially different stance on enforcing federal cannabis laws. The memo directed prosecutors to adhere to federal law when pursuing cases related to cannabis, granting them more leeway to target individuals and businesses involved in the cannabis industry, even in states where cannabis is permitted.[22]

The impact of the Sessions Memo was immediate and widespread across the cannabis industry, especially concerning banking. It introduced uncertainty and apprehension among enterprises, many of which were already navigating a gray area. Banks were already cautious about offering services to the cannabis industry due to the ban on cannabis.

The switch from the Cole Memo to the Sessions Memo was a setback for the cannabis industry and banking. Despite this setback, the cannabis industry has continued to expand and adapt, buoyed by changing public perceptions of cannabis and the growing recognition of its benefits.

The Role of the Cole Memo in Current Cannabis Banking Practices

Despite being revoked in 2018, the Cole Memo's influence continues to guide banks in their dealings with CRBs. The memo laid out priorities for prosecutors when it came to enforcing cannabis laws, giving states that had legalized cannabis a framework to operate with decreased fear of federal intervention as long as they followed strict regulatory guidelines. Although the Cole Memo is no longer policy, the industry's continued adherence to its principles demonstrates a practical approach toward navigating the intricate legal environment surrounding cannabis.

The removal of the Cole Memo emphasizes the necessity for regulations and laws to support the growing cannabis sector. In its absence, financial institutions remain cautious and conservative, still guided by the memo's principles. Cannabis bankers must stay alert and proactive, ensuring their compliance frameworks are not only strong but adaptable to changing regulations. Upholding standards of compliance and risk management is essential for integrating cannabis businesses into mainstream finance.

The significance of compliance, due diligence, and risk management in cannabis banking practices is underscored by the legacy of the Cole Memo. Even though the memo has been rescinded, its influence persists in shaping how banks deal with challenges and opportunities within the cannabis industry. Bankers in the cannabis industry need to stay updated and flexible; they should use the core principles of the Cole Memo to manage the challenges of this changing sector.

PRACTICAL CHALLENGES IN CANNABIS BANKING

The financial burden of compliance is a challenge for institutions in the cannabis industry. Meeting compliance requirements demands resources including personnel, advanced monitoring systems, and ongoing training initiatives. These costs can be daunting for banks and may discourage financial institutions from involvement in the cannabis sector altogether. While investing in compliance can help mitigate risks, it also eats into profit margins, making the business less appealing.

The Compliance Burden on Financial Institutions

Despite the obstacles, some financial institutions have effectively managed the world of compliance to offer banking services to the cannabis industry. These banks often use technology to improve their compliance processes, using software to monitor transactions and detect any activities. They also prioritize building relationships with regulators and key players in the industry, promoting an open and transparent approach to meeting regulatory requirements.

Complying with regulations poses a challenge for institutions operating in the cannabis sector. Nonetheless, by committing to compliance measures, staying vigilant about updates, and smartly utilizing technology, banks can effectively tackle these hurdles and take advantage of opportunities in the cannabis market.[23]

Common Operational Hurdles for Banks Servicing Cannabis Clients

In terms of operations, banks encounter difficulties in processing transactions, including handling cash, due to the prohibition on cannabis. Many cannabis businesses primarily deal in cash, leading to security concerns and logistical and compliance hurdles for banks. Managing large amounts of cash necessitates robust cash handling protocols while also heightening the risks of theft and fraud.

Moreover, there is a lingering stigma surrounding the cannabis industry that presents another obstacle for banks. Despite increasing acceptance and legalization in states, cannabis remains a contentious subject. Banks may face challenges related to their reputation when deciding whether to serve cannabis-related clients. Concerns about how the financial institution is perceived by other customers or stakeholders can affect a bank's choice to engage with the cannabis market.

Banks face not only risks to their reputation, but financial uncertainties when dealing with the cannabis industry. Despite its expansion, the cannabis market remains relatively new and unpredictable. Fluctuations in the market, regulatory changes, and legal obstacles can all affect the stability of cannabis companies, creating risks for banks.

Additionally, the lack of banking services to cannabis businesses has a ripple effect on the entire industry. Companies in the cannabis industry, without banking support, may resort to practices like storing large amounts of cash on site or using less secure third-party services. These practices not only endanger the businesses themselves but also pose risks to the wider community. Banks that do provide services to the cannabis sector play a role in mitigating these risks by offering regulated financial solutions, which has significant value to community safety.

Serving the cannabis industry presents hurdles ranging from legal environments and compliance standards, to managing cash transactions and safeguarding reputations. Despite these challenges, there are promising opportunities for banks that are willing to invest resources in understanding and addressing these obstacles as the industry continues its growth and development. By acquiring knowledge and implementing risk management plans, banks can significantly contribute to the growth of the cannabis sector while maintaining a focus on security and adherence to regulations.[24]

FUTURE OUTLOOK AND LEGISLATIVE CHANGES

Financial institutions in the cannabis sector are closely watching for changes in federal policies that could impact cannabis banking. Currently, one of the challenges facing CRBs is the classification of cannabis as a Schedule I substance under the CSA. However, there are signs indicating that federal policies may be shifting soon, which could have implications for banking. Rescheduling cannabis from Schedule I to Schedule III would mark a significant shift in US drug policy, reflecting a growing recognition of its medical value. Currently, under Schedule I, cannabis is classified alongside substances like heroin and LSD, indicating a high potential for abuse and no accepted medical use. This classification severely restricts research and limits medical access. Moving cannabis to Schedule III, where it would be grouped with drugs like anabolic steroids and ketamine, acknowledges its medicinal benefits and potentially eases regulatory hurdles. This change would facilitate more extensive research into cannabis's therapeutic potential, allowing scientists to conduct studies with fewer legal barriers and fostering a deeper understanding of its health impacts.

Another possible upcoming change involves the approval of the SAFER Banking Act that has been introduced in Congress in various forms. If passed, this legislation would provide a safe haven for financial institutions to serve CRBs without fear of prosecution. The aim of the SAFER Banking Act is to address concerns about safety arising from cash operations within the cannabis industry, where businesses currently lack access to regular banking services. By establishing a regulatory framework, this Act would likely encourage more financial institutions to participate in serving the cannabis market, promoting greater financial inclusivity and security.

Furthermore, there is increasing support at the federal level for broader reforms related to cannabis. Efforts, like the Marijuana Opportunity Reinvestment and Expungement Act (MORE Act) and the Cannabis Administration and Opportunity Act (CAOA), aim to not only decriminalize but also remove cannabis from scheduling altogether. These proposed laws seek to address injustices of cannabis prohibition, while setting up a framework for CRBs to function just like many other legal entities. If these broad reforms are approved, they could resolve many of the uncertainties and operational hurdles faced by those in the cannabis banking sector.

The changing political landscape indicates a shift in policies. With growing backing for cannabis legalization, more states are adopting laws for recreational and medical cannabis use, leading to mounting pressure on federal legislators to align state and federal approaches to cannabis. Additionally, alterations in policies could have implications for services linked to cannabis banking. Clearer regulatory guidelines may encourage increased investment in technologies and insurance products related to the industry. These advancements could offer CRBs with much needed solutions, including specialized payment processing systems, risk management tools, and comprehensive insurance protection. As the public's views on marijuana change, we might see a rise in financial technology advancements designed specifically for the requirements of the cannabis sector.

Potential upcoming shifts in government regulations could have an impact on the banking industry related to cannabis. Laws such as the SAFER Banking Act and broader reforms proposed by initiatives like the MORE Act may offer much needed clarity and safeguards for financial institutions catering to CRBs. The changing attitudes toward marijuana legalization, both politically and publicly, further indicate the likelihood of these changes. With adjustments in policies, traditional banks may increasingly engage with the cannabis banking sector, offering improved services and creating a safer environment for CRBs and the communities in which they operate.

Predictions and Strategies for Cannabis Banking Services

Plans for institutions interested in offering banking services to the cannabis industry revolve around navigating a changing regulatory environment and seizing new opportunities. With the continuous growth of the cannabis industry comes a heightened demand for banking options, including lending and deposit services. Financial institutions looking to step into this market need to ready themselves for the challenges and advantages it brings.

One significant forecast is that more states will likely legalize cannabis for recreational purposes, leading to an increased need for banking services tailored specifically to CRBs. This trend is expected to pick up pace as public support for cannabis legalization rises and state governments acknowledge the advantages. By establishing compliance frameworks and specialized banking solutions for CRBs, financial institutions can position themselves as leaders in the industry, capturing a portion of this expanding market.

Financial institutions are advised to explore collaborations to handle the complexities of cannabis banking. Working with experts specializing in cannabis law, industry associations, and technology providers can offer insights and resources. These partnerships enable banks to stay updated on regulatory changes, exchange practices, and access innovative solutions tailored to the cannabis sector.

It is essential for banks to educate their employees and stakeholders about various aspects of cannabis banking. Regular training sessions on updates, industry trends, and the specific requirements of banking CRBs will equip staff members to better serve this market segment. Transparent communication with stakeholders regarding the bank's approach to cannabis banking can build trust, reduce reputational risk, and garner support for these initiatives.

Financial institutions venturing into cannabis banking must take a strategic stance. By anticipating shifts, investing in compliance measures and technology upgrades, establishing partnerships, and providing comprehensive training programs, banks can effectively manage the complexities of this evolving market.

As the cannabis industry expands, banks that establish themselves as trustworthy allies for CRBs will be able to capitalize on the lucrative opportunities in this swiftly growing and changing industry.

CONCLUSION

Staying informed and adaptable is key to achieving success. The cannabis industry is in a state of flux with new laws and regulations cropping up, and for bankers, this entails staying aware of the updates to ensure compliance and seize new opportunities. Despite legalization in many states, it remains prohibited at the federal level, leading to a continuously shifting legal environment that demands ongoing attention. Subscribing to industry publications, participating in events like conferences and webinars, and engaging with professionals are all valuable ways to stay current. Networking within the industry can offer insights and help keep you ahead of important developments. Knowledge is indeed power in banking. It acts as your tool for navigating market uncertainties.

Being agile requires readiness to adjust swiftly to changes as they arise. This may involve tweaking compliance procedures or embracing technologies that streamline compliance obligations more effectively. Being adaptable and responsive is essential in cannabis banking, ensuring your institution can effectively manage any developments compliantly. It's not just a plan but also a mindset that prioritizes flexibility and quick decision-making to react to market changes.

Creating a compliance framework is paramount and this framework should not only follow regulations but also be flexible for future modifications. Imagine it as constructing a house on a foundation of withstanding tremors; regularly assessing and enhancing your compliance procedures will bolster your financial institution's resilience by:

- Embracing technology that streamlines compliance tasks can enhance efficiency and reliability, minimizing the chances of errors.
- Encouraging learning within your organization. Motivate your team to stay inquisitive and proactive regarding industry shifts. Routine training sessions can ensure everyone is well informed and prepared to tackle obstacles. An informed and agile team serves as an asset in navigating the intricacies of cannabis banking.
- Effective communication and collaboration can significantly improve how your institution adapts to industry changes.

Lastly, it's crucial to recognize that staying informed and agile involves more than reacting; it's about proactively anticipating changes. Keeping an eye on patterns, market dynamics, and technological progressions, and adjusting your strategies ahead of time to adapt to these shifts, will give you an edge over competitors. It's like playing chess; thinking ahead and being ready for a variety of outcomes will provide you with an advantage.

The significance of staying well informed and flexible in cannabis banking cannot be emphasized enough. By enhancing your knowledge, promoting adaptability within your team, and proactively preparing for changes, your financial institution can successfully manage cannabis banking with confidence. Approach the challenge with an open mindset and you'll discover possibilities where others perceive obstacles.

NOTES

1. Financial Crimes Enforcement Network. "BSA Expectations Regarding Marijuana-Related Businesses." U.S. Department of the Treasury, February 14, 2014. https://www.fincen.gov/news/news-releases/fincen-issues-guidance-financial-institutions-marijuana-businesses.
2. U.S. Congress. "Agriculture Improvement Act of 2018." Public Law No: 115-334, December 20, 2018. https://crsreports.congress.gov/product/pdf/IF/IF11088.
3. Ibid. at 1.
4. Ibid.
5. Ibid.
6. Ibid.
7. "USA PATRIOT Act," U.S. Department of the Treasury, https://home.treasury.gov/about/general-information/orders-and-directives/treasury-order-180-01.
8. "Customer Due Diligence Requirements for Financial Institutions," Financial Crimes Enforcement Network, https://www.fincen.gov/resources/statutes-and-regulations/cdd-final-rule.
9. Ibid. at 7.
10. Lozzi, Mark. "3 Pillars of Cannabis Banking compliance." *Cannabis Industry Journal*. Accessed July 23, 2024. https://cannabisindustryjournal.com/column/3-pillars-of-cannabis-banking-compliance.
11. Ibid.
12. Ibid.
13. Ibid.
14. "State Medical Cannabis Laws," National Conference of State Legislatures, https://www.ncsl.org/research/health/state-medical-marijuana-laws.aspx.
15. "Laws and Regulations." California Cannabis Portal. Accessed July 23, 2024. https://cannabis.ca.gov/cannabis-laws/laws-and-regulations.
16. "Washington State Marijuana Laws," Washington State Legislature, https://apps.leg.wa.gov/rcw/default.aspx?cite=69.50.101.

17. "Marijuana Enforcement Tracking Reporting & Compliance," METRC, https://www.metrc.com.
18. Marijuana Policy Project. "Cannabis Tax Revenue in States that Regulate Cannabis for Adult Use." https://www.mpp.org/issues/legalization/cannabis-tax-revenue-states-regulate-cannabis-adult-use.
19. Cole, James M. "Memorandum for All United States Attorneys: Guidance Regarding Marijuana Enforcement." U.S. Department of Justice, August 29, 2013.
20. "Guidance Regarding Marijuana Enforcement." U.S. Department of Justice, August 29, 2013.
21. Hudak, John. "Why Sessions is Wrong to Reverse Federal Marijuana Policy," Brookings, January 10, 2018. https://www.brookings.edu/articles/why-sessions-is-wrong-to-reverse-federal-marijuana-policy.
22. Ibid.
23. "Cannabis banking: Risk tolerance, CRBs, and compliance," Crowe LLP, https://www.crowe.com/insights/fincrime-in-context/cannabis-banking-risk-tolerance-crbs-and-compliance.
24. "Navigating the Hazy Landscape: Challenges and Solutions in Cannabis Payment Processing," Goodwin Law, https://www.goodwinlaw.com/en/insights/publications/2024/03/insights-finance-ftec-navigating-challenges-solutions-cannabis-payment-processing.

CHAPTER FOUR

Understanding Cannabis Businesses

 CANNABIS BUSINESS OVERVIEW

It cannot be understated how crucial it is for bankers to have an in-depth understanding of the cannabis industry. This goes far beyond just following rules and regulations, it also involves grasping the intricacies of a market that operates within its own unique set of challenges and opportunities.

To begin with, bankers must have a grasp of the network of federal and state laws that govern the cannabis sector. This includes knowing the distinctions between hemp and marijuana, understanding the regulations in states, and being aware of how ongoing federal restrictions can affect the industry. Without this knowledge bankers risk facing compliance issues, damaging their reputation, and potentially facing enforcement consequences.

Unlike traditional businesses, cannabis companies encounter difficulties related to managing cash flow, ensuring security measures, and handling supply chains. Bankers should be able to identify these challenges and devise customized solutions tailored to meet the requirements of their cannabis clientele.

Keeping up to date with industry trends and market dynamics is vital. The cannabis sector is known for its fast growth, innovative practices, and constant changes. Bankers need to stay informed about product categories emerging in the market, changing consumer preferences, and any potential disruptions so they can anticipate their clients' needs by offering relevant financial expertise. Establishing relationships and trust within the cannabis community is key to achieving success.

To truly succeed in this growing market, bankers must grasp the culture, values, and obstacles encountered by cannabis entrepreneurs. Building connections allows bankers to gather knowledge, spot risks early on, and nurture enduring collaborations that are advantageous for both the financial sector and the cannabis industry. Essentially having an insight into the cannabis industry is not merely a requirement but a vital strategy for bankers aiming to excel in this expanding industry.

THE CANNABIS INDUSTRY

Market Size and Growth Projections

The cannabis sector has seen progress in the last decade, since recreational cannabis became legal in some states in 2014, shifting from a niche market to a thriving industry with a significant economic influence. This evolution is primarily due to the increasing legalization efforts for both medical and recreational purposes, leading to a growing market. With more states and countries embracing the cannabis industry, it's now poised for expansion, catching the attention of investors, entrepreneurs, and consumers alike.[1]

In the United States, the cannabis industry has grown in revenue and consumer base. Recent data indicates that the legal cannabis market was valued at around $17.5 billion in 2020 and is forecasted to reach $58 billion by 2030 in sales, plus additional $145 billion in economic benefits indirectly associated with those retail sales (Figure 4.1).

This growth is driven by the rising number of states permitting cannabis use and the potential federal legalization could further boost this growth by establishing regulations and broadening market access. According to a Gallup poll, 70% of American adults support the legalization of marijuana.[2]

U.S. cannabis industry total economic impact

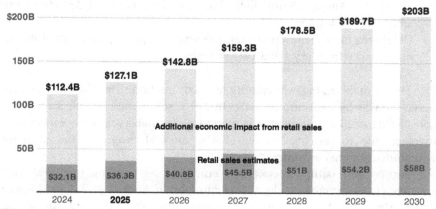

FIGURE 4.1 Total impacts projected to US economy from sales revenue and externalities.

Source: "MJBiz Factbook: Marijuana industry will add $112.4 billion to US economy in 2024," https://mjbizdaily.com/marijuana-industry-will-add-112-4-billion-to-us-economy-in-2024-mjbiz-factbook. Accessed 6/3/2024. Reprinted with permission with MJBiz.

More information about cannabis legalization[3]:

- 54% of Americans live in a state where the recreational use of marijuana is legal – less than a dozen years after Colorado and Washington became the first states to allow the drug for recreational purposes.
- 74% of Americans live in a state where marijuana is legal for either recreational or medical use.
- California was the first state to legalize medical marijuana in 1996.
- 79% of Americans live in a county with at least one cannabis dispensary.
- There are nearly 15,000 cannabis dispensaries in the United States. Dispensaries (businesses that sell cannabis products) are common not only on the West Coast and Northeast, but also in interior states like Michigan, Oklahoma, and Colorado.
- California has far more dispensaries than any other state: 3,659 at the time of this analysis, more than double the amount in the second-highest ranking state. A quarter of all marijuana dispensaries in the US are in

California, and nearly all Californians (99.5%) have a dispensary in their county. Los Angeles County alone has more dispensaries (1,481) than any state except California itself.
- Oklahoma has the most marijuana dispensaries per capita of any state: 36 dispensaries for every 100,000 residents.

The cannabis industry is gaining momentum. Countries like Canada have paved the way by legalizing cannabis in 2018, setting an example for nations considering similar measures. The worldwide cannabis market is expected to increase due to the legalization efforts, medical progress, and growing acceptance among consumers.[4]

Europe and Latin America are emerging as bustling markets, with countries like Germany just legalizing cannabis in April of 2024, and Mexico considering cannabis legalization, having decriminalized the recreational use of cannabis in 2021. Several factors drive the growth forecasts for the cannabis sector and there is a rising acknowledgment of cannabis for both recreational and medical use.[5] Ongoing research reveals the advantages of cannabis, leading to medical adoption and a shift in public attitudes. Additionally, advancements in cultivation techniques, extraction methods, and other product innovation have led to a variety of high-quality products that cater to diverse consumer tastes. Innovations such as cannabis-infused beverages, edibles, and topicals are diversifying the market beyond flower and vape offerings. Also, cannabis businesses are understanding the value of branding for women and are recognizing the unique needs of this growing base of consumers.

Investment interest in the cannabis industry has grown alongside market expansion. Major corporations and institutional investors are increasingly entering this space due to recognizing its long-term potential and profitability. Venture capital investments, mergers and acquisitions activities, along with initial public offerings (IPOs) are becoming more prevalent as confidence in the industry's sustainability grows. The increase in funding also requires adherence to regulations and effective risk management to maintain positive progress.[6]

While the future looks promising, the cannabis sector is confronted with obstacles that could hinder its growth path with uncertainty surrounding regulations in the United States as just one barrier. Challenges related to taxes, market saturation, and increasing competition from markets present additional potential threats.

The cannabis industry is set for expansion in the coming years due to increased legalization, consumer approval, and market advancements. The anticipated market size and revenue forecasts underscore the possibilities of this growing industry. Nevertheless, stakeholders must understand the frameworks and tackle various obstacles to fully capitalize on the industry's potential. As the sector progresses, further continuous research efforts, strategic investments, and adaptable policies will play a role in shaping the future of this exciting industry.

Current Market Valuations: A Banker's Perspective

Certain cannabis companies, such as those involved in operations across states and new product categories like edibles and beverages, have experienced a surge in their market worth in recent years. However, the industry faces fluctuations too, with some companies seeing a decrease in their values due to obstacles, disruptions in the supply chain, and intense competition.[7]

A variety of factors play a role in shaping these market values, such as revenue growth, profitability, brand recognition, market share, and the evolving regulatory requirements. Companies that offer a range of products and have established themselves in several legal markets usually command higher valuations.[8] The possibility of legalization in the US also hangs over the industry, with significant effects on valuations leading to increased consolidation and investment activities.

Future Growth Estimates

The cannabis industry is set to expand in the years ahead, offering a promising opportunity for professionals in the field. As per MJBizDaily, revenue in the cannabis market in the United States is forecasted to reach almost US$40 billion in 2024. "The United States sees a growing trend in cannabis investments, with increased focus on regulatory developments and market expansion."[9]

For professionals in the cannabis industry, growth projections highlight the significance of comprehending industry trends, and making strategic decisions accordingly thereby positioning themselves for long-term success. However, it's crucial to recognize that despite growth prospects for the cannabis industry's future, issues such as disruptions in supply chains, banking challenges, and changing consumer preferences could influence its trajectory.

Despite the obstacles, the future prospects for the cannabis industry appear promising. By staying up to date on market trends, adjusting to legal and industry shifts, and fostering creativity, professionals in the cannabis banking sector can successfully establish themselves as reliable allies and trusted advisors for companies in this growing field.

KEY MARKET SEGMENTS

Medical Cannabis

The medical marijuana sector is a part of the cannabis industry, providing opportunities and challenges for those in the cannabis banking field. According to MJBizDaily, it is estimated that medical marijuana sales will hit $12.3 billion by 2025 and $14.1 billion by 2028, highlighting its importance within the growth of cannabis markets[10] (Figure 4.2).

An important aspect of the medical marijuana sector is its emphasis on patients and their specific health needs. This results in a market dominated by strains with cannabidiol (CBD) and lower tetrahydrocannabinol (THC) levels, as well as specialized formulations aimed at addressing various conditions such as chronic pain, anxiety, epilepsy, and multiple sclerosis.[11]

Navigating medical marijuana requires understanding the market. Unlike the recreational market, medical marijuana is typically subject to regulations that involve patient registration, product testing procedures, and oversight by healthcare providers. Due to the nature of medical marijuana, there is an increased need for education to ensure patients make informed decisions about products and potential risks involved.[12]

The medical marijuana industry may not see the same expansion as the recreational market, but it stands as a steady and strong sector with loyal patients. With studies on the healing properties of marijuana progressing, and

U.S. Medical Cannabis Sales Estimates: 2022–2028
MJBiz Factbook projections for medical markets, in billions of dollars.

2022	2023	2024	2025	2026	2027	2028
$10.7	$11.1	$11.6	$12.3	$12.9	$13.5	$14.1

Estimates are high end of range.
Chart: © 2023 MJBiz, a division of Emerald X, LLC • Created with Datawrapper

FIGURE 4.2 Estimates and projections of medical cannabis sales.

Source: "U.S. Cannabis Retail Sales Estimates: 2022–2028," https://mjbizdaily.com/us-cannabis-sales-estimates. Accessed 6/22/2024. Reprinted with permission with MJBiz.

the increased likelihood of rescheduling, there is potential for advancements and new products in the field. For professionals working with cannabis businesses, this offers a chance to establish connections with medical cannabis companies by offering customized financial services that aid in their development and enhance patient care.

Recreational Cannabis

The segment of the cannabis industry focused on recreational use is experiencing significant growth and change, offering lucrative opportunities for those involved in cannabis banking. This expansion is being driven by the increasing legalization of adult use cannabis in states across the country and the growing societal acceptance of cannabis as a leisure activity. Staying aware of consumer trends and evolving regulations in the market is essential. Unlike the medical sector, recreational cannabis often faces regulatory restrictions that require more innovation in product development and marketing strategies.[13]

The growth of the market offers bankers the opportunity to create specialized financial offerings that meet the specific requirements of this industry. This involves offering banking services for dispensaries, growers, producers, and other seed-to-sale enterprises in the sector. By establishing connections with seasoned professionals in the industry and staying up to date on current trends, cannabis bankers can establish themselves as reliable allies and compliance partners for businesses in this dynamic and fast-paced field.

Industrial Hemp and CBD

The market for hemp and CBD is an expanding sector in the wider cannabis industry, offering unique opportunities for cannabis bankers. Industrial hemp, unlike its THC counterparts, contains only trace amounts of the psychoactive compound, making it legal to grow and process in the United States under the 2018 Farm Bill. This has paved the way for a variety of hemp-derived products, such as CBD, a compound known for its therapeutic advantages. The surge we are experiencing in the cannabis industry is primarily fueled by the rising demand for CBD products across industries such as pharmaceuticals, cosmetics, food and beverage, and personal care.[14]

For bankers, grasping the nuances of the hemp and CBD market requires an in-depth understanding of market forces and predictions. The changing perspective of the FDA regarding CBD products introduces an element of unpredictability for companies involved in this industry. Despite these obstacles, the industrial hemp and CBD sector offers an exciting prospect for experts specializing in cannabis. Given its range of uses and increasing consumer interest, this field is set for expansion and advancement. By keeping informed about changes, comprehending the requirements of hemp and CBD enterprises, and providing customized financial services, banking professionals in the cannabis industry can play a crucial role in fostering the development of this vibrant market sector.

 SEED-TO-SALE: THE CANNABIS LIFE CYCLE

For cannabis bankers, it is crucial to grasp the journey from seed-to-sale and at its core, cultivators are key to the "growth" of the cannabis industry (pun intended). As Tier 1 businesses that work directly with cannabis through the agricultural growth cycle, their perspective on the future viability of the industry is critical to its overall survival since a pessimistic view could endanger the product growth cycle for hundreds of CRBs whose businesses depend on the ongoing cultivation and expansion of products and brands.

To that end, MJBizDaily found that 57% of cultivators had moderate to strong positive views of their businesses' own growth over the next year, while almost 50% had similarly positive views of the cannabis industry overall (Figure 4.3).

With cultivators having a positive take on both their CRBs and the industry overall, other businesses within the seed-to-sale process have strong reasons to continue investing and expanding. This intricate process covers every aspect of the cannabis plant's life starting from cultivation (seed) and processing to testing, distribution, and finally selling to consumers (sale). Each stage is closely monitored and tracked by a software system, usually Metrc and BioTrackTHC. The Metrc system is widely adopted, currently used by 24 states and Washington D.C.[15] It's a comprehensive, web-based platform that tracks cannabis plants and products from cultivation to distribution (seed-to-sale), ensuring compliance with state regulations, and providing transparency in the supply chain. Another major player, BioTrackTHC is currently used by 12 states. It offers similar tracking capabilities to Metrc, ensuring regulatory compliance, and facilitating data collection for government agencies.[16] For financial institutions offering banking services in this industry, a deep understanding of the seed-to-sale cycle is not just advantageous, but absolutely necessary for effective compliance.

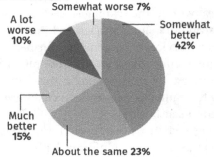
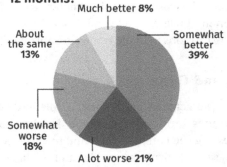

FIGURE 4.3 Overall industry outlook from practitioners remains strong.

Source: MJBizDaily 2023 Factbook, pg. 38, Chart 3.05, https://insights.mjbizdaily.com/factbook-2024. Reprinted with permission with MJBiz.

As per the National Conference of State Legislatures (NCSL), most legal cannabis states utilize seed-to-sale tracking systems to oversee and regulate the industry.[17] These systems meticulously document each plant's identifier, monitoring its movement throughout the supply chain. For bankers, this information is invaluable as it offers insights into inventory management, compliance adherence, and overall business operations. By comprehending how seed-to-sale tracking functions, bankers can effectively evaluate the risks and opportunities linked with providing banking services and loans to enterprises.

The seed-to-sale life cycle serves as a framework for comprehending the types of businesses within the cannabis sector. Cultivators, processors, manufacturers, distributors, and retailers all have roles that necessitate financial products and services. For example, a farmer might seek funding for buying land and equipment, while a store owner might need loans to handle cash flow and inventory. By understanding these unique needs, financial institutions serving the cannabis industry can customize their services to suit various types of seed-to-sale businesses.

In this upcoming section we will explore the process from planting to selling in the cannabis industry, examining each phase closely and considering how it impacts banking. We will also talk about the obstacles and possibilities that arise from tracking products throughout the seed-to-sale pipeline, and how financial professionals can use this information to make informed banking decisions. Throughout the course of this chapter, you will gain an understanding of the cannabis business cycle and its significant role in shaping the choice of financial institutions to bank, or not to bank, cannabis.

Seed Selection and Genetics

The choice of seeds and genetics plays a major role in determining the final product. For institutions involved in cannabis lending, understanding this aspect is key to assessing the potential risks and rewards. Selecting seeds goes beyond picking any seed; it involves consideration of factors like strain type, genetic background, and intended purpose, leading to potentially new and exciting products for cannabis consumers.[18]

Growers meticulously pick seeds based on their goals – whether it's to increase yield, enhance profiles, or create distinct terpene profiles. The genetics chosen influence the plant's growth patterns, potency levels, taste, and scent. These factors ultimately impact the end product's market value and appeal to consumers. For financial institutions, grasping a cultivator's seed selection approach can offer insights into their production targets, risk appetite, and chances for success despite changing preferences and market dynamics.[19]

Apart from strain attributes, maintaining consistency is vital in cannabis cultivation. Stable genetics ensure predictable traits and results, enabling growers to uphold harvests and provide a dependable product. Unstable genetics can lead to variations in yield quality and potency levels that pose risks for both growers and their financial backers. Bankers can enhance their evaluation of a cultivator's dedication to quality control (QC) and capacity for delivering outcomes by grasping the significance of plant stability.[20]

Understanding Cannabis Strains

In the cannabis industry, it is crucial for professionals working with cannabis businesses to have a grasp of the various strains available. These strains aren't different versions of the same plant; they each have distinct qualities that impact their effects, uses, and ultimately their market worth. For bankers, being able to differentiate between these strains is vital for evaluating the viability of cultivation ventures and creating valuable solutions for cannabis companies.[21]

Cannabis strains are typically grouped into three categories: indica, sativa, and hybrid. In general, indica varieties are known for their sleep-inducing properties making them popular choices for managing pain, insomnia, and anxiety. Sativa strains, on the other hand, are valued for their uplifting and invigorating effects that can enhance creativity, focus, and mood. Hybrid strains combine traits from both indica and sativa plants offering a wider range of effects based on their genetic composition.[22]

Beyond these classifications, each strain has a chemical makeup, primarily determined by its levels of cannabinoids and terpenes. Cannabinoids like THC and CBD play a role in producing therapeutic effects in the plant. Terpenes contribute to the strain's scent, taste profile, and potential synergies with cannabinoids. It's crucial for bankers to understand the details of these profiles when they assess the quality and market potential of a grower's products.[23]

By exploring the world of cannabis strains, bankers can develop an understanding of the variety and complexity within the plant. This knowledge not only enriches their comprehension of the industry, but it also empowers them to make well-informed decisions when evaluating creditworthiness, compliance risks, and potential return on investment. A knowledgeable cannabis banker is better prepared to meet the industry's demands and contribute to its progress and prosperity.

Importance of Genetics and Breeding

In the cannabis world, the importance of genetics and breeding cannot be emphasized enough. This fundamental aspect of growing directly influences the quality, reliability, and profitability of cannabis products. For those in the cannabis banking industry, recognizing the importance of genetics and breeding is essential for evaluating the long-term sustainability and prosperity of cultivation endeavors.[24]

The process of selection and breeding serves as a catalyst for introducing enhanced cannabis strains. By choosing parent plants with traits like high cannabinoid levels, resistance to diseases, or distinct terpene profiles, breeders can produce offspring with improved characteristics. This method results in the development of strains that cater to various consumer preferences, and also plays a vital role in enhancing crop yield, strength, and overall product quality.[25]

Investing in genetics and breeding programs is a move for cannabis enterprises that can lead to substantial rewards. An established breeding program can create strains that set a company apart from its rivals, boost brand recognition, and command premium prices in the market. Furthermore, superior plants can cause yields with lower production costs and therefore increased profitability. When evaluating a cultivator's creditworthiness, cannabis financiers should carefully consider their investment in genetics and breeding programs.[26]

A strong breeding initiative showcases a dedication to excellence, creativity, and lasting viability. It indicates that the grower is not only just dependent on strains but is also proactively enhancing their offerings and adjusting to changing market needs and consumer preferences. Recognizing the significance of genetics and breeding allows financiers to make informed choices that bolster the advancement of top-notch cannabis goods and promote the expansion and resilience of the sector.

CULTIVATION AND GROWING TECHNIQUES

The heart of the cannabis industry revolves around the cultivation process, where a blend of science, art, and nature comes together to create the sought-after flowers and extracts of the plant. For professionals in the cannabis sector, grasping the complexities of cultivation and the various growing methods used by growers is key to assessing risk, evaluating investment opportunities, and designing solutions tailored to meet the unique requirements of this industry. This section delves into cannabis cultivation, exploring techniques and factors impacting crop yield and quality, and financial considerations for cultivators and their banking partners.

From farming to state-of-the-art indoor hydroponics setups, the cannabis industry embraces a diverse range of cultivation practices, each with its own strengths and limitations. Understanding these approaches offers insights into a grower's operational capabilities and efficiency, and also highlights potential risks and obstacles they might encounter. Elements like climate conditions, energy usage, pest management strategies, and environmental sustainability all significantly influence the success of a cultivation venture and consequently can impact its viability. By reviewing how a farmer conducts their operations, their skills, and their risk management abilities, financial institutions can evaluate the prospects of the farm and its potential for expansion and long-term viability. This understanding also helps banks create customized solutions that meet the requirements of farmers, fostering a collaborative partnership that promotes the sustainable growth of the cannabis industry. In this section, we will delve into farming techniques, analyze their impacts, and offer perspectives on the factors affecting the effectiveness of cannabis farming endeavors.

Indoor vs. Outdoor Cultivation

Growers and investors must think about the choice between indoor and outdoor cultivation methods. Each approach has its advantages and challenges that can affect the success of a cannabis business. It's essential for those involved in banking to understand these distinctions when evaluating the risks and potential returns of cultivation operations.

Indoor cultivation offers more control, allowing growers to adjust factors like light, temperature, humidity, and CO_2 levels for consistent high-quality yields. Indoor facilities are less prone to pests and diseases, reducing crop losses and enhancing productivity. However, the need for technology comes with costs, and initial investments in infrastructure such as lighting, HVAC systems, and automation technologies can be substantial. Operational expenses like energy consumption also tend to be higher in indoor settings.[27]

On the other side, outdoor cultivation takes advantage of sunlight and outdoor conditions to lower operational expenses significantly. The appeal of outdoor farming lies in its ability to scale operations. Yet, success in outdoor farming heavily relies on factors like location; changes in seasons, unpredictable weather patterns, and natural disasters can all jeopardize crop health and yield inconsistency. Outdoor farms are also more prone to pest infestations and diseases, leading to losses and the need for enhanced pest control measures, which can be costly.[28]

Choosing between outdoor and indoor farming has implications on financial forecasts and risk evaluations. While indoor farming requires investment, it offers a more stable yield that aids in financial planning and loan management. Consistently producing high-quality cannabis indoors can also fetch premium prices in the market, potentially boosting profit margins. On the other hand, outdoor farming may demand lower upfront costs and lower operational expenses, making it an attractive option for businesses aiming for rapid expansion. However, the inherent uncertainties of environmental dynamics should be carefully factored into projections and risk assessments.[29]

Ultimately deciding whether to fund an outdoor or indoor farming venture should depend on an evaluation of the business model, location specifics, and market objectives. Bankers in the cannabis industry must assess the requirements and capacities of cultivation businesses, consider their ability to handle challenges, and secure funding for developing infrastructure and potential expansion down the road. By grasping the intricacies of both indoor and outdoor cultivation, bankers can make informed choices that aid in the progress and sustainability of their clients in the cannabis sector.

Sustainable and Organic Practices

Sustainability and organic methods are becoming more popular in the cannabis industry as consumers seek eco-friendly products, and regulations incorporate sustainability standards. For those in the cannabis banking sector, understanding these practices is key to assessing the viability and market position of cultivation businesses in the long term. Embracing organic approaches not only lessens environmental impact, but also boosts brand credibility and potentially allows for higher pricing in the market.[30]

In cultivation, sustainable practices cover a range of strategies aimed at reducing harm. These include water use through drip irrigation systems, collecting rainwater, and recycling wastewater. Energy conservation is also vital with many growers turning to renewable energy sources like wind power to lessen their reliance on other fuels. Employing pest management methods that do not use chemical pesticides is another aspect of sustainable practices that benefits both the environment and business by cutting costs through decreased resource consumption and improved efficiency.[31]

Organic cannabis farming involves utilizing fertilizers such as compost, manure, and bone meal to enrich the soil and support plant growth. Soil health plays a crucial role in farming, where techniques like crop rotation, cover cropping, and using beneficial microorganisms help sustain soil fertility and structure. These approaches enhance plant resilience and product quality, making organic cannabis highly desirable in the market. For financiers, investing in operations that follow organic standards can be a smart choice due to the rising consumer desire for organic goods.[32]

Supporting cannabis businesses that prioritize organic practices can bring a variety of financial benefits. These enterprises are better equipped to comply with changing regulations and consumer preferences leaning toward sustainability. Adopting organic practices can lead to cost savings that enhance profitability while reducing risks. By backing these companies, financial institutions involved in cannabis can help uphold the industry's sustainability goals and adhere to the growing emphasis on environmental, social, and governance (ESG) principles in finance.

Harvesting and Curing Processes

The process of curing is a stage in the production of cannabis, which plays a vital role in determining the quality, potency, and market worth of the final product. For individuals involved in cannabis banking, understanding the nuances of curing is crucial for assessing the effectiveness and product standards of cultivation businesses. Effective curing enhances the consumer experience by enriching flavor and aroma, and also ensures that the cannabis retains its strength and purity, thus upholding its value in a competitive market.[33]

Curing entails carefully drying harvested cannabis flower in a controlled setting to gradually reduce moisture content. This procedure typically occurs in a room with regulated temperature and humidity levels usually maintained at around 60–70 °F with humidity levels between 55% and 65%. The objective is to prevent drying that could lead to degradation of cannabinoids and terpenes – compounds for the plant's therapeutic properties and unique flavors.[34]

Throughout the curing phase it is essential to monitor and adjust factors such as adequate ventilation, which plays a role in preventing mold growth or mildew formation, and thus could jeopardize the crop's integrity and pose health hazards to consumers. Regularly checking and gently handling the cannabis buds is crucial for ensuring adequate drying and preventing contamination. This level of care and attention can be demanding in terms of effort and time, impacting expenses and production schedules. Nonetheless, investing in curing methods results in higher-quality cannabis that can command premium prices in the market.[35]

For those involved in the cannabis industry, the curing process presents both risks and opportunities. Cured cannabis can lead to product wastage, decreased potency, and compromised safety standards, impacting a company's public image and financial health. On the other hand, companies excelling in curing can produce products that set them apart from competitors and build increased demand. Therefore, evaluating a company's curing procedures, facilities, and quality control measures is crucial for cannabis professionals conducting diligence. Companies with effective curing processes are likely to deliver high quality products that enhance consumer satisfaction and drive loyalty.[36]

There are advancements in curing technology and techniques that offer avenues for innovation and efficiency. Products such as automated curing systems, advanced humidity control devices, and real-time monitoring technologies can improve the curing process. For bankers, having a grasp of these advancements and how they are integrated into a company's operations can offer valuable insights into that company's dedication to excellence and its potential for growth.[37]

To sum up, the curing process plays an important role in production, directly impacting product quality and market appeal. For financiers, having in-depth knowledge of curing methods and the ability to evaluate a company's curing practices are essential for making informed investment choices. By focusing on companies that prioritize and excel in curing processes, bankers can back operations that are well equipped to deliver top-notch cannabis products, ensuring stability and competitive edge in the expanding cannabis industry.

PROCESSING AND EXTRACTION

Methods of Processing Cannabis

The phase beyond growing cannabis plants – processing and extraction – is crucial for the industry, directly impacting product variety and revenue streams. This complex process involves turning raw cannabis flower into a variety of products like concentrates, edibles, topicals and more. Understanding the implications of processing and extraction is essential for cannabis bankers to assess their client's business models and risk profiles accurately.

Setting up processing and extraction facilities requires investments in equipment, technology, and skilled labor. These facilities must adhere to regulations concerning safety protocols, environmental standards, and quality control measures. Consequently, processors and extractors often require financial support for equipment purchases, working capital loans, and real estate loans for expanding their facilities.[38]

The processing and extraction area plays a role in the cannabis supply chain by creating high-value products that fetch higher prices than raw flower. By diversifying cannabis forms, processors cater to consumer preferences, broadening market reach and revenue opportunities in the industry. However, there are challenges such as regulations, fluctuating input costs, changing consumer needs, values, and preferences.[39]

Cannabis bankers must consider these obstacles when assessing the well-being and growth prospects of processing and extraction companies. Furthermore, the process of extraction itself is intricate and often expensive. Various methods, like CO_2 extraction, hydrocarbon extraction, and ethanol extraction, come with their pros and cons in terms of effectiveness, purity, and cost. The selection of an extraction method can greatly influence the caliber and worth of the end product, impacting a company's profitability, sustainability, and competitive edge in the market. For bankers, having a grasp of the extraction techniques and their financial impacts is vital for evaluating the operational efficiency and product standards of potential banking clients.

Extraction Techniques and Their Applications

The process of extraction is where the real magic happens in transforming raw cannabis flower into a variety of products. There are a multitude of methods, each with its own pros and cons, allowing for the production of a range of products tailored to specific consumer preferences. For someone working in the cannabis industry, having a grasp of these methods is crucial for assessing the capabilities and financial aspects of processors and extractors.[40]

Using solvents like ethanol and hydrocarbons for extraction is known for its efficiency and flexibility. These methods involve using solvents to dissolve cannabinoids and terpenes from the plant material, resulting in products such as oils, waxes, and shatter. Solventless extraction techniques like rosin pressing and ice water extraction focus on purity without using harmful chemicals. Rosin pressing entails applying heat and pressure to extract a resin in cannabinoids and terpenes. Ice water extraction separates trichomes from plant material through agitation and filtration. These approaches yield top-notch concentrates like rosin and bubble hash that are often preferred by cannabis enthusiasts for their taste and purity.[41]

Selecting the extraction method holds importance for cannabis companies as it influences the quality of products, expenses incurred in production, and adherence to regulations. Some enterprises might opt for a combination of extraction methods to offer a wider range of products and meet varying consumer demands. For professionals involved in cannabis banking, grasping the intricacies of these methods and their respective expenses and the types of products they generate can offer perspectives on a company's approach and financial sustainability.

Quality Control (QC) and Testing Standards

In the cannabis industry, quality control and testing standards are paramount for ensuring consumer safety, product consistency, and regulatory compliance. For cannabis bankers, understanding these standards is crucial for evaluating the risk profile and operational integrity of processors and extractors. Robust QC and testing protocols safeguard consumers and protect a company's reputation and financial stability.[42]

Quality control begins at the cultivation stage, where meticulous attention is paid to growing conditions, nutrient management, and pest control. However, it extends far beyond cultivation, encompassing the entire processing and extraction workflow. This includes stringent sanitation practices, equipment calibration, and meticulous documentation of every step in the production process. By adhering to rigorous QC standards, businesses can minimize the risk of contamination, ensure product consistency, and maintain compliance with state and federal regulations.[43]

Testing is a critical component of quality control in the cannabis industry. State-licensed laboratories play a vital role in analyzing cannabis products for potency, purity, and the presence of contaminants such as pesticides, heavy metals, residual solvents, and microbial impurities. These tests ensure that products meet regulatory safety standards and provide accurate information to consumers. For cannabis bankers, reviewing a company's testing protocols and lab results can offer valuable insights into their commitment to quality and compliance.[44]

By understanding the importance of quality control and testing standards, cannabis bankers can make informed banking decisions and support businesses that prioritize consumer safety and product integrity at every step in the seed-to-sale supply chain. Additionally, bankers can play a role in advocating for industry-wide adoption of best practices and encouraging businesses to exceed minimum regulatory requirements. This collaborative approach can help build consumer trust, strengthen the industry's reputation, and ultimately contribute to the long-term success and sustainability of the cannabis market.

MANUFACTURING AND PRODUCT DEVELOPMENT

Creating Edibles, Topicals, and Concentrates

In the world of cannabis manufacturing and product development, there is a lot of room for creativity and innovation. It's a space where raw cannabis is transformed into an assortment of products, each offering its own unique qualities and effects. For those in the cannabis industry, having a grasp of this process is essential for evaluating a business's potential, market reach, and financial feasibility.

Crafting edibles is like an art form and typically involves infusing fats or oils with cannabinoids, which are then used in a creative medley of food and drink items. The options are varied, from brownies and gummies to chocolates and infused beverages. Each type of edible has its onset time and effects, catering to a range of consumer preferences. Understanding the details of production can assist professionals in assessing a company's manufacturing capabilities and product uniqueness.[45]

Topicals offer a way to experience the benefits of cannabis without any psychoactive effects. These products are applied directly onto the skin and are often used for pain relief, reducing inflammation, or addressing skin issues. Developing topicals involves infusing cannabinoids into creams, balms, ointments, and even bath products. Having insights into the formulation and production techniques for topicals can give banking experts an important understanding of a company's products and its potential in markets.[46]

Concentrates are known for their potency, providing doses of cannabinoids and terpenes in forms like shatter, wax, and live resin. These items are usually made using extraction methods involving solvents or solventless processes that require specific tools and expertise. The concentrate market is highly profitable, often commanding premium prices and attracting cannabis enthusiasts, making it an important sector for financial institutions to comprehend. Evaluating a company's extraction methods and quality control protocols can assist financiers in gauging their production capabilities and product consistency.[47]

Safety and Compliance in Product Development

In terms of production and creating new products, ensuring safety and following regulations are essential priorities. For banking professionals in the cannabis industry, understanding the rules and quality control measures that oversee this sector is crucial.

Safety measures start with the cultivation of cannabis plants. It's vital to grow them in controlled environments, free from substances like pesticides, heavy metals, and mold. During the manufacturing process, maintaining cleanliness standards is necessary to prevent contamination and uphold product quality.[48]

Compliance doesn't stop at production; it extends throughout every stage. Cannabis items must undergo testing at accredited labs to confirm their potency, purity, and safety levels. These tests ensure that products meet requirements for content, terpene profiles and are free from harmful impurities. Manufacturers must follow rules on labeling and packaging to provide details on ingredients, dosage instructions, and potential side effects.[49]

Conducting diligence assessments on companies' safety practices is a vital part of the cannabis banker's role in assessing risk and ensuring compliance. This involves reviewing operating procedures, quality assurance records, and laboratory test results. Ensuring safety and following rules not only reduces risks, but also shows how much a company cares about customers' health, and how they can work within the heavily regulated cannabis industry. When backing companies that focus on safety and rules, bankers can help build a lasting industry that gains approval from both customers and regulators.

Packaging and Labeling Requirements

The way cannabis products are packaged and labeled extends beyond aesthetics, as it involves adhering to regulations to ensure consumer safety and establish a brand identity. Packaging requirements vary depending on the state location, with a focus on preventing consumption by children, deterring tampering, and providing customers with accurate information. Child-resistant packaging is essential and typically involves containers that can be resealed with locks or have delayed openings. Packaging features like seals or shrink wraps are also necessary to indicate if a product has been tampered with. In some individual states, specific packaging for edibles is mandated to make them less appealing to children.[50]

Labeling standards are equally stringent, requiring certain information to be included on cannabis products. This encompasses details such as product name, weight, THC and CBD levels (cannabinoid content), dosage instructions, warnings, and a symbol denoting the presence of cannabis. Some states may also stipulate batch numbers, expiration dates, and details about the manufacturer or distributor. Accurate labeling is crucial not only for compliance, but also for building consumer trust and facilitating informed decision-making, helping build the stability of the industry.[51]

A critical aspect of due diligence for cannabis bankers is evaluating how a company packages and identifies its products. Ensuring compliance with regulations, verifying childproof packaging and tamper evidence, and confirming the presence of information on labels are important steps. This in turn enhances consumer confidence and promotes long-term growth.

DISTRIBUTION AND SUPPLY CHAIN MANAGEMENT

Cannabis Supply Chain Overview

The cannabis industry's supply chain is a network that covers every aspect of the product's path, from growth to use. For professionals in the cannabis banking industry, having an understanding of the supply chain is essential for assessing operational efficiency, risk management, and financial health of companies in this field.

It all starts with cultivation, where licensed growers carefully tend to cannabis plants in controlled settings. After harvesting, the plants go through processing where they are dried, trimmed, and cured to improve their quality and potency. Next comes manufacturing, where the processed cannabis is turned into products like flower, edibles, concentrates, and topicals. Testing labs play a key role here by ensuring that products meet quality and safety standards before entering the distribution chain.[52]

Distribution's role in the supply chain consists of handling the transportation of cannabis products from manufacturers to retailers. This stage requires coordination and compliance with regulations to ensure that products are monitored throughout their journey. Retailers like dispensaries and delivery services act as the touchpoint for consumers by offering them a range of cannabis products.[53]

Throughout the supply chain there are players like growers, processors, manufacturers, labs for testing, distributors, sellers, and regulators. Each of them has a role in ensuring that cannabis products are made, distributed, and used safely and responsibly. It's important for cannabis bankers to understand what each stakeholder does to evaluate the health and risks of businesses in every step from seed-to-sale. By grasping how the cannabis supply chain operates intricately, bankers can make informed lending choices, manage risks effectively, and support the growth of this vibrant industry.[54]

Logistics and Transportation Challenges

Logistics and transportation within the cannabis industry pose challenges that greatly affect supply chain efficiency and security. Due to the varying regulations of cannabis across states and its federal prohibition, transporting cannabis products involves dealing with safety and logistical obstacles. For professionals working with cannabis-related businesses, understanding these challenges is vital for evaluating risks and financial sustainability.

A key issue in logistics is navigating the state regulations. Each state that has legalized cannabis has its own rules on how to transport these products, including packaging requirements, security measures, and documentation. For instance, some states may demand GPS tracking on all vehicles carrying cannabis, while others might require security procedures or transport documentation. This regulatory complexity not only raises compliance costs but also demands a deep understanding of each state's legal framework to prevent penalties and ensure continuous operations and compliance.[55]

Another significant obstacle is ensuring the safety of cannabis products during transportation. Since cannabis holds value, it becomes a target for theft and diversion. Transporting quantities over distances exposes businesses to considerable security threats. To reduce these risks, companies need to invest in enhanced security measures for their vehicles, like real-time GPS tracking and secure communication systems. Drivers and transportation staff should undergo training to handle threats and ensure the safe delivery of goods. While crucial for safety, these security measures contribute to the complexity and cost of logistics operations.[56]

The federal cannabis ban adds another layer of complexity to transportation logistics. Cannabis businesses are prohibited from transporting products across state lines. This restriction forces them to set up supply chains within each state leading to inefficiencies and increased costs. For instance, a company operating in more than one state must replicate its production, storage, and distribution facilities to comply with laws. The absence of interstate trade not only hampers economies of scale but also raises operational expenses and logistical and safety hurdles.[57]

The challenges of logistics solutions in the cannabis industry compounds these difficulties. Unlike sectors with established logistics networks and service providers, the cannabis industry is still building its infrastructure. Many traditional logistics firms are reluctant to enter this market due to uncertainties and associated risks. Cannabis companies often depend on service providers or build their own logistics capabilities, which can be pricier and less effective compared to using established logistics networks.[58]

Managing the logistics and transportation of cannabis products involves navigating through regulations, ensuring security measures, and overcoming inefficiencies caused by federal restrictions. These hurdles significantly affect the cost structure and operational effectiveness of cannabis companies. For cannabis bankers, understanding these challenges is crucial for assessing risks and opportunities in the cannabis supply chain. By tackling these obstacles, the industry can progress toward establishing a secure distribution system that ultimately promotes the growth and sustainability of cannabis enterprises.

Ensuring Compliance in Distribution

Ensuring that cannabis products follow regulations is crucial for upholding the legality and reliability of the supply chain. The cannabis industry's regulatory environment is intricate, requiring businesses to follow state and local rules. These regulations cover an array of needs like monitoring and reporting security measures and accurate documentation.[59]

A pivotal aspect of compliance in distribution involves establishing tracking and reporting systems. Regulations dictate that every movement of cannabis products be monitored from seed-to-sale, guaranteeing that all transactions are recorded accurately. This transparency helps prevent hijackings and ensures product origins can be traced effectively. As mentioned earlier in the chapter, many states mandate the use of tracking software such as Marijuana Enforcement Tracking Reporting Compliance (Metrc), which offers real-time insights into the whereabouts and status of cannabis products throughout the supply chain.[60]

Implementing security measures is another element in ensuring compliance within cannabis distribution. Regulations usually demand security procedures be used to deter theft and unauthorized access to cannabis products. Physical security measures, like surveillance cameras, alarm systems, and secure storage facilities, along with personnel protocols such as background checks and training for employees handling cannabis products, are crucial for maintaining compliance and safeguarding the integrity of the supply chain in the cannabis industry. In addition, it is important to audit these security measures to ensure they are being followed consistently.[61]

Proper documentation and recordkeeping play an important role in ensuring compliance in the distribution of cannabis. Businesses need to keep records of all transactions, including purchase orders, transport manifests, and delivery receipts. These records should be easily accessible for inspection by authorities and should accurately record the movement and handling of cannabis products. Failure to maintain proper documentation can lead to penalties like fines and license suspension.[62]

Ensuring cannabis products are distributed in compliance with regulations requires dealing with a maze of intricate rules. By setting up systems for tracking and reporting, enforcing security measures, and sticking to detailed documentation procedures, companies can limit risks and reduce penalties linked to noncompliance. For financial professionals dealing with cannabis businesses, having a grasp of these compliance rules is essential for evaluating the feasibility and long-term success of ventures, which ultimately promotes the development and credibility of the industry.

RETAIL AND DISPENSING

Setting up a Cannabis Retail Operation

Starting a cannabis business involves a series of important steps, beginning with acquiring the required licenses and permits. The cannabis industry is tightly regulated, with each state having its own laws and processes for licensing. Aspiring retailers need to work through this framework to obtain a retail license, which typically entails submitting applications that include background checks, business strategies, and financial disclosures. It's crucial to stay updated on the regulations in each state where you operate and adhere to all rules and zoning ordinances.

Choosing the location for your cannabis store becomes a pivotal choice because the location can greatly influence the success of your store by factors such as customer traffic, visibility, and accessibility. Consideration should be given to demographics, competition levels, and proximity to establishments that attract foot traffic. Additionally, complying with zoning laws is essential; many areas have restrictions on how close a cannabis store can be located near schools, parks, or other sensitive sites.[63]

The next step involves planning your store layout to create a functional space for customers. The layout should encourage a movement of customers from entering the store to making purchases ensuring that their shopping experience is pleasant and efficient. Careful positioning of product displays, checkout counters, and customer service areas is essential. A well-designed store layout not only improves the shopping experience but also keeps operations running smoothly. It's crucial to think about the appeal and branding aspects too, as a well-planned store can reinforce brand identity and lead to customer loyalty.[64]

When it comes to staffing a business, hiring competent and friendly employees is key for delivering top-notch customer service and educating clients about the products. Staff training should cover product knowledge, compliance with regulations, customer service etiquette, and security measures. Trained staff can elevate the customer experience, ensure adherence to requirements, and contribute to the overall success of the enterprise.[65]

Effective inventory management is another key element in establishing a successful retail venture. Retailers need supply chains and inventory systems to maintain product availability and handle stock levels efficiently. This involves choosing suppliers, implementing inventory tracking mechanisms, and preparing for fluctuations in product demand. Efficient inventory management aids in keeping products in stock, minimizing waste, and boosting profitability.[66]

Establishing a business requires a sequence of intricate and interconnected tasks, including obtaining permits, choosing a suitable site, organizing the store layout, hiring staff, and handling inventory. Every aspect is essential for the business's prosperity. For financial institutions dealing with cannabis businesses, comprehending these procedures is vital for evaluating the feasibility and risks involved in banking cannabis ventures.

Customer Experience and Point-of-Sale Systems

In the cannabis retail industry, it's crucial to create a top-notch customer experience, especially due to the competitiveness of the sector. Customers come in with various levels of knowledge and expectations about cannabis products. It's important to make their visit welcoming, informative, and efficient. A good customer experience begins as soon as they walk through the door. This includes having knowledgeable staff, a clean store layout, and an overall vibe that makes customers feel at ease and appreciated. By engaging with customers and educating them about the products, you can boost satisfaction levels, build loyalty, and encourage repeat business. For those in banking, recognizing the significance of customer experience can offer valuable insights into the potential success and longevity of a retail operation.[67]

One key tool for enhancing customer experience is the Point-of-Sale (POS) system. A robust POS system handles transactions and integrates functions like inventory management, customer relationship management (CRM), and compliance reporting in cannabis retail settings. Advanced POS systems provide sales data that help retailers understand customer preferences and purchasing habits better. This information can be leveraged to personalize the shopping experience by suggesting products based on previous purchasing habits or informing customers about arrivals that align with their interests.[68]

Another important aspect of POS systems in cannabis retail is their ability to streamline the transaction process. Effective and dependable POS systems help reduce wait times, minimize errors, and ensure a seamless checkout experience. This efficiency is especially critical in stores where fast and accurate service is vital for maintaining customer satisfaction.

Incorporating loyalty programs into POS systems is another important feature for the competitive cannabis market. These programs encourage repeat business by rewarding customers for their purchases. By integrating loyalty programs with POS systems, retailers can track customer purchases automatically, apply rewards, and customize marketing efforts. For instance, a customer who frequently buys a specific type of product might receive promotions or discounts on similar items. This not only enhances customer retention but also boosts spending per visit.[69]

The connection between customer experience and POS systems plays a vital role in the success of retail operations. A good POS system can improve customer satisfaction by offering transactions, useful data analysis, and loyalty programs that are well integrated. When dealing with cannabis businesses, it's crucial for bankers to assess the effectiveness and features of a store's POS system to understand how efficiently they operate and track compliance. By backing retailers who value customer service and employ cutting-edge POS systems, banks can play a role in supporting the expansion and endurance of the retail industry.

Security and Compliance Measures in Retail

Security and compliance are important aspects of running a retail store due to the valuable nature of the products and the complex regulations in place. It is essential for a cannabis dispensary to follow security measures to follow the law and to safeguard against theft, diversion, and other illicit activities.

One key security feature in retail is using surveillance systems. These systems typically consist of high-quality cameras strategically positioned throughout the store covering entryways, exits, sales areas, and storage spaces. Continuous monitoring and recording are vital, as state laws often mandate that retailers retain video footage for a set period of time. These surveillance setups act as both deterrents against unlawful behavior and sources of evidence in case of any security incidents.[70]

Alongside surveillance, physical security measures play a role. This includes entry points, secure storage facilities, and alarm systems. Many cannabis stores hire security personnel to oversee operations and address risks. Secure storage areas equipped with vaults or safes are utilized for storing cannabis products when the shop is closed. To prevent theft and unauthorized access to tightly controlled inventory, it's important for retailers to follow security procedures.[71]

Regulatory Requirements for CRBs

Beyond security, compliance with regulatory requirements involves meticulous recordkeeping and reporting. Cannabis retailers are required to keep records of all transactions, inventory movements, and security incidents. These records are subject to regulatory audits to ensure compliance with local laws. Retailers must adopt inventory tracking systems as mandated by state regulations because these systems ensure that all cannabis products are monitored. These systems also guarantee traceable transactions from seed-to-sale, ensuring transparency and proper compliance.[72]

Employee training plays a role in maintaining security and compliance in retail operations. Staff members must receive training on security protocols, regulatory guidelines, and proper product handling practices. Regular training sessions help keep employees updated on the regulations and industry best practices, enhancing security while promoting a culture of compliance and accountability within the organization.[73]

Strong security and compliance practices are critical to running a retail cannabis dispensary. Cutting-edge surveillance systems, strict physical security measures, thorough recordkeeping, and comprehensive staff training all play roles in safeguarding the business and meeting regulatory requirements. It's vital for bankers to assess these factors to gauge the feasibility and risks involved in financing retail ventures. By backing businesses that prioritize security and compliance, banks can contribute to nurturing an accountable cannabis industry.

CONCLUSION

Bankers looking to provide services to the cannabis industry must have an understanding of its unique regulations, market dynamics, and operational risks and challenges. By developing a deep understanding into the intricacies of this industry, bankers can effectively navigate compliance requirements, anticipate client needs, and foster lasting relationships.

The cannabis market is experiencing undeniable growth, making a significant positive economic impact due to increasing legalization efforts, consumer acceptance, and ongoing technological innovations. To stay competitive and offer compliant solutions, bankers need to stay updated on market trends, legal changes, and technological advancements. The potential for legalization brings both opportunities and uncertainties that require constant attention and adaptability.

For bankers to truly understand the cannabis industry they must go beyond compliance; they must also recognize the challenges that cannabis businesses face. These challenges include managing cash flow, implementing security measures, navigating supply chains, and ensuring consistent product quality. By providing solutions that address these needs, bankers can establish themselves as trusted partners in supporting the growth and success of cannabis companies. Building relationships and earning trust within the cannabis community are critical elements for success.

NOTES

1. "US Cannabis Sales Estimates," *MJBizDaily*. Accessed July 23, 2024. https://mjbizdaily.com/us-cannabis-sales-estimates.
2. "Public Support for Marijuana Legalization," *Gallup*, 2024, https://news.gallup.com/poll/323582/public-support-marijuana-legalization.aspx.
3. "Most Americans Now Live in a Legal Marijuana State and Most Have at Least One Dispensary in the County," Pew Research Center, February 29, 2024, https://www.pewresearch.org/short-reads/2024/02/29/most-americans-now-live-in-a-legal-marijuana-state-and-most-have-at-least-one-dispensary-in-their-county.
4. "US Cannabis Sales Could Total $71b in 2030 Without Federal Legalization," New Frontier Data, 2023, https://newfrontierdata.com/cannabis-insights/u-s-cannabis-sales-could-total-71b-in-2030-without-federal-legalization.
5. "Cannabis and Marijuana," American Medical Association, 2024, https://www.ama-assn.org/topics/cannabis-marijuana.
6. "Beginner's Guide to Investing in Marijuana Stocks and The Booming Cannabis Industry," *Business Insider*, 2024, https://www.businessinsider.com/personal-finance/investing/cannabis-investments.
7. "Marijuana Investors Bet Big on Long Term Growth Over Short Term Earnings as Market Value Rises," *Business Insider*, April 15, 2024, https://markets.businessinsider.com/news/stocks/marijuana-investors-bet-big-on-long-term-growth-over-short-term-earnings-as-market-value-rises-by-39-1033251052.
8. "Market Insights, Cannabis," Statista, March 2024, https://www.statista.com/outlook/hmo/cannabis/united-states.
9. "US Cannabis Sales Estimates," *MJBizDaily*, April 2023, https://mjbizdaily.com/us-cannabis-sales-estimates.
10. "Cannabis (Marijuana) and Cannabinoids: What You Need to Know," U.S. Department of Health and Human Services, https://www.nccih.nih.gov/health/cannabis-marijuana-and-cannabinoids-what-you-need-to-know.
11. Ibid.
12. Ibid. at 9.
13. "Hemp Research Needs Roadmap," U.S. Department of Agriculture, https://www.usda.gov/topics/hemp.
14. "Metrc," Metrc, 2024, www.metrc.com.
15. "BioTrackTHC," BioTrackTHC, 2024, www.biotrack.com.
16. "Cannabis Overview," National Conference of State Legislatures, https://www.ncsl.org/research/civil-and-criminal-justice/marijuana-overview.aspx.
17. "Choosing the Right Cannabis Seeds: A Comprehensive Guide for Growers," FloraFlex, 2024, https://floraflex.com/default/blog/post/choosing-the-right-cannabis-seeds-a-comprehensive-guide-for-growers.

18. Ibid.
19. Ibid.
20. "Beginner's Guide to Marijuana Strains," Healthline, 2024, https://www.healthline.com/health/beginners-guide-to-marijuana-strains.
21. Ibid.
22. Ibid.
23. "Understanding the Importance of Cannabis Genetics in Breeding," FloraFlex, 2024, https://floraflex.com/default/blog/post/understanding-the-importance-of-cannabis-genetics-in-breeding1.
24. Ibid.
25. Ibid.
26. "Indoor vs. Outdoor Grown Cannabis: Does It Make a Difference," Canna Culture Collective, 2024, https://cannaculturecollective.com/indoor-vs-outdoor-grown-cannabis-does-it-make-a-difference/#features-of-outdoor-grown-plants.
27. Ibid.
28. Ibid.
29. "Cannabis and Sustainability: Eco-Friendly Practices in Cannabis Cultivation," FloraFlex, 2024, https://floraflex.com/default/blog/post/cannabis-and-sustainability-eco-friendly-practices-in-cannabis-cultivation.Cannabis and Sustainability: Eco-Friendly Practices in Cannabis Cultivation - Blog
30. Ibid.
31. Ibid.
32. "The Ultimate Guide to Drying and Curing Cannabis for the Best Results," Leafly, 2020, https://www.leafly.com/learn/growing/harvesting-marijuana/drying-curing-cannabis.
33. Ibid.
34. Ibid.
35. Ibid.
36. Ibid.
37. "The Evolution of Ethanol Extraction Methods in Cannabis," *Cannabis Science and Technology*, 2021, https://www.cannabissciencetech.com/view/the-evolution-of-ethanol-extraction-methods-in-cannabis.
38. Ibid.
39. Ibid.
40. Ibid.
41. "Elevating the Green: The Crucial Role of Quality Control and Testing in the Cannabis Industry," *Cannabis Science and Technology*, December 1, 2023, https://www.cannabissciencetech.com/view/elevating-the-green-the-crucial-role-of-quality-control-and-testing-in-the-cannabis-industry.
42. Ibid.
43. Ibid.
44. "How to Make Edibles with Concentrates and Dabs," Leafly, 2024, https://www.leafly.com/learn/consume/edibles/how-to-make-edibles-cannabis-concentrates.
45. "How to Make DIY Cannabis Topicals," Leafly, 2024, https://www.leafly.com/news/strains-products/how-to-make-diy-cannabis-topicals.
46. "Cannabis Glossary: Concentrates," Leafly, 2024, https://www.leafly.com/learn/cannabis-glossary/concentrates.

47. "Regulatory Compliance and Quality Control Testing Solutions in Cannabis & Hemp," PerkinElmer, 2024, https://www.perkinelmer.com/category/regulatory-compliance-and-quality-control-testing-solutions-in-cannabis-hemp.
48. Ibid.
49. "Requirements for Cannabis Product Labeling by U.S. State," Cannabis and Cannabinoid Research, 2021, https://www.ncbi.nlm.nih.gov/pmc/articles/PMC9070747.
50. Ibid.
51. "Cannabis Supply Chain," Indica Online, 2022, https://indicaonline.com/blog/cannabis-supply-chain.
52. Ibid.
53. Ibid.
54. "Cannabis Supply Chain Challenges in the USA: Navigating Complexities in a Rapidly Growing Industry," *Supply Chain News*, 2024, https://www.supplychaintechnews.com/index.php/supply/cannabis-supply-chain-challenges-in-the-usa-navigating-complexities-in-a-rapidly-growing-industry.https://www.supplychaintechnews.com/index.php/supply/cannabis-supply-chain-challenges-in-the-usa-navigating-complexities-in-a-rapidly-growing-industry.
55. Ibid.
56. Ibid.
57. Ibid.
58. Pinsent Masons, "Regulatory Compliance in the Global Supply Chain," Pinsent Masons, September 7, 2020, www.pinsentmasons.com.
59. Ibid.
60. Ibid.
61. Ibid.
62. "How to Open a Dispensary Guide," FlowHub, 2024, https://flowhub.com/how-to-open-dispensary-guide.
63. Ibid.
64. Ibid.
65. Ibid.
66. "Getting Started with Cannabis Point of Sale Systems," Dutchie, 2024, https://business.dutchie.com/papers/guides/getting-started-with-cannabis-point-of-sale-systems.
67. Ibid.
68. Ibid.
69. "The Complete Guide to Dispensary Security," Flowhub, 2020, https://flowhub.com/dispensary-security-guide.
70. Ibid.
71. Ibid.
72. Ibid.
73. Ibid.

CHAPTER FIVE

Risk Management for Cannabis Bankers

INTRODUCTION

Bankers looking to enter the cannabis industry face a set of rules and regulations weighing growing opportunities against considerable risks. A crucial aspect of making this decision involves the board and top executives in determining how much risk the bank is willing to take to achieve its strategic goals. This risk tolerance reflects the level and areas of risk that the bank is willing to take on with cannabis banking, where a deep understanding of regulatory, operational, and reputational risks is essential.

Understanding Risk at the BOD Level

The board of directors plays a major role in defining how much risk exposure the bank is comfortable with when it comes to dealing with the cannabis sector. They need to assess whether engaging in cannabis banking aligns well with the financial institution's objectives. This assessment includes evaluating revenue streams, opportunities for market growth, and how well it fits with the bank's mission and values. The board's oversight ensures that the bank has a risk management framework to address the challenges posed by cannabis banking. This involves examining the regulatory environment, which can differ significantly between state and federal legalities, as well as understanding exactly what complying with laws like the Bank Secrecy Act (BSA) and Anti-Money Laundering (AML) regulations entails.

Leadership executives in positions such as the Chief Executive Officer (CEO), Chief Financial Officer (CFO), and Chief Risk Officer (CRO) play a role in translating the board's risk preferences into practical policies and procedures that stand up to internal and external audits. Their responsibility involves guaranteeing that the bank is equipped with the tools, technology, and skills to effectively handle accounts related to cannabis businesses. This entails establishing due diligence processes, continuous monitoring systems, and robust reporting mechanisms to meet FinCEN guidelines and other regulatory standards. Additionally, it is essential for the leadership team to promote a culture of compliance across the organization by ensuring that all staff members receive training to identify and manage risks associated with cannabis banking.

Both the board of directors and key executives need to assess the risks to their reputation posed by engaging in cannabis banking activities. In states where cannabis is legal, there may be concerns from the public and stakeholders regarding the bank's participation in this industry. Open communication and interaction with stakeholders – including shareholders, clients, and community organizations – are crucial for shaping perceptions and establishing and maintaining trust. Through strategic risk assessment and robust risk management practices, both the board of directors and the C-Suite can position the bank to leverage growth opportunities in the cannabis industry while upholding important compliance standards and safeguarding its reputation.

The BOD and C-Suite should ask themselves some questions before considering banking cannabis:

1. Do we understand each area of risk in banking cannabis (compliance, operational, reputational, and legal)?
2. What part (or all) of the seed-to-sale supply chain will our institution focus on?
3. Do we have or can we acquire the necessary compliance expertise to understand and manage the unique aspects of the cannabis business?
4. How well do we understand the compliance that CRBs face, like state licensing and regulatory requirements of cannabis businesses, and are we prepared to follow them?

For any financial institution looking to bank cannabis, these questions must be considered at the senior executive/board level, and the answers must be used to create the bank's risk appetite for moving forward with cannabis banking.

Establishing Risk Policies and Procedures

Risk assessment in the cannabis industry requires a more nuanced approach compared to traditional industries. Banks must consider not only the legal implications of serving businesses associated with a substance that is federally illegal but also the potential for these businesses to be targets for financial crimes. Effective risk assessment for cannabis clients involves understanding the specific business activities, analyzing transaction patterns, and constantly monitoring for any changes in the business's risk profile. This heightened level of scrutiny ensures that banks can detect and act on potential risks promptly, maintaining the integrity of their operations and complying with regulatory expectations.

Risk Assessment Process

Policies and procedures serve as the foundation for how a bank conducts its business, including its interactions with cannabis-related businesses (CRBs). During a cannabis banking audit, the auditors will thoroughly examine the bank's policies, procedures, and internal controls pertaining to CRB relationships to ensure that they are comprehensive, well defined, and effectively implemented. The auditors will start with looking at the bank's risk assessment process specific to its CRB relationships, which involves evaluating how the bank identifies, measures, and manages the risk associated with providing banking services to CRBs.

The risk assessment should consider various factors, including:

- Regulatory compliance risks
- Reputational risks
- Operational risks
- Legal risks

Auditors will review the methodology used to assess these risks and determine the appropriate level of due diligence and monitoring required for your CRB customers. It's critical to understand that the banks aren't just assessing these risks, but maintaining an audit trail of the risk assessment, whether that's been done online or on paper.

Due Diligence Procedures

The bank's auditor is going to scrutinize the bank's due diligence procedures for onboarding your CRB customers. What does this include? It includes examining the documentation and information collected from CRB customers during the account opening process to verify their identities, understand the nature of their business activities, and assess their risk profile.

Due diligence procedures during account opening involve:

- Reviewing business license permits
- Financial statements
- Ownership structures
- Operating agreement
- Compliance with state and local regulations

Also, auditors will assess the adequacy and consistency of the bank's due diligence practice in mitigating the risks associated with the CRB relationships, which are established at the board level. The auditor will ensure that the financial institution is within the parameters of its risk assessment and risk appetite. Ongoing monitoring is critical, and as it relates to the audit function, the auditors will evaluate the bank's procedures for ongoing monitoring of CRB accounts. This involves reviewing how the bank monitors CRB transactions and activities to detect those suspicious or potentially illicit behaviors and filing suspicious activity reports (SARs) accordingly. Ongoing monitoring may include reviewing transactional activity, conducting periodic reviews of customer information, and assessing changes in CRB customers' business operations or regulatory status. The auditor will assess the effectiveness of the bank's monitoring systems and processes in identifying and addressing potential risks associated with CRB accounts in a timely manner.[1]

INTERNAL CONTROLS AND AUDITS

At the heart of every audit, especially in the cannabis industry, is regulatory compliance. The multifaceted legal environment of cannabis banking elevates the importance of audits for financial institutions dealing with CRBs. This is largely due to the intricate weave of regulations spanning federal, state, and local levels. Auditors and examiners bear the critical responsibility of thoroughly assessing and ensuring that a bank's operations align with the comprehensive spectrum of regulatory requirements.

Federal Regulations

In terms of federal regulations, auditors are responsible for scrutinizing the bank's compliance with the federal regulations – specifically the Cole Memo, which lays out the guidelines of the audit and responsibilities for any institution that is banking CRBs, including any business in seed-to-sale, encompassing Tiers 1, 2, and 3, which is covered in detail in Chapter 1. The primary framework for cannabis banking at the federal level includes FinCEN, the Financial Crimes Enforcement Network guidance issued in 2014 around the Cole Memo, which outlines the expectations for banks, credit unions, and any financial institution to provide products and services to CRBs. The role of the auditor and the examiner in cannabis banking is to assess whether the bank has implemented and followed the FinCEN guidance appropriately.[2]

Next, the BSA imposes requirements on financial institutions with the intention of combating money laundering, terrorist financing, human trafficking, etc. In terms of cannabis banking, auditors are responsible for evaluating the bank's compliance with the BSA provisions, such as the implementation of effective AML programs, conducting Customer Due Diligence (CDD) and Enhanced Due Diligence (EDD), and then filing currency transaction reports (CTRs) on those large cash transactions involving CRB customers.[3]

State and Local Regulations

When dealing with state and local regulations, there's a patchwork quilt of regulations currently across the United States that varies greatly depending on where you are located geographically, and auditors are responsible for examining the bank's compliance with the state and local regulations that govern CRB banking. The regulations obviously vary significantly from one jurisdiction to another, from state to state, and often conflict with states that border a state that hasn't fully legalized cannabis. For example, Wisconsin has not legalized medical or recreational cannabis, but is bordered by Illinois, Minnesota, and Michigan – all of which have legalized the recreational use of cannabis. It's important that auditors and examiners not just focus on the state in which they are based, but that they're also understanding and taking into consideration bordering states that might also have an impact on transactional or operational activities of local bank branches. Auditors must ensure that the bank is aware of and is compliant with all the relevant state and local laws, including the licensing requirements for CRBs.

The latest federal regulation the industry received was issued more than 10 years ago with the Cole Memo, so it's more likely that state and local regulations are the ones that change without you noticing. Ensuring that you are on your state's monitor list for getting newsletters and updates for any regulatory changes that might take place and making changes to the financial institution's policies to comply, is paramount for staying aware of changing regulations.

Internal Controls

The auditor is going to review the bank's internal controls governing its CRB relationships to ensure that they are robust and effective in mitigating those risks.

Internal controls may include:

- Segregation of duties
- Authorization procedures
- Transaction limits
- Reconciliation processes specific to CRB accounts

Is your bank following those processes? Auditors will assess the design and implementation of these internal controls for effectiveness to prevent and to detect both internal and external fraud.

COMPLIANCE WITH POLICIES AND PROCEDURES

We'll explore the practical application of policies and procedures, specifically how they're implemented and overseen when engaging with actual CRBs. It's clear that Tier 1 CRBs present the highest risk, yet comprehensive due diligence is essential across all tiers of CRBs. In the audit process, it's vital for the bank to grasp each facet of the CDD program that will be under scrutiny. The risk assessment of the bank serves as the blueprint and foundation upon which all due diligence is built, guiding the identification and grading of risk factors associated with each CRB customer. This initial step informs the depth of CDD measures and the rigor of ongoing monitoring to ensure that the bank remains in compliance while effectively managing its risk exposure.[4]

Finally, it's crucial to understand the Know Your Customer (KYC) requirements that originated from the PATRIOT Act in the 2000s. These regulations shed light on the origins and types of funds entering your bank through various businesses. They require institutions to confirm their customers' identities, grasp their business nature, and effectively manage risks related to crimes. Auditors play a role in assessing the bank's KYC processes to ensure they are comprehensive and suitable for both individual customers and businesses served by the bank. This involves confirming customer identities, understanding their involvement in cannabis-related activities, and evaluating risk levels to determine due diligence measures while staying within the institution's risk tolerance limits. The bank's board of directors and executive team set the level of risk for the institution with auditors, ensuring that risk assessments align with these standards.[5]

Regarding Policies and Procedures

The risk assessment process we've covered so far outlines how internal structures support auditing procedures and how well the bank's compliance program complies with its policies, alongside federal, state, and local regulations. Now let's delve into how we put this into practice and oversee it in real-world scenarios with cannabis businesses. During the audit, the bank must grasp the elements of your CDD program that the auditor will review. The bank's risk assessment serves as the groundwork and guiding principle for this process. Auditors will review the bank's methodology and documentation for assessing the risk posed by CRBs.

Based on factors such as business activities, typical questions to ask for CDD compliance would be:

- What type of business are they doing? (what part of seed-to-sale are they?)
- Where are they located? (one state? multiple states?)
- What is the ownership structure? (BSA, beneficial ownership, etc.)

The overall financial stability of the business will be assessed in this stage of the process including defining high risk, moderate risk or low risk based on the institution's individual risk assessment. The financial institution will want to thoroughly understand the operations of each CRB they decide to bank. Some financial institutions might choose to only bank Tier 2 or 3 CRBs at first, before deciding to take on (or not!) Tier 1. Your internal audit might uncover that a Tier 2 is now getting into some planting touching businesses and needs to be reclassified as Tier 1. Even if the customer profile risk assessment is low, if that's outside the parameters that the bank's senior leadership has set up for establishing customer risk, the auditor needs to note that as an exception.[6]

The risk assessment must be thorough and systemic, enabling the bank to categorize its customers into those risk tiers, and then apply appropriate due diligence in its policies and procedures. During the account opening process, it's the bank's responsibility to examine the documentation collected from those customers during the onboarding process and account opening to verify identities, understand the nature of their business operations, and be able to determine if the risk assessment matches the documentation that the institution has on hand. This includes reviewing the documentation for items such as the appropriate business licenses, the permits, local and state articles of incorporation, and tax documentation, which are all a part of the account opening process. The auditors must assess the adequacy and accuracy of the customer information collected to ensure compliance with all regulatory requirements, and to determine the effective risk assessment profile is set.

Ongoing Monitoring

The auditor's role is to verify that SARs are identified and filed correctly, especially when transactions deviate from expected patterns. Consider a dispensary – a Tier 1 CRB – that typically deposits $100,000 weekly. If deposits unexpectedly surge to $1 million a week after six months, this is a substantial deviation that merits attention. The bank must vigilantly track such anomalies. Even if regular reporting is in place, a transaction spike well beyond average levels necessitates further investigation. The bank's procedures for continuous monitoring will be assessed to ensure they are effective in detecting patterns of suspicious activity that could suggest illegal actions. While this doesn't automatically imply wrongdoing, the high-risk nature of CRBs demands that all irregularities are taken seriously. This scrutiny involves examining both past and present account data and other pertinent information to spot potential warning signs. These can include disproportionately large cash deposits, changes in the frequency of transactions, irregular payment patterns, or activities that don't align with the business's declared operations. The bank must maintain comprehensive monitoring systems to identify, scrutinize, and act on these red flags, which typically includes filing SARs with regulatory bodies when warranted.[7]

CUSTOMER DUE DILIGENCE (CDD) AND ENHANCED DUE DILIGENCE (EDD)

Customer Risk Assessments

In cases where CRB customers are deemed to pose a higher risk of money laundering, especially Tier 1, the bank should always be monitoring for illicit activities spelled out in the Cole Memo where the money sources are not clear and transparent. The auditor's responsibility is to assess the bank's procedures for conducting the EDD on these higher risk activities, which can involve additional verification checks, more detailed documentation, etc. The financial institution should have clear criteria for determining when EDD is necessary and documented procedures for implementing these measures accordingly.

Finally, in terms of compliance with regulatory requirements, the auditor must verify whether the bank's process for CRB customers, with all applicable local, state, and federal regulatory requirements, including those outlined by FinCEN and the state authorities, are being followed. This includes ensuring that the bank follows the best practices within the industry and updates its CDD procedures in response to regulatory changes, and then maintains accurate records of CDD activities for audit and regulatory reporting purposes. Overall, the audit of CDD for CRB customers is essential for ensuring that the institution effectively identifies, assesses, and manages the risks associated with serving these clients. Auditors play a critical role in evaluating the adequacy and compliance of the bank's practices, helping to strengthen the institution's risk management framework to protect against financial crime and violations.[8]

TRANSACTION MONITORING

Transaction Monitoring Systems

It's time to discuss a crucial impact of risk management for financial institutions serving CRBs: transaction monitoring. Because CRBs operate in an industry with inherent risks of financial crime due to high levels of cash and lots of compliance hurdles, during a cannabis banking audit, auditors will thoroughly assess the bank's transaction monitoring systems to ensure they are robust, effective, and compliant with regulatory requirements.

Next, let's focus on transaction monitoring systems, which are in place to evaluate the capacity to identify and flag potentially suspicious activity related to the CRB accounts. This activity includes examining the technology infrastructure, software solutions, and analytical tools used by the bank to monitor the transaction data from the CRB accounts in real time, or near real time. The transaction monitoring system should be sophisticated enough to handle the volume and complexity of these transactions, and thus should be regularly updated to reflect changes in regulations and emerging financial crime trends. The auditor is going to assess the effectiveness of your transaction monitoring rules in the scenarios employed by the bank to detect suspicious activity related to a CRB account. This involves reviewing the criteria used to trigger the alerts for potentially suspicious transactions, such as unusual transaction amounts, frequencies, or patterns that deviate from typical account behavior.

Transaction Monitoring Rules and Scenarios

The bank should have a comprehensive set of transaction monitoring rules tailored to the unique risks of the CRB customers, including those related to:

- Cash-intensive activities
- Large cash transactions
- Structuring layering
- Other money laundering techniques commonly observed in the cannabis industry

Auditors are going to evaluate the thresholds and parameters set by the bank for triggering these alerts within the transaction monitoring system. This includes reviewing the criteria used to determine when a transaction exceeds a predefined threshold or meet certain risk parameters that warrant further investigation. Thresholds may vary based on factors such as transaction amounts, customer profiles, transaction types, and geographic locations. The bank should periodically review and adjust these thresholds to ensure they remain effective in capturing suspicious activity without generating an excessive number of false positives.[9]

Alert Generation and Escalation

Next, auditors are going to assess the bank's processes for generating alerts within the transaction monitoring system, and the escalation process for further review and investigation. This includes evaluating the timeliness and accuracy of alert generation, the completeness of alert documentation, and the procedures followed by bank personnel for reviewing and disposition alerts. The bank should have documented protocols for investigating alerts, including identifying the root cause of the alert, gathering additional information as needed, and then determining whether to file a SAR.

Integration with Compliance Processes

Finally, full integration with the compliance process will be examined. The auditors will verify whether the transaction monitoring system is effectively integrated with the bank's broader compliance processes, including KYC procedures, CDD and EDD activities, and SAR reporting. This process includes assessing the flow of information between different systems and departments within the bank to ensure that transaction monitoring alerts are promptly addressed and resolved in accordance with regulatory requirements, the bank's risk assessment, and internal policies. Overall, the auditing of transaction monitoring for CRB accounts is essential for ensuring that financial institutions can effectively detect and mitigate the risks of financial crime associated with serving clients in the cannabis industry in accordance with the FinCEN guidance. Auditors play a critical role in evaluating the adequacy, effectiveness, and compliance of the bank's transaction monitoring systems and processes, which will help strengthen the institution's risk management framework and protect against illicit financial activities.[10]

REPORTING AND FILING

The implementation of SARs shifted some burden of identifying potential illicit activity from individual front-line employees to a more collective effort across the bank. Typically, the compliance department within a bank manages the SAR identification and filing process. Nevertheless, it remains crucial for front-line staff to be vigilant and report any unusual or suspicious behavior as a part of their regular responsibilities.

Suspicious Activity Reports (SARs)

Auditors play a key role in evaluating the bank's protocols for pinpointing and investigating activities that may prompt, or have led to, the filing of a SAR, particularly regarding CRB accounts. The auditor's examination includes reviewing whether SARs were appropriately filed with the FinCEN and other regulators. This review also scrutinizes the thoroughness and precision of the SARs, ensuring that all fields are filled out completely and accurately reflect the suspicious transactions flagged. They must verify that the SAR contains all necessary details, and that the narrative clearly describes the suspicious nature of the activity.[11]

Auditors act as a critical checkpoint to confirm the accuracy of these filings before they are submitted to federal authorities. Incorrect information can expose the bank not only to federal scrutiny but also to potential fines for noncompliance and issues of timeliness. Auditors must assess whether SARs are filed within the 30-day window and CTRs within 15 days. Ensuring that filings are not only timely but also prioritized correctly is an essential part of an auditor's responsibilities. They must review and verify that the bank has effective procedures in place for escalating and prioritizing these reports to meet deadlines and address any reporting delays.

Risk Assessment in AML

Risk assessment plays a role in an AML program tailored for cannabis banking. This involves conducting an analysis to identify and assess the risks linked to money laundering and other financial crimes to the cannabis industry. The unique position of cannabis, as a product legalized in state jurisdictions but illegal under federal law, adds complexity to the banking sector. This dual regulatory environment calls for vigilance in risk assessments by bankers considering legal disparities and the increased potential for illicit activities.

Identifying AML risks within cannabis banking begins with understanding the behaviors of CRBs. This includes examining their cash handling procedures, client base, supply chain, and operational locations. Due to the industry's reliance on cash transactions, the risk of money laundering is inherently elevated. Cannabis bankers must also factor in the status of the product in their operating states and monitor any regulatory changes that could impact their exposure to risks. Given the operations of CRBs spanning from seed-to-sale, each aspect may carry varying levels of AML risk. Assessing levels of risk is not a one-off activity but an ongoing process that adapts along with shifts in the business environment.

Financial institutions need to classify CRBs based on their risk level, usually using a risk-based approach that involves scrutiny, for higher risk clients. The evaluation considers factors like how a CRB manages its own AML controls, its financial track record, the transparency of its transactions, and the strength of its recordkeeping practices. Banks commonly use risk scoring models to measure and prioritize risks, ensuring that resources are effectively allocated to oversee and handle these accounts.[12]

To address identified risks, cannabis bankers must execute customized strategies. These strategies may involve:

- Implementing due diligence procedures for high-risk clients
- Providing regular training to staff on identifying suspicious activity

- Reporting SARs
- Setting up advanced monitoring systems to detect irregularities in transaction patterns.

Additionally, banks should ensure that their risk management plans can adjust easily to changes at both state and federal levels.

Effective risk management strategies for cannabis bankers should encompass:

- EDD: conduct background checks and ongoing monitoring for high-risk CRBs that go beyond standard due diligence protocols.
- State and Federal Compliance: stay informed about updates, at state and federal levels, to adapt risk assessment and mitigation strategies accordingly.
- Advanced Monitoring Systems: use monitoring systems that can identify patterns that may signal money laundering activities.
- Continuous Staff Training: conduct training programs for bank employees to keep them alert and knowledgeable about AML risks and reporting obligations.
- Open Communication Channels: establish clear communication channels among the compliance team, frontline staff, and management to enable swift and appropriate responses to potential risks.

By implementing a comprehensive and adaptable risk assessment process and employing risk reduction measures, financial institutions serving the cannabis industry can proactively manage their AML risks. This proactive approach is crucial for ensuring compliance, safeguarding the integrity of transactions, and sustaining banking services to the cannabis sector.[13]

Staying ahead of emerging risks is another important aspect of managing AML programs. This proactive approach involves more than just responding to regulatory changes; it requires a forward-thinking strategy that considers potential future developments in the cannabis industry and broader financial sector. By engaging with thought leaders, participating in industry forums, and leveraging advanced data analytics, cannabis bankers can identify trends and patterns that may pose new risks. This foresight allows for the early implementation of controls and measures to manage these risks effectively, keeping the bank's AML program at the forefront of best practices in cannabis banking.

MANAGING HIGH-RISK BANKING

The significance of AML measures within the cannabis banking industry goes beyond requirements – it serves as a crucial foundation that upholds the financial structure of the sector. Adhering to AML guidelines enables financial institutions to effectively cater to CRBs while upholding the integrity of the broader financial system. With the cannabis industry's growth and maturity, the role of AML in preventing illicit activities and financial crimes becomes increasingly vital. Compliance with AML rules enhances the legitimacy of the cannabis sector in regulators and the public's eyes. It also establishes trust and dependability essential for continued development and acceptance.

In managing AML risks, recommended practices involve conducting risk assessments, regularly updating customer diligence procedures, implementing advanced transaction monitoring systems, and providing staff training on AML protocols at all organizational levels to foster a culture of compliance. Additionally, maintaining communication with authorities and staying aware of changes in AML regulations and cannabis laws aids in early risk detection and mitigation.

Looking ahead, cannabis financial professionals need to stay proactive by adjusting their AML strategies to address the complexities of a rapidly evolving market. Keeping pace with industry advancements means adopting technologies like artificial intelligence, machine learning, and blockchain to improve the efficiency and effectiveness of AML practices. This approach will help cannabis banking experts meet requirements and mitigate risk, while also preparing for future changes in the industry, thus solidifying their position as reliable stewards of compliance and risk control.

Risk Assessment in High-Risk Industries

Evaluating risks in industries like cannabis that are deemed high risk requires a grasp of the dangers and weaknesses within the sector. Professionals serving CRBs must conduct investigations, continually assess business operations to ensure compliance with regulations, and prevent any involvement in money laundering or other illegal financial activities. This includes monitoring transaction trends, staying informed about industry developments, and understanding the intricacies of the cannabis market. The goal is to protect the bank's interests and uphold the integrity of the broader financial system.

For bankers working with CRBs, overcoming these obstacles involves:

- Implementing cybersecurity measures to safeguard customer information and maintain confidentiality during identity verification processes.
- Developing identity verification procedures for individuals without access to banking services.
- Performing risk evaluations geared toward understanding the characteristics of the cannabis industry and its complexities.
- Addressing identity verification challenges in cannabis banking calls for problem solving and a readiness to adjust banking practices according to the changing regulatory requirements of this emerging industry.

Achieving success in this sector not only meets basic requirements but also cultivates a safer and more welcoming banking atmosphere for cannabis enterprises.[14]

In discussions about risks with banking the cannabis industry, the focus often shifts to how the PATRIOT Act and KYC regulations play a role. These regulations are key to ensuring that financial institutions in the cannabis sector operate legally, with integrity and transparency. The PATRIOT Act, known for its rules against money laundering, requires banks to conduct checks on all clients, especially those involved in banking CRBs, which face complex legal challenges.

Being diligent and adaptable is now more important than ever for bankers dealing with cannabis-related transactions. Diligence ensures every aspect, from bringing in clients to handling individual transactions, meets stringent compliance requirements. Adaptability is equally crucial as banks must be ready to respond to changes in laws and market trends affecting the cannabis industry. The ability to adjust compliance practices promptly and proactively is essential, especially as state and federal laws continue to change and impact banking operations.

Looking ahead, it seems likely that there will be developments in compliance requirements for banking services related to cannabis. Given the possibility of changes at the federal level and ongoing state approvals for cannabis use, banks need to stay vigilant and be prepared to adjust their policies in accordance with the PATRIOT Act and KYC regulations to meet forthcoming requirements. The significance of their contribution in fostering a cannabis market cannot be overstated and their commitment to compliance leadership will remain crucial.[15]

REPORTING AND RECORDKEEPING OBLIGATIONS

Keeping records and submitting reports play a significant role in the regulatory structure of cannabis banking, acting as the foundation of a strong compliance system. In the cannabis banking sector where scrutiny is high, maintaining records is crucial. It involves creating a history of activities that validates the legitimacy of the business and aids in monitoring and reporting transactions in line with laws like the BSA and the PATRIOT Act.

Introduction to Reporting and Recordkeeping

The purposes of reporting and recordkeeping for cannabis bankers are multifaceted. Primarily, these best practices help financial institutions identify and report suspicious activity, which is vital for preventing money laundering and terrorist financing. Accurate recordkeeping sets up an audit trail for every transaction for internal audits and regulatory inspections. For bankers this means surpassing legal requirements to establish systems capable of handling the complexities of cannabis-related transactions, often involving significant cash amounts, under intense scrutiny.

Effective reporting and recordkeeping support informed decision-making and risk management strategies. Keeping records allows banking professionals in the cannabis industry to review transaction trends, evaluate client risk levels, and adapt their compliance strategies as needed. This proactive method meets requirements and also enables banks to promptly address any inquiries or investigations from authorities. In a sector marked by changing regulations, having access to, and insight into, thorough records is crucial for staying compliant and upholding the credibility of financial services offered to cannabis enterprises.[16]

Regulatory Requirements for Reporting

For those working in the cannabis banking sector, understanding and complying with reporting requirements play a role in their day-to-day activities. A deep comprehension of the BSA is essential as it outlines guidelines for reporting types of transactions. The BSA aims to combat money laundering and financial fraud by mandating institutions to keep records and submit reports on transactions that may indicate illicit activities. To adhere to regulations, cannabis bankers must ensure that all cash transactions exceeding specified limits are reported through CTRs and any suspicious activities regardless of amount are reported via SARs.

Apart from federal requirements, there are state reporting obligations that must be followed that can vary significantly across states. Cannabis bankers need to stay updated on the requirements in each state where they operate as these can impact both the nature and extent of their reporting responsibilities. This may involve disclosures at the state level, reporting to state bodies regulating cannabis operations, and compliance with financial rules specific to the cannabis industry.[17]

Cannabis bankers grapple with the challenge of balancing reporting requirements with the intricacies of the cannabis sector. This emphasizes the importance of:

- Implementing compliance programs tailored specifically for banking.
- Remaining vigilant and adaptable to address changes in reporting regulations.
- Investing in transaction monitoring systems to facilitate timely reporting.

By meeting these reporting obligations carefully, institutions involved in the cannabis industry ensure both compliance and the credibility and steadiness of the financial system supporting the cannabis market.

Recordkeeping Best Practices

In cannabis banking, where regulation is stringent and adherence is imperative, maintaining recordkeeping practices is crucial. A defined recordkeeping policy acts as a guide for keeping precise records of transactions and client interactions. This policy should detail the types of records to store the format and storage location, legal retention periods and protocols for record retrieval and disposal. It needs to follow the requirements of the BSA, which mandate that financial institutions retain records that could be valuable in regulatory inquiries.

Technological advancements have enhanced the efficiency and security of record management. Employing software for record management can assist cannabis bankers in ensuring audit ready recordkeeping. These systems can automate record categorization, storage, and retrieval processes, reducing the likelihood of errors. They often include security measures to safeguard information – an important aspect considering the nature of data handled by cannabis bankers. The appropriate software can facilitate compliance by enabling access to records during audits or investigations.

Audits and Compliance Assessments as Sound Recordkeeping Practices

It is essential to conduct checks to confirm that the recordkeeping policy is being followed and that the record management system is working correctly. Internal audits can help in identifying and addressing any issues, and preparing the bank for external regulatory inspections. Compliance checks are crucial to ensure that recordkeeping practices meet evolving requirements in the cannabis banking sector. Regular reviews also promote a culture of compliance within the institution, reminding employees of the vital role recordkeeping plays in the bank's risk management strategy.

For those involved in cannabis banking, adherence to these recordkeeping practices is vital:

1. Develop a recordkeeping policy that's strong and kept up to date with current regulations.
2. Invest in record management software to improve the accuracy, security, and accessibility of records.
3. Conduct audits and compliance checks to maintain adherence to recordkeeping standards continuously and be prepared for external audits.

By incorporating these practices, cannabis bankers can strengthen their institutions against compliance challenges and establish a benchmark of operational integrity.

CONCLUSION

For banks that have not yet made the decision to take the steps necessary to begin banking CRBs, the aspects of managing risk and risk exposure are at the forefront of the minds of most financial executives and board members. The Association for Cannabis Banking (ACB) polled bankers across the industry for their opinions on "what keeps them up at night." The bifurcated results highlighted two distinct tranches of concerns, based on whether or not the institution currently banks CRBs.

Banks that have rejected, or are still on the fence about banking cannabis, cited risk-related issues as their primary hurdles. These barriers include federal illegality, BSA, regulations, etc. However, while "risk" is still on the minds of bankers at institutions that have been banking CRBs, the hurdles are much more traditional in terms of pricing, competition, and positioning that are more common with other legal industries (Figure 5.1).

Conclusion • 107

Institutions That Do Not Bank Cannabis (MRBs)

For institutions not yet banking MRBs, concerns were heavily weighted to the legality, regulations, compliance and risk hurdles that lie ahead

- Illegality
- Compliance challenges
- Board objections
- BSA risks
- Archaic banking system
- Increased scrutiny
- Regulations
- Overhead costs
- Education/training

Institutions That Already Do Bank Cannabis (MRBs)

For institutions that already cleared the primary hurdle and now bank MRBs, future hurdles still include regulatory concerns, but also emphasize business, finance and operational challenges

- Competition once legal
- Profitability and fees
- Increased regulations
- Medicinal vs. recreational use MRBs
- Cash flow management
- Monitoring local/town ordinances
- Managing access to fed services (ACH, wire, etc)
- Education/training

FIGURE 5.1 Decision hurdles bankers confront about banking cannabis.

Source: Adapted from American Cannabis Bankers Association and RiskScout. © 2024. All Rights Reserved.

Regardless of where institutions stand on banking cannabis, risk is still critical when it comes to ensuring compliance, consistency, and oversight. To that end, it's clear that recordkeeping and reports are key to effective risk management and mitigation. These practices essentially serve as the foundation of a bank's compliance program, acting as a shield against violating regulations and financial crimes. Even for banks that are not currently seeking CRBs to bank, thorough and precise recordkeeping is vital for accurate reporting, creating an audit trail for investigating transaction histories. This meticulous approach is especially critical in an industry with changing risks and intense scrutiny. Being able to provide records when requested by regulators isn't simply about following rules – it also reflects the bank's operational reliability and dedication to openness.

Proactive Planning for Compliance

Looking forward, proactive planning for compliance hurdles is crucial for those involved in cannabis banking. It requires looking to anticipate shifts in regulations and getting ready for technological progress that can improve reporting and documentation procedures. Banks need to be willing to allocate resources for implementing technologies and providing training to stay competitive in the evolving industry and to have an understanding of the advanced compliance solutions available. Being proactive in these aspects will set apart institutions serving the cannabis sector, enabling them to tackle hurdles with assurance and uphold their reputation as reliable and compliant entities in this distinctive, dynamic, and expanding market.

 NOTES

1. Financial Crimes Enforcement Network. "Guidance." Accessed July 23, 2024. https://www.fincen.gov/resources/statutes-regulations/guidance.
2. Wikipedia. "Cole Memorandum." Last modified April 19, 2024. https://en.wikipedia.org/wiki/Cole_Memorandum.
3. Office of the Comptroller of the Currency. "Bank Secrecy Act (BSA)." Accessed July 23, 2024. https://www.occ.treas.gov/topics/supervision-and-examination/bsa/index-bsa.html.
4. Ibid. at 1.
5. Ibid. at 3.
6. Ibid. at 1.
7. Ibid. at 3.
8. Ibid. at 1.

9. Ibid. at 3.
10. Ibid.
11. Ibid. at 1.
12. Ibid. at 3.
13. Ibid.
14. Ibid.
15. Ibid.
16. Ibid.
17. Ibid.

CHAPTER SIX

Understanding the Payments Landscape in Cannabis Banking

 INTRODUCTION TO CANNABIS PAYMENTS

Payment processing plays a role in the operations of many businesses, and this holds particularly true in the cannabis industry. The restrictions stemming from cannabis laws have limited the banking and payment options available to cannabis-related businesses (CRBs). Efficient and compliant payment processing is vital for the success of cannabis companies and to thrive in this sector, cannabis bankers must assess the challenges and available solutions related to payment processing. Reliable payment systems not only ensure business operations, but also enhance customer satisfaction while providing essential financial data for robust accounting practices.

This chapter will explore the complexities of payment processing within the cannabis industry. It will discuss how transactions are executed, delve into the hurdles posed by high-risk payment processing, and examine how federal regulations influence payment processing capabilities. Given the high risk associated with cannabis, conventional methods such as credit card and debit card processing come with complexities, underscoring the crucial role of compliant and reliable merchant services for these establishments. Cannabis bankers must tread carefully through these waters, balancing efficiency with adherence to regulatory requirements.

The upcoming sections will give cannabis professionals a grasp of the payment environment they work within. Through examining methods, impacts, and services designed for risky accounts, this chapter seeks to provide financial experts with the insights needed to assist cannabis enterprises in setting up safe, effective, and law-abiding payment processing systems. Additionally, it will present a glimpse into trends and advancements that could transform the payment scene in the cannabis industry.

THE BASICS OF CANNABIS TRANSACTIONS AND PAYMENTS

The cannabis industry, despite its expansion and increasing acceptance in most states, faces challenges when it comes to conducting banking and payment transactions due to its complex legal status. Unlike industries that commonly use credit cards, online payments, and bank transfers, these traditional payment methods are not always available for cannabis businesses. As a result, transactions within the cannabis sector vary greatly from cash payments to solutions developed out of the absence of banking services.

Heavy Reliance on Cash

Historically, cash transactions have been prevalent in the cannabis industry because federal banking regulations make it challenging for businesses to access banking and treasury services. This reliance on cash has implications for dispensaries and other cannabis-related establishments. It can make them vulnerable to theft and complicate sales tracking and the tax collection processes. Additionally, managing payroll, paying bills, and reinvesting in business growth become more complicated. Dealing primarily in cash also poses challenges for cannabis bankers who must implement security measures and enhanced accounting practices to handle the influx of cash deposits and, to-date, these challenges remain.

Nevertheless, the resilience and creativity of the cannabis industry have led to payment methods emerging as alternatives to reduce dependence on cash. Some companies have started using closed loop payment systems, which are networks where customers deposit money into an account that can only be spent at specific stores. There are also apps and digital platforms from parties that help facilitate transactions between consumers and businesses within legal boundaries. These digital solutions mitigate the risks associated with handling cash and aid in maintaining a more accurate financial record.

The cannabis payment sector has also seen the integration of technology and cryptocurrencies providing a degree of anonymity and freedom from banking systems. While these digital currencies offer solutions to banking challenges, they also bring additional considerations for regulations and compliance. It is crucial for bankers to stay informed about these emerging technologies and understand their impact on reporting and anti-money laundering (AML) efforts.

For bankers, managing transactions and payments requires a mix of financial knowledge and adaptability:

- Handling Cash: Establishing solid procedures for securely storing, handling, and transporting large amounts of cash.
- Embracing Technology: Keeping updated on new payment technologies that meet regulatory requirements.
- Compliance and Reporting: Ensuring all payment methods comply with strict regulations, like the Bank Secrecy Act (BSA).

To provide enhanced services to their clients, it is important for bankers to understand the various transaction types and payment methods used in the cannabis sector. This in-depth knowledge enables them to support business operations while complying with regulations.

High-Risk Payment Processing

The complexities of processing payments using debit cards in the cannabis industry poses a challenge. While debit cards are commonly used for consumer purchases due to their convenience and security features, cannabis businesses face difficulties because of the laws categorizing cannabis as federally illegal. This continually conflicting situation creates an obstacle for bankers in the cannabis industry, who must handle transactions while carefully following a set of regulatory rules and risk management protocols.

Establishing a risk management strategy for transactions within the cannabis industry requires compliance with laws like the BSA and AML regulations. Banks need to set up processes for verifying customers and monitoring transactions to detect and report any suspicious activities. Every transaction should be carefully checked to ensure its authenticity and detailed records should be kept for an audit trail that regulators or law enforcement can review when needed.[1]

When it comes to handling debit card transactions in the cannabis industry, different banks have taken different approaches. Some have developed their own payment systems that operate within networks, providing some level of protection from the wider federal financial system. Others have partnered with third-party processors specializing in high-risk sectors to facilitate debit card transactions using their expertise and infrastructure. There are also businesses using cashless ATMs or point-of-banking systems, allowing customers to use debit cards for cash withdrawals during transactions.

However, Visa issued a memo warning against the use of "cashless ATMs" by cannabis companies. In December of 2021, Visa sent a compliance memo to banks that process transactions for cannabis merchants, stating that the practice of miscoding POS transactions as ATM withdrawals is prohibited. This practice, popular among cannabis dispensaries, involves using POS terminals that mimic standalone ATMs but do not dispense cash. Instead, they process purchases as ATM cash disbursements, often rounding up amounts to create the appearance of a cash disbursement. Visa warned that such transactions could lead to non-compliance assessments, penalties, or other enforcement actions. "Cashless ATMs are primarily marketed to merchant types that are unable to obtain payment services – whether due to the Visa Rules, the rules of other networks, or legal or regulatory prohibitions," Visa's memo reads. "Therefore, supporting this scheme affects the integrity of VisaNet and the Plus network, as well as the Visa payment system."

For banks dealing with high-risk debit card processing in the cannabis sector, key factors include:

- Forming partnerships with payment processors experienced in high-risk markets who understand the challenges of the cannabis industry.
- Regularly updating risk management procedures to adapt to changing regulations and market conditions.
- Ensuring transparency and traceability in all payment processing operations, through recordkeeping practices.

Cannabis bankers must exhibit sharpness, creativity, and initiative when dealing with debit card processing. Potential legislative shifts in the future could reshape how debit card processing is handled within the cannabis sector, but for now, it is essential for cannabis bankers to conscientiously operate within the current structure, leveraging innovation and strategic collaborations to offer payment processing services to their cannabis clientele.

The Impact of Federal Regulations on Payment Processing

Federal regulations have an impact on how banking services are provided to the cannabis industry, especially when it comes to payment processing. Even though many states have legalized cannabis in some form, it is still classified a Schedule I controlled substance at the federal level. Currently the Drug Enforcement Administration (DEA) is working toward rescheduling marijuana to a Schedule III controlled substance. This classification under the Controlled Substances Act (CSA) casts a shadow over transactions involving cannabis, affecting how banks and payment processors operate within this industry. The conflict between state laws permitting its use and federal laws prohibiting it creates a confusing regulatory environment for processing payments in the cannabis sector.

The influence of regulatory guidance on banking and payments in the cannabis industry is crucial because it sets the rules for institutions determining their risk tolerance levels and compliance strategies. For example, under the BSA, banks are required to implement AML measures, conduct thorough investigations and report any suspicious activities that could indicate money laundering or other illegal financial practices. Therefore, banks need to be extremely cautious when handling payments related to cannabis to avoid violating regulations, which could lead to consequences such as substantial fines, reputational risk, and legal repercussions.

Payment processors and banks that opt to work with cannabis companies often encounter challenges due to regulatory requirements. Navigating through AML regulations, the potential for facing enforcement actions, and the constant uncertainty of changes in federal policies or enforcement priorities can pose significant challenges and threats. Financial institutions often find themselves at a crossroads, having to decide between denying services to cannabis businesses or investing in costly compliance measures to manage the challenges associated with serving these high-risk clients. For payment processors, the risks go beyond compliance as they must also weigh the reputational and operational implications of serving an industry that remains federally illegal.

Despite these hurdles, there are strategies for maneuvering through regulations in payment processing. Some financial institutions have implemented diligence procedures that surpass the basic BSA and AML requirements, ensuring a comprehensive understanding of each cannabis business they serve, thereby applying Enhanced Due Diligence (EDD) best practices. This may involve continuous transaction monitoring to verify alignment with expected business activities, reporting mechanisms for tracking and documenting all transactions, and establishing partnerships with legal and compliance professionals specializing in cannabis law and accounting.

Certain banks and payment processors have adopted methods such as blockchain and cryptocurrency to facilitate transactions in a way that could potentially reduce their payment processing risks. Although these approaches come with challenges and controversies that we discuss in detail in Chapter 9, they show a rising interest in payment and banking options within the cannabis sector.

Important factors for banks navigating the payment processing environment include:

- Staying informed about changes in federal enforcement policies and adjusting compliance strategies accordingly.
- Promoting a culture of compliance and risk awareness within the organization.
- Exploring technologies and approaches for payment processing that meet compliance standards while supporting the needs of cannabis businesses.

With the growth of the cannabis industry, there is optimism that federal regulations will develop in a way that addresses the gap between state and federal laws. Until this reform happens, bankers handling cannabis must delicately juggle meeting their clients' needs while also following the network of regulations that oversee their activities.

Merchant Services for High-Risk Accounts

In the growing cannabis sector, the concept of "merchant services" takes on a new meaning. Merchant services encompass a variety of services utilized by businesses, such as handling credit and debit card transactions, payment gateways, and point-of-sale systems. However, with cannabis banking, these services need to be customized to address the challenges and regulatory intricacies of an industry that's legal in numerous states but illegal at the federal level in the United States.

When choosing a merchant service provider for a cannabis enterprise, the criteria go beyond what's typical for most retail operations. Cannabis companies should seek vendors who understand the nuances of the industry. This includes possessing an understanding of regulations, being able to handle fees or reserves typically associated with high-risk accounts, and being proactive in anticipating legislative changes that could impact service delivery. Additionally, it's essential for these providers to have security measures in place to safeguard financial information due to heightened cybersecurity risks in high-risk sectors.[2]

Effectively managing high-risk merchant accounts necessitates adhering to best practices. The top priority is making sure to follow all the rules like the BSA and AML laws. Cannabis businesses and their banking partners need to keep records and make sure every transaction is clear and can be traced. Another good idea is to have continuity plans in case something changes with one of the processors so that banking operations can keep running smoothly. It's advisable for CRBs to look for service providers who offer support and guidance on navigating the complexities of banking in the cannabis industry, and many times, the banks servicing cannabis have relationships with high-risk merchant services providers, so this is a great place to start.

For those involved in cannabis banking, managing merchant services for high-risk accounts means:

- Ensure all rules are followed carefully.
- Watch for signs of fraud in transactions.
- Staying connected with service providers to make sure their services meet the business's changing needs.

By following these guidelines, companies in the cannabis industry and financial institutions can establish a strong foundation for successful and secure operations. As the market evolves, it will be those CRBs and banks that balance prudence with creativity in their merchant services strategies that will succeed.

PAYMENT METHODS AND RISK CONSIDERATIONS

It's important to understand the multiple obstacles in handling payments that CRBs encounter due to regulations categorizing cannabis as a Schedule I controlled substance. Despite these challenges there are payment alternatives to choose from, each with its own risk factors. While cash remains an option, it brings about security concerns and operational difficulties because of the large cash volumes involved.

To address these issues many CRBs have opted for various payment methods. Card transactions can be processed through third-party payment services that convert the transaction into a pre-defined format. However these services often entail fees and the potential for federal scrutiny. ACH transfers and digital wallets offer electronic payment avenues with enhanced security and convenience, but necessitate robust compliance structures to ensure adherence to regulations. Cryptocurrencies are emerging as a potential payment solution, providing anonymity and low transaction costs. Nevertheless their volatility and regulatory ambiguity incorporate risks. Each payment method presents its own unique challenges and advantages requiring CRBs to assess their choices to strike a balance between accessibility, cost effectiveness, and regulatory conformity.

In the following section, from the "Cannabis Payments Guidelines," Emerging Markets Coalition (2022),[3] we'll delve into multiple payment types and some of the pros and cons of each for CRBs.

Risk Assessment

An important step in the decision to use one or more payment mechanisms over another is to ensure that your organization has examined the risks for each. This process can be formal or informal and is dependent on the complexity and unique needs of each organization. Please note that the services available vary by state and service providers that cross borders must have done so with a well-thought-out state law compliance plan.

Some of the key risk considerations to examine may be:

- Reliability of the system – will this payment mechanism be available 99% of the time? Is there a risk of discontinuance?
- Ease of use for employees – is this option the most efficient use of employee's time? Does it require additional training or is it difficult to use?
- Customer understanding and adoption – will there be a need to educate the customer, or do they understand how it works?
- Opportunity for internal or external fraud or theft – does this method of payment increase security risks? Does it introduce opportunities for fraud?
- Reputational risk – will customers be adversely impacted? Will the company's financial institution approve this payment mechanism?
- Cost – is the cost relatively close to what a non-cannabis mechanism pays?

 BUSINESS-TO-CONSUMER PAYMENTS

Credit Cards

Although no explicit prohibition of card acceptance by cannabis retailers is found in operating rules for either Visa or Mastercard, it is widely publicized that both networks do not allow them. Discover and American Express are more explicit in their position. While cannabis sales are illegal at the federal level, we do not expect the payment brands to allow their cards to be used at dispensaries. It is understood that the major card brands' position is due to the fact that cannabis is currently illegal at the federal level. Therefore, many acquiring FIs will not knowingly risk their network standing by accepting cannabis transactions. Where credit card transactions are accepted, it sometimes appears that the underlying acquiring financial institution was unaware they were processing cannabis transactions, as was the case in the Eaze Technologies scheme. This increases the risk of any participant in the payment being implicated, therefore delaying acceptance of credit cards for cannabis transactions is deemed best practice.

Debit Cards

The use of financial institution debit cards for cannabis transactions has emerged as a solution by some payment processors, intended to avoid the challenges presented by acceptance of major national card brands. There are more than a dozen regional PIN debit networks with varying degrees of tolerance to state legal cannabis transactions. However, it should be noted that currently there is no debit network that has publicly endorsed cannabis transactions. Participants in PIN debit card acceptance are cautioned to ensure transparency – that the underlying financial institution is aware of the true nature of the transactions and that transactions are processed in the businesses name at the correct address.

Checks

The CRB should have a financial institution relationship and operating checking account to facilitate acceptance of checks and ACH as payment for goods. The CRB should utilize processes and systems like other heavily cash-based businesses, such as check cashing, to mitigate fraud risk associated with accepting checks as payment. This is usually done using a third-party service.

- All checks should be deposited with the financial institution daily.
- All checks should be properly endorsed for deposit only with the business's name and account number. Ideally, all checks should be scanned and deposited using the financial institution's remote deposit capabilities.
- Low-volume businesses may be able to use the mobile remote deposit application.

- High-volume businesses may employ a check scanner with financial institution-supplied software (local or cloud-based) to scan higher volumes of checks.
- Follow your financial institution's procedures for retaining scanned (physical) checks before destroying them.

Cashless ATMs

Cashless ATMs, also referred to as Point of Banking, is a debit card payment that is coded the same as an ATM transaction, but that occurs using debit card processing equipment rather than a cash-dispensing ATM. To reflect an ATM cash withdrawal, the equipment will round up the purchase amount to the nearest $5 increment. The cardholder can accept the change back or can choose to designate the change as a tip. Not only is the cashless ATM a cumbersome process, but it can also cause inadvertent consumer harm. The cardholder is likely to incur an out-of-network ATM fee, or in some cases an over-the-counter cash advance fee for a transaction that is actually a point-of-sale purchase.

This payment method warrants additional caution, as it could be deemed a violation under the UDAAP (Unfair, Deceptive, or Abusive Acts and Practices) Act. Visa has provided clear guidance that coding a retail purchase as an ATM transaction (with cashless ATM) is prohibited on its network.

Digital Payments

There are payment providers in the market that have created digital first payment solutions for cannabis transactions. Similar to Venmo, CashApp, or PayPal, the payment provider's technology creates a connection between the consumer financial institution account and a digital wallet that allows for the consumer to pay a merchant via their primary financial institution account. Digital payments can support a transaction in store, via eCommerce, ordering delivery. There are multiple digital native payment products available in the market including Consumer-to-Merchant direct payments, Buy Now, Pay Later, and Crypto solutions.

Consumer-to-Merchant

Digital wallet payments from the consumer to the merchant are a more modern approach to payments as compared to card-based payments, as there is no physical card. This payment type does not require specialized equipment or software integrations as the fintech company manages technology requirements with POS or other providers. The consumer visits a website or downloads the payment app on their smartphone to enroll. After identity verification, the consumer connects their financial institution account via secured authentication, using mobile/online banking credentials, or by entering their routing number and account number. After enrollment, the consumer pays for cannabis products via a QR code scanned by the merchant that includes product receipt information. The transaction settles with the merchant after it is deducted from the consumer's account.

Buy Now, Pay Later

The buy now, pay later market is exploding, and there are some innovative providers that have applied this product to cannabis purchases. The product allows a transaction to be paid for in 4 equal installments, the first of which is due at the time of purchase. Best practice for these types of programs is for the consumer to not be charged interest for the loan, but instead for the transaction to be funded by the merchant. This means that, like paying merchant processing charges, the merchant will be settling for the whole purchase amount, less a discount, at the point of sale. Subsequent bi-weekly payments are collected from the consumer by the payment processor and underlying lender. While slightly more costly, the consumer's increased purchasing power leads to a larger average ticket.

Crypto

Crypto is a complex payment type, requiring expertise in systems, compliance, and tax. The best form of crypto payments is to leave the complex process of connecting to consumer wallets, moving funds, settling, reporting, compliance, etc. to a professional fintech company. Dispensaries seeking to execute in-house programs expose themselves to a multitude of unique challenges related to tax, reporting, volatility, etc.

However, crypto-based payments can be seen as an advantageous strategy because they are more anonymous when compared to other payment types. This is something consumers may see as an advantage. When a consumer pays with crypto, they typically transfer US dollars into a wallet or purchase crypto from an exchange. The consumer then will use that crypto they purchased by transferring it via a fintech partner to a merchant account that has been verified. Typically, the merchant remitted funds in US dollars a few days later into their financial institution's account.

BUSINESS-TO-BUSINESS PAYMENTS

Automated Clearing House

ACH or Automated Clearing House transactions are electronic payments similar to wire transactions but typically used for smaller transaction amounts and are a lower cost to the user. Unlike the wire system (see below), it is a batch push-and-pull system, meaning both debits and credits can be sent. The NACHA (National ACH Association) Operating Rules governs it and has two operators: the Federal Reserve and the Electronic Payment Network (EPN) without the restrictions of card network brands or their terms of service, and with well-defined rules for bank transaction clearing. At the time of this publication, NACHA has taken a neutral stance on the use of ACH for cannabis transactions, noting the issue of the federal legal status and various state legal statuses. Only an ACH Originator, which is either a business, non-profit, or government entity, can originate transactions to consumer, business, and government accounts. Banks and credit unions take on the due diligence responsibilities as Originating Depository Financial Institutions (ODFIs) to onboard and give access to originating ACH transactions. ACH transactions also have a return process that includes insufficient funds for several other reasons, so transactions are not final like they are for wires.

ACH is widely used for business-to-business payments in all other industries. Due to limited access, many business-to-business payments within the cannabis industry are still done via cash. ACH business-to-business payments require one of the cannabis businesses to be onboarded with an ODFI, including all the due diligence required. Once this access has been granted, the cannabis originator can make payments to other cannabis businesses and government agencies, like taxing authorities. All transactions, whether to a business, non-profit organization, or a government agency, need to follow the NACHA Operating Rules, and the rules and guidelines set by the ODFI.

Wire

Wire transfers are credit payments from one bank account to another using the electronic wire system. These payments are fast, secure, and final. These processes move funds from a financial institution to the Federal Reserve Bank's Fedwire system for domestic wires, and if international wires are used, will use international correspondent banks, which can delay the process. Wires are typically used for business-to-business, large dollar payments due to the increased fees associated with this payment method. The advantage for using wires is that there are not the same risks for insufficient funds or returns like there are with checks or ACH. It also is only a credit push system, so the payment must originate from the payor to the payee.

Checks

Checks are written, signed, and dated with a specific amount from a checking account with a MICR (Magnetic Ink Character Recognition) line consisting of routing and account information. Traditionally, checks have been physical, but with the passage of Check 21, images of checks are allowed to be used for processing through the check system, and some even convert to ACH using specific codes. Checks are used primarily for business-to-business transactions, tax, and license payments, and can even be used by consumers. There are risks of insufficient funds and returns with checks, and longer processing times than ACH or wires. There are also increased risks of check fraud due to advancements in image technology.

Bill Payments

Bill payments are a service of most financial institutions that allow for electronic payments of bills such as utilities, lending payments, and more. Bill payments will either send physical checks to lockboxes or will use digital endpoints to electronically make payments.

Real-Time Payments are the newest payment rail set up by The Clearing House to allow payments to be made in real time digitally. FedNow is another real-time payment option that the Federal Reserve launched in 2023. Both are considered higher risk due to payment speed, and there are not many providers or options available to cannabis operators currently.

CONCLUSION

The path of cannabis banking has faced payment hurdles from the onset due to its position of straddling state legalization and federal prohibition. Challenges have included access to banking services, risks tied to cash transactions, and strict regulatory oversight. However, the industry has shown resilience by adapting strategies such as embracing creative payment methods, partnering with state institutions, and collaborating with specialized payment processors for high-risk sectors. The innovative approaches taken reflect an industry poised for growth, despite grappling with compliance complexities and financial operations.

Successful financial institutions and payment processors are those that not only embrace innovation but also prioritize compliance efforts. This entails following regulations, as well as proactively preparing for changes, implementing robust tracking systems, and maintaining transparency in all transactions. Diligence in compliance practices, along with innovation, has helped manage risks and establish a sense of stability in this emerging and ever-changing industry.

Looking ahead, the payments landscape in banking is set to undergo changes. Potential legislative reforms, like the passing of the SAFER Banking Act or rescheduling, could mark a chapter in providing more mainstream financial services to cannabis companies. Technological advancements in blockchain and AI are expected to bring advanced solutions that can streamline operations, improve customer service, and ensure compliance with evolving regulations.

Payment processors and financial institutions that are adaptable and forward looking are likely to lead the way in this field, showing that combining compliance with innovation can create efficient payment systems. Therefore, staying ahead of technological developments will be essential for all involved in cannabis banking as the industry moves toward acceptance and integration into the global financial sector.

NOTES

1. Financial Crimes Enforcement Network. "Guidance." Accessed July 23, 2024. https://www.fincen.gov/resources/statutes-regulations/guidance.
2. Flowhub. "Dispensary Payment Processing Guide." Accessed July 23, 2024. https://flowhub.com/dispensary-payment-processing-guide.
3. Emerging Markets Coalition. "Cannabis Payments Guidelines." 2022. https://emcoalition.org/cannabis-payments-guidelines.

CHAPTER SEVEN

Cannabis Lending

 DESCRIBING THE CURRENT LENDING NEEDS

The rise of cannabis markets has sparked a growing industry. However, securing funding remains a major challenge for many cannabis companies. Traditional banks have been cautious about entering the market due to the federal illegality of cannabis, leading to a sometimes-sparse lending environment. Despite the hurdles, an increasing number of lenders are understanding the potential and stepping up to provide loan options tailored to meet the specific needs of cannabis entrepreneurs.

Complexities of Cannabis Lending

Cannabis lending has its own complexities. The federal prohibition presents compliance obstacles, requiring lenders to evaluate and manage the unique risks associated with the industry. These risks encompass changes in regulations, uncertainties in operations, and concerns about reputation.

Despite the challenges, there is a growing demand for cannabis lending as the industry expands and matures. Lenders are attempting to create innovations that service the special requirements of cannabis businesses by offering loan products for real estate investments, inventory financing, equipment acquisitions, and working capital needs. These loans typically feature terms and conditions tailored to address industry risks such as interest rates and stricter collateral requirements.

TYPES OF LOANS AVAILABLE TO CANNABIS BUSINESSES

The rise of cannabis markets has sparked a revolution leading to the growth of cannabis lending as a key driver for industry expansion. With traditional financial institutions staying cautious due to restrictions, a new wave of non-bank lenders is seeing the potential and stepping in to fill the funding gap. Driven by the increasing acceptance and legalization of cannabis across states, there has been an increase in the demand for capital in the cannabis industry. Cannabis businesses at all stages of seed-to-sale, from cultivation and manufacturing to retail and distribution, require funding for expanding operations, investing in infrastructure, and meeting consumer demand with adequate inventory. Cannabis lenders have become partners by offering loans, lines of credit, and other financial tools that can be difficult to access within the traditional banking system.[1]

The Rise of Cannabis Lending

Cannabis lending offers promising opportunities, but it also comes with its share of challenges. Lenders have to navigate through a maze of state regulations, deal with industry risks, and follow strict underwriting standards. Specialized loans are available for purposes such as real estate, equipment financing, managing inventory, and supporting working capital. These financial options empower business owners to tackle money-related obstacles and drive their business growth.

The future of lending in the cannabis industry looks promising. With mainstream players entering the scene, there may be increased competition, lower interest rates, and improved access to funding for entrepreneurs in the cannabis field. The possibility of rescheduling and even federal legalization on the horizon could significantly impact the landscape by unlocking new investment opportunities and fostering innovation within the cannabis lending industry.

Legalization and Market Growth

In the United States, it is projected that the legal cannabis market will reach almost $40 billion by 2025 (Figure 7.1).

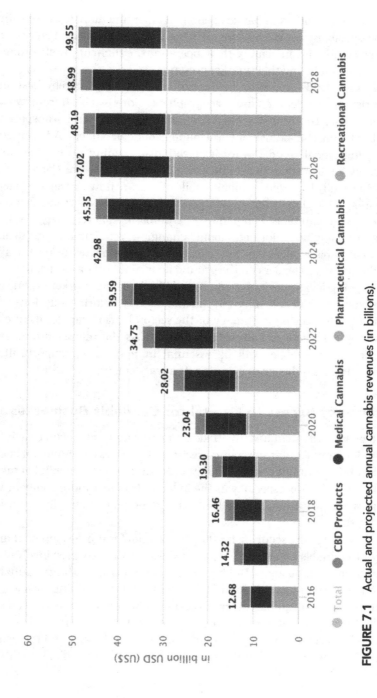

FIGURE 7.1 Actual and projected annual cannabis revenues (in billions).

Source: Adapted from Statista, Cannabis Revenue March 2024, https://www.statista.com/outlook/hmo/cannabis/united-states#revenue

For lenders, this offers a chance to enter an emerging market with positive growth prospects. By providing support to cannabis enterprises, lenders can assist these companies in scaling their operations, enhancing their product offerings, and broadening their market presence.

Legalization lends credibility to the cannabis industry, thereby lowering perceived risks for lenders. As more geographic regions establish frameworks for cannabis use, the industry becomes more organized and transparent, thereby simplifying risk assessment and management for lenders. Additionally, the increasing global trend toward legalization is opening up markets and opportunities for investments around the globe. Countries like Canada and Germany have fully legalized cannabis, while others are now considering steps to legalization. This global shift creates possibilities for lenders to support and collaborate with cannabis companies operating in different regions and countries. By staying informed about changing regulations and being proactive, cannabis lenders can take advantage of the growing market and position themselves as leaders on the ground floor of this dynamic field.

The ongoing legalization of cannabis and its resulting market expansion offer prospects for lenders involved in the industry. By tailoring solutions and recognizing the increasing legitimacy of the sector, lenders can contribute to the growth and success of cannabis businesses. As the market progresses, adopting lending strategies will be essential in maximizing opportunities within the cannabis industry and driving its advancement.

Importance of Access to Capital for Cannabis Businesses

Starting a business in an industry with demand for your product can be exhilarating. But for cannabis entrepreneurs, securing the necessary financial backing can feel like an unfair and uphill battle. Having access to capital is more critical than ever before, especially as the industry becomes more competitive, and mergers and acquisitions could lead to larger players potentially dominating the industry.

Let's delve into why securing funding is essential for the development and longevity of cannabis enterprises. First, let's discuss the expenses involved in launching a cannabis business. Unlike most other industries, getting a cannabis venture off the ground goes beyond finding a location and setting up shop. It entails investments in equipment for cultivation, obtaining expensive licenses, and establishing operational structures for expenses like inventory and on-site security. These costs can quickly escalate to millions of dollars, and the usual tax write-offs available to most businesses are not necessarily available to CRBs.

Without support, numerous aspiring cannabis businesses find themselves at a standstill even before they have a chance to thrive.[2]

Another crucial aspect in starting a cannabis business is compliance. The cannabis sector operates under regulations that make doing business complex and financially demanding. Businesses must adhere to state and local laws through audits, security enhancements, and sometimes facility modifications to meet standards. These ongoing compliance efforts necessitate continual access to capital, rather than just one-time financial injections at start-up time.

Expansion is another aspect where capital plays a major role; however, venturing into additional territories comes at a cost. It entails establishing operations, hiring employees, promoting the business through marketing channels, and of course, always complying with regulations. For a cannabis company aiming to seize opportunities for expansion, having financial support to facilitate this expansion is vital. Without it, there is a risk of falling behind competitors who possess the required funds for growth.[3]

Effective cash flow management is also essential when it comes to accessing capital. Access to capital enables enterprises to handle their cash flow more effectively, meet supplier and vendor payments promptly, and invest in necessary inventory without constantly worrying about liquidity issues.

There is innovation happening in the cannabis sector, from introducing product varieties, like edibles and topicals, to implementing advanced cultivation methods. To remain competitive and satisfy consumer needs, cannabis companies must invest in research and development efforts. Capital access empowers them to innovate swiftly and introduce products to the market efficiently.

Having access to capital isn't just necessary for competitive enterprises; it's absolutely essential because it:

- Fuels growth
- Ensures adherence to regulations
- Facilitates expansion
- Fosters innovation
- Provides a safety net to stay afloat

As the industry progresses, securing funding will be instrumental in determining which businesses flourish and which ones struggle to stay alive. For those involved in cannabis banking, recognizing this dynamic is pivotal for promoting industry growth and aiding these businesses in realizing their fullest potential.[4]

OVERVIEW OF THE LENDING LANDSCAPE

When it comes to securing financing for cannabis businesses, there's no one-size-fits-all solution. Each type of lender brings something unique to the table, and understanding the differences can help cannabis entrepreneurs make the best choice for their needs. Let's dive into the various types of lenders – banks, credit unions, and private lenders – and explore what they each offer.

Types of Lenders (Banks, Credit Unions, Private Lenders)

Banks are what most people think of first when considering a loan. Traditional banks are well-established and offer a wide range of financial products, from loans and lines of credit to treasury and cash management services. However, for cannabis businesses, getting a loan from a traditional bank can be quite challenging as many banks are hesitant to work with the cannabis industry due to compliance costs, risk appetite, and potential legal repercussions. Rescheduling on the horizon will likely cause more banks to consider entering cannabis lending due to the strengthening of seed-to-sale enterprises through their enhanced financial positions.

Credit unions and community banks are another viable option and can often provide more products and services to the cannabis industry. Credit unions are member-owned financial cooperatives, which means they might be more flexible and willing to work with cannabis businesses, especially if those businesses are local and therefore part of their community. Because credit unions and community banks are generally smaller and more community-focused, they can offer a more personalized banking experience that leads to growth and prosperity for the communities they serve. However, they may not have the same range of services or the large lending capacity that larger banks offer.

Then there are private lenders who can be real lifesavers for CRBs. Private lenders include individuals, private equity firms, venture capitalists, and specialized lending companies that are more willing to take on the risks associated with the cannabis industry. These lenders are often more flexible and can offer customized financing solutions that are specifically designed for the unique needs of cannabis businesses. They might offer higher interest rates due to the risk, but they also tend to move faster than traditional banks, providing much-needed capital without the lengthy approval processes. Private lenders can be particularly useful for start-ups or businesses that need quick, albeit sometimes more expensive, access to funds.[5]

Each type of lender has its pros and cons. Banks offer stability and a comprehensive suite of services but may be difficult to access for cannabis businesses. Credit unions and community banks provide a more personal touch and can be more flexible but might lack the extensive resources of larger banks. Private lenders provide flexibility and speed, but often come with higher costs and the possibility of giving up equity. For cannabis businesses, the best approach might involve a combination of these lenders to meet different needs at different stages of growth.

Loan Products (Term Loans, Lines of Credit, Equipment Financing)

When it comes to financing a cannabis business there are loan options that cater to different needs. Understanding these choices can help bankers provide solutions to their clients and support the growth of this thriving industry. Let's delve into term loans, lines of credit, and equipment financing to see how each can make a difference for cannabis enterprises.

Term loans represent one form of financing. Imagine needing a lump sum for launching a project such as constructing a cultivation facility or opening another dispensary. Through a term loan, a business receives a sum of money and repays it over an established period, typically with a fixed interest rate. This predictability can be extremely beneficial for cannabis businesses, enabling them to manage their finances with a predictable repayment plan in place. It's a good choice for one-time investments that can significantly enhance the business's capabilities and growth prospects.[6]

Next are lines of credit, which function as financial safety nets. Unlike term loans, lines of credit provide businesses with access to funds as required on demand, and up to a limit. This can be especially handy for cannabis businesses to handle unpredictable fluctuations in cash flow. Perhaps there's a chance to secure discounted inventory, or maybe an unforeseen expense arises in a cannabis enterprise due to a regulatory change in packaging or labeling requirements, for example. With a flexible and convenient line of credit, the business can easily access funds without going through the hassle of applying for a loan each time.[7]

Equipment financing is designed specifically for buying equipment, which can be an expensive cost in the cannabis industry. Whether it's cultivation lights, inventory systems, processing machines, or retail point-of-sale systems, these loans cover the equipment costs needed to operate a business efficiently. The advantage of equipment financing is that the equipment itself acts as collateral, making it easier to secure the loan for businesses facing challenges with other types of financing. This kind of loan enables cannabis businesses to stay current with cutting-edge technology, enhancing efficiency and productivity, which is especially important as competition continues to increase in this growing industry.[8]

Selecting the loan product depends on the requirements and circumstances of the cannabis business. For one-time investments, term loans offer a regular repayment plan, while lines of credit provide flexibility. When it comes to securing the equipment needed for operations, opting for equipment financing is often the best choice. By having a grasp of these alternatives, bankers can offer expert advice to their clients, enabling them to make well-informed decisions that are in line with their business objectives and provide a path to stabilization and growth.

Ultimately, providing a range of loan options can have an impact on the success of cannabis enterprises. Through customized solutions, bankers not only aid in the growth and success of their clients, but also nurture enduring relationships based on trust and mutual gain. It's about finding the best match for each business, thereby ensuring they possess the financial resources required to thrive in this dynamic and ever-changing industry.

Interest Rates and Fees

Let's dive into a topic that's always top of mind when it comes to loans, interest rates and fees. For lenders working with cannabis businesses, understanding and defining these terms is key because they not only impact how affordable the loan is for the borrower but also shape the profitability and risk management for the lender.

Interest rates essentially represent the cost of borrowing money and can vary widely based on multiple factors. In the high-risk cannabis industry, interest rates tend to be higher compared to other more traditional and established industries. Lenders must balance this heightened risk with interest-appropriate rates helping to offset potential losses. Nonetheless, striking a balance is crucial – setting rates too high could deter borrowers, while setting them too low might not adequately cover risks for the lender.

Fees are another important aspect of lending, and these may include application fees, origination fees, processing fees, or even prepayment penalties. For cannabis businesses, understanding these fees upfront is vital to steer clear of any surprises in the future that could bring unforeseen cash challenges. From the perspective of the lender, fees play a role in covering the expenses related to processing and managing loans, particularly considering the added compliance and due diligence needed in the cannabis sector. The key lies in being transparent – clearly outlining all fees to borrowers fosters trust and nurtures a relationship between lenders and borrowers.[9]

Ultimately, it's all about striking a balance where both parties – the lender and borrower – feel confident and secure. For lenders this involves evaluating risks, establishing interest rates and fees transparently, and being upfront about the terms. As for cannabis businesses, it's important to comprehend these expenses and how they align with their overall business and financial management plans. Through collaboration, lenders and cannabis enterprises can develop financing solutions that promote growth and sustainability.

As Tony Repanich, president and CEO of Shield Compliance, states, "a financial institution's existing traditional commercial lending program can be extended to the cannabis banking space using almost the same criteria that it would evaluate any other loan."

Regulatory Considerations

Let's delve into something that's incredibly important for anyone involved in cannabis lending – regulation. The regulatory requirements can feel like walking a tightrope, yet it's crucial for staying compliant and reducing risks. For lenders, grasping the nuances of cannabis regulations is not just about following the law – it's also about supporting your clients and understanding their specific needs in a heavily regulated setting.

The following section comes from Shield Compliance.[10]

BSA/AML Risks Associated with Cannabis Lending

Implementing a compliant cannabis banking program requires considerable planning and an understanding of all potential risk areas. Guidance from FinCEN outlines how to manage some BSA/AML compliance risks. There are additional underlying risks associated with the cannabis industry because of how it has evolved. These risks are related to the industry's high cash concentration, the abundance of legacy cash, the potential for bad actors to try to attach themselves to legal businesses, and the ongoing strength of the illicit market.

Whether you are taking a CRB as a deposit and loan client or as a loan-only client, enhanced BSA/AML procedures and KYC due diligence will need to be conducted to ensure funds coming into the FI are from legal sources. Having control over the entire relationship is the best way to monitor cash for BSA/AML purposes and manage compliance risks, which aligns well with the relationship-driven culture of many community banks and credit unions. If you are not the primary depository, you will need to have controls in place to make sure that you understand the source of repayment coming from a qualified cannabis deposit account outside of your financial institution. Lastly, depending on who the primary borrower is, an investor or ancillary company versus a plant-touching entity, ongoing SAR filing may also be required.

Navigating matters in cannabis lending demands an attentive approach. By grasping and abiding by state regulations, establishing AML protocols, and promoting a culture of adherence to rules, lenders can effectively maneuver through the intricacies of the cannabis sector.

The following new lender checklist is part of "The Shield Compliance Cannabis Lending Guide."[11]

- If you currently serve CRBs, consider the impact of lending to your cannabis banking program.
- Create a cannabis lending team that is comprised of internal team members and external experts.
- Assess the strengths and weaknesses of your existing commercial lending program.
- Identify which loan products or services can be extended to the cannabis industry.
- Evaluate ways you can create compliance efficiencies using automated solutions, including those designed to support banking CRBs.
- Modify your risk assessment and internal policies to account for the BSA/AML, credit, and reputational risks associated with the cannabis industry.
- Determine your position on lending to entities that do not bank with your financial institution.
- Set policy on lending thresholds based on how much exposure you want to this industry as a percentage of capital. This could include setting limits on loans to a single entity.
- Establish requirements for guarantors or secondary sources of repayment.
- Define your exit strategy.

CONCLUSION

As we conclude our examination of cannabis lending, it's evident that the industry is poised for growth and change. The emergence of cannabis markets has led to an industry with forecasts pointing toward positive market growth in the upcoming years, especially with rescheduling on the horizon. While obtaining funding remains a challenge, more lenders, including traditional banks, are acknowledging the potential upside of the cannabis industry and are stepping forward to provide customized loan options tailored to meet the specific requirements of cannabis entrepreneurs.

Cannabis lending presents its complexities. The federal illegality poses compliance challenges, compelling lenders to carefully handle the unique risks associated with these businesses. These risks encompass regulatory shifts, operational uncertainties, and concerns about reputation. Consequently, lenders often impose criteria for risk evaluation, necessitating research and robust risk management strategies. Although this may appear daunting, it is crucial for mitigating the high-risk nature of cannabis lending and ensuring success.

Despite these obstacles, there is a rising demand for cannabis lending as the industry continues to grow and evolve. Lenders are adapting to the needs of cannabis enterprises by offering loan products tailored for real estate ventures, inventory financing, equipment purchases, and working capital requirements – all are much needed banking services for any industry. These loans are usually designed with terms and conditions to address the risks that are common in the cannabis industry, such as higher interest rates and stricter collateral requirements.

While challenges exist in the state of cannabis lending, there are also opportunities for those prepared to manage its complexities. By understanding the risks involved, adhering to regulations, and offering additional products, lenders can contribute significantly to the growth and sustainability of the cannabis sector. As the market progresses, taking steps forward with informed lending practices will be crucial to seize the expanding opportunities within this dynamic new industry. It's crucial for lenders and cannabis enterprises to forge a path through collaboration, innovation, and shared progress to achieve growth of the industry.

NOTES

1. Bloomberg Law. "Finance Professional Perspective: Debt Financing in the Cannabis Industry." Accessed July 2, 2024. https://www.bloomberglaw.com/external/document/XFAEEE8000000/finance-professional-perspective-debt-financing-in-the-cannabis-.
2. Ibid.
3. Ibid.

4. Ibid.
5. Order.co. "Cannabis Financing." Accessed July 2, 2024. https://www.order.co/blog/finance/cannabis-financing/.
6. Ibid.
7. Ibid.
8. Ibid.
9. SH Financial. "An Expert Guide on How to Get Cannabis Business Loans." Accessed May 5, 2024. https://shfinancial.org/an-expert-guide-on-how-to-get-cannabis-business-loans/.
10. Shield Banking. "The Shield Compliance Cannabis Lending Guide." Accessed June 23, 2024. https://www.shieldbanking.com/post/the-shield-compliance-cannabis-lending-guide.
11. Ibid.

CHAPTER EIGHT

Marketing Strategies for Cannabis Bankers

 IMPORTANCE OF MARKETING IN CANNABIS BANKING

Marketers in the field of cannabis banking must tread carefully, balancing promotion with adherence to rules and servicing the needs of cannabis-related businesses (CRBs) that often struggle to access traditional banking services. Creating marketing plans in this environment involves understanding the complexities and the business realities of CRBs. For those in cannabis banking, emphasizing compliance and the ability to handle aspects of operations securely and legally is crucial. This approach can establish trustworthiness amidst uncertainties for CRBs seeking stability and expertise from their banking partners.

As the industry matures and continues to gain acceptance, cannabis bankers who invest in strategic, compliant, and educational marketing efforts may gain a competitive edge. They are the ones who have developed connections with their intended audience, gained a reputation for leading thinking and dependability, and offered the cannabis community the banking services needed to succeed in a constantly changing legal environment.

Marketing plays an important role in the cannabis banking sector and effective marketing strategies should highlight the bank's expertise with issues that CRBs encounter. A targeted marketing approach conveys to clients that the bank not only comprehends the nuances of complying with federal guidelines, like FinCEN requirements, but also provides customized financial solutions addressing industry-specific challenges and needs. This can position the financial institution as a leader in cannabis banking, a factor in an industry that highly values trust and expertise.

Impactful marketing within banking works to dispel misconceptions surrounding the cannabis industry. By showcasing achievements, compliance successes, and secure banking practices of CRBs, financial institutions can help legitimize the industry to both the public and policymakers. This effort could potentially lead to reduced pressures and open doors for enhanced financial services. Therefore, the role of marketing in banking goes beyond business development. It plays a crucial part in shaping the future of the industry and creating an environment conducive to the growth of CRBs.

UNDERSTANDING YOUR MARKET

For bankers in the cannabis industry, grasping the market starts with pinpointing the intended target market – individuals who own and manage businesses related to cannabis seeking banking services. These customers need tailored solutions that address the requirements of the cannabis industry, like managing large cash volumes, handling transactions, and adhering to state and federal laws.

The target audience also encompasses businesses supporting the cannabis sector, such as law firms, accounting firms, security companies, and logistics providers specializing in cannabis-related activities. While these enterprises may not directly deal with cannabis products, they operate within the industry's network and may encounter banking and regulatory hurdles.

To effectively market to these groups, cannabis bankers must delve into the details of the cannabis market by evaluating not just the scale and revenue prospects of these entities, but also the risk profiles and regulatory frameworks under which they function. This entails keeping up to date with modifications at both state and federal levels that could impact a CRB's financial processes and regulatory requirements.

Organizations like the Association for Cannabis Banking (ACB) offer education, information, research, and updates that are essential for financial institutions operating in the cannabis industry. Further, in the expanding cannabis industry, it is crucial for banks to understand the customer base of their CRB clients. This knowledge allows them to anticipate CRBs' service requirements. Given that cannabis is a developing field, bankers should explore collaborations with industry experts and participate in specialized conferences and workshops to gain deeper insights into the market. Engaging with industry experts, think tanks, and research bodies focusing on cannabis policy and economics can greatly enhance a banker's grasp of the industry. By integrating industry research, customer perspectives, and regulatory expertise, cannabis bankers can successfully cater to audience segments, customizing their services to address the unique needs and complexities of the cannabis market.[1]

Understanding the cannabis market means understanding:

- Brand positioning for trust and compliance
- Messaging and communication strategies
- The role of corporate social responsibility (CSR)

Brand Positioning for Trust and Compliance

Establishing a cannabis banking brand requires a thought-out strategy that places emphasis on trust and adherence to regulations. When positioning a brand for cannabis banking, it's not just about standing out in the market with visually dazzling images; it's also about building a reputation as a reliable and knowledgeable partner for CRBs.

Trust plays a role in all banking relationships and in the complex cannabis sector it carries even more weight. A cannabis bank brand should reflect dependability and honesty, assuring CRBs that their funds, transactions, and compliance matters are handled with the utmost care. The visual elements and messaging of the brand should convey professionalism and an emphasis on safeguarding assets, presenting the bank as a stabilizing presence in the industry.[2]

Equally important for branding within cannabis banking is compliance. Given the delicate balance CRBs must maintain, this sector must exhibit unwavering dedication to following regulations. A company that showcases a stance toward following rules and regulations can position itself as a trusted advisor in the view of potential customers.

To strengthen trust and compliance within the brand, educational programs can play an important role. By offering workshops, online seminars, and best practices tailored to the cannabis industry, a financial institution can establish itself as an expert and primary source of important information. These endeavors not only assist potential clients in navigating their own compliance issues but also emphasize the institution's knowledge and dedication to the field. Given the emerging nature of cannabis banking, it is crucial for a bank's branding to embody adaptability and forward thinking. This signals to CRBs that the bank will grow alongside the industry, foreseeing and adjusting to challenges and opportunities quickly. The brand should represent a balance between caution and innovation, assuring potential clients that their banking partner is both adept at risk management and creative in exploring solutions.[3]

Creating a story that spans all platforms from the bank's website to its presence on social media and engagements at industry gatherings is essential. A trusted brand serves as a marketing tool and also plays a fundamental role in shaping the strategic positioning of the bank's cannabis offering.[4]

Messaging and Communication Strategies

Brand creation requires more than market awareness. It also demands strong messaging and strategic communication strategies. When it comes to cannabis banking, the messaging approach needs to find the balance between showcasing innovative services and highlighting dedication to following regulations and ensuring security.

At the heart of a banking brand's messaging should be a focus on reliability and expertise within the cannabis industry. Given the scrutiny from regulators, communication efforts should consistently underline the bank's ability to navigate legal frameworks, its commitment to compliance, and its proactive stance in protecting its clients' interests. This message can be effectively conveyed through channels like expert articles, industry analyses, and educational content that address issues faced by CRBs.[5]

The tone of communication is crucial, and it should reflect the professionalism and seriousness expected in banking services, while remaining engaging for the audience of cannabis entrepreneurs. This involves using language that explains standards and banking procedures without oversimplifying complex concepts. Although social media and digital marketing are tools for communicating a banking brand message, they must be used cautiously due to advertising limitations related to cannabis products and services.[6]

Banks need to make sure that the content they share online, whether on their websites or social media, follows the rules for financial services marketing and specific regulations on advertising in the cannabis industry. Content marketing plays a role by promoting the bank through valuable and informative material that positions it as a trusted figure in cannabis finance. Consistency is

> **CannaFirst Financial**
> 306 followers
> 3d ·
>
> Elevate your business with CannaFirst Financial, a premier Cannabis Bank with knowledgeable ACBA certified professionals who specialize in cannabis banking.
>
> Our team at CannaFirst Financial is committed to guiding you through regulatory compliance and safeguarding your financial assets.
>
> CannaFirst Financial is proud to serve Alabama & Mississippi businesses like cannabis cultivators, processors, dispensaries, secure transporters, state testing laboratories, and integrated facilities.
>
> Visit Our Website
> www.cannafirst.com
>
> CannaFirst Financial Is Powered By Merchants & Marine Bank,
>
> Member FDIC.

FIGURE 8.1 Actual testimonial from financial institution banking cannabis.

key across all communication platforms to reinforce brand identity. Every marketing material, from website content to business cards, should mirror the bank's values and core messages.[7]

For example, CannaFirst Financial has created social media ads on LinkedIn that showcase the bank's knowledge of the industry, discussing the bank's commitment to compliance, highlighting their professional certifications through the Association for Cannabis Banking (ACB), and sharing enthusiasm as well as a welcoming message for serving the cannabis industry (Figure 8.1).

Creating a communication strategy for banking demands planning and a thorough understanding of both the target audience and regulatory challenges. By building a brand known for reliability, knowledge, and adherence to regulations, cannabis banks can establish an important and predictable presence in the market.

The Role of Corporate Social Responsibility (CSR)

Establishing a brand goes beyond offering services and products; it involves utilizing CSR at the core of the brand's identity. For bankers, CSR serves as a tool to enhance their brand, setting them apart in a competitive and intricate niche market. By participating in CSR projects, banks can showcase their dedication to standards, community involvement, and environmental conservation. Additionally, educating stakeholders about consumption and backing community programs addressing the effects of drug policies can strengthen a bank's reputation as a community-focused establishment.[7]

Another important area where cannabis banks demonstrate responsibility is by supporting the economic progress of the communities they serve. By promoting community development and economic inclusivity, banks can establish local connections and improve their reputational and social standing.

Initiatives focused on employees are also crucial, such as advocating for diversity and inclusion in the workforce and organizing volunteer programs that benefit the community. These internal CSR efforts can enhance employee involvement and satisfaction, leading to a solid brand reputation and improved customer service.

DIGITAL MARKETING TECHNIQUES

Marketing for cannabis banking requires the strategic use of digital marketing strategies to connect with and create interest with CRBs. Digital marketing provides a range of impactful methods for banks to establish their visibility and reputation in this market. Important tactics involve content marketing, including creating blog articles, reports, and online seminars that tackle the financial obstacles encountered by CRBs. These resources play a role in establishing expertise and fostering trust within the sector.

Digital marketing techniques for cannabis bankers include[8]:

- Website and SEO best practices
- Content marketing for thought leadership
- Leveraging social media responsibility

Website and SEO Best Practices

Having an online presence and utilizing digital marketing strategies are key elements for attracting and serving clients. A crucial starting point for marketing is the bank's website, which often serves as the initial point of contact for potential clients. The website should convey professionalism and expertise, while reflecting the brand's dedication to security, compliance, and customer service. It should be user-friendly with navigation that enables visitors to access information about services offered, regulatory compliance, and how the bank can cater to their specific needs related to cannabis businesses.[9]

Implementing SEO best practices plays a role in enhancing the visibility of the website to individuals seeking cannabis banking solutions. This process involves conducting keyword research to understand what potential clients are searching for and strategically incorporating those keywords into the website's content. Using keywords associated with cannabis banking, regulatory requirements, financial services in titles, meta descriptions, and headers can help boost search engine rankings and attract traffic to the site.[10]

In SEO strategies, producing high-quality content that addresses the challenges and inquiries of the cannabis industry is paramount. This content helps position a bank as an authority in this field and also engages audiences effectively. Having a blog or a section dedicated to resources that gets updated regularly with the industry news, updates on regulations, and financial advice for cannabis businesses can improve not only SEO but also offer valuable insights to customers while showcasing the brand's knowledge. Companies like Cadence SEO are helpful in ensuring that websites can be searchable and that opportunities to be discovered online are maximized.

Factors like website speed, mobile friendliness, and ensuring consistent hosting are crucial for successful SEO. With Google giving importance to user experience in ranking websites, it's essential to ensure that your site loads quickly and works seamlessly on both desktop and mobile devices. Additionally, using Secure Sockets Layer (SSL) website encryption provides reassurance to customers that their online interactions with the bank are secure – an important element in gaining trust in banking services. In terms of marketing for cannabis banking institutions, the focus should be on creating a platform that goes beyond just being a digital business card – it should serve as a valuable resource that fosters trust and credibility among potential clients. By incorporating these recommended strategies, cannabis bankers can effectively target their desired audience, showcase their expertise, and expand their client base.[11]

Content Marketing for Thought Leadership

In the cannabis banking sector, showcasing expertise through content marketing is a good method to establish trust and bring in clients. This involves developing and sharing relevant and consistent content to engage and retain an audience to drive customer engagement. For bankers, content marketing not only promotes their services but also educates their audience on intricate regulatory requirements, financial best practices, and cannabis laws, a true win-win situation.

By creating educational content, cannabis bankers can address the unique concerns and inquiries of cannabis companies. This could involve producing materials such as papers on financial compliance, blog posts discussing recent regulatory updates, or comprehensive guides on managing finances within the legal framework of the cannabis sector. Disseminating content, such as media, webinars, and podcasts, across platforms enables banks to reach a wider audience while positioning themselves as leading authorities in this field.[12]

Tailored content marketing for cannabis banking can include showcasing case studies and success stories that illustrate the bank's proficiency in navigating challenges within the cannabis industry. This method not only highlights the bank's knowledge, but it also exhibits the practical impact of its services. By focusing on stories that align with the values and interests of cannabis businesses, bankers can create a bond with their audience. Incorporating SEO into the content marketing strategy is crucial to ensure that users seeking information can easily find the valuable content produced. This includes conducting keyword research to pinpoint the terms and queries potential clients use and creating content that seamlessly integrates these terms, ultimately enhancing the bank's visibility in search engine rankings.

It is essential to emphasize that in an industry like cannabis banking, where regulatory compliance is paramount, all content must undergo scrutiny to guarantee accuracy and compliance with legal standards. The trust established through thought leadership can be swiftly eroded by content that does not meet these requirements.

By implementing a thorough content marketing strategy, cannabis bankers can strengthen their reputation as industry leaders fostering trust with their audience and establishing a robust digital presence aligned with their business objectives. This approach informs clients and cultivates loyalty and confidence in the bank's ability to address the distinctive challenges of the cannabis sector.

Leveraging Social Media Responsibility

For professionals working in the cannabis banking sector, using media as part of their marketing strategy requires a careful and thoughtful approach. While social media platforms offer opportunities for building a brand and engaging with customers, they also pose challenges due to the regulatory environment surrounding the cannabis industry. It's crucial for cannabis bankers to manage these platforms with caution, ensuring that their content complies with platform rules as well as federal and state laws.[13]

When utilizing social media, cannabis finance professionals should concentrate on providing content that adds value to their audience without directly promoting the sale or use of cannabis. This could involve:

- Sharing updates on industry developments
- Changes in legislation
- Advice for CRBs
- Insights into the aspects of the industry

By positioning themselves as sources of education, banks can interact with their audience in a manner that showcases their expertise and supportiveness without violating advertising regulations. Maintaining an eye on public conversations and participating responsibly is also essential. By listening to what their audience is concerned about or interested in, bankers can tailor their content effectively. However, it's vital to maintain a professional demeanor and avoid getting involved in discussions that might suggest approval of illegal activities.

Banks should establish a compliance monitoring system to ensure that all social media content is current, accurate, and compliant with the regulatory updates. With the spread of misinformation online, it is crucial for cannabis bankers to contribute positively and accurately to industry discussions.

Prioritizing data privacy is also essential. While engaging with customers and the public on platforms, banks must prioritize safeguarding information and complying with privacy regulations. They should educate clients about the risks of sharing details and set clear guidelines on discussing client information in public digital spaces.[14]

By embracing these strategies, cannabis bankers can leverage social media to expand their brand's reach effectively, while at the same time fostering thought leadership and community engagement.

NETWORKING AND PARTNERSHIPS

Building connections and forming alliances are strategies that drive the success of cannabis bankers. In an industry known for its regulations and rapid changes, creating ties with cannabis companies is not just about marketing; it's a core business practice that can determine the future sustainability of a bank operating in the cannabis industry.

Establishing and nurturing connections with cannabis businesses demands an understanding of the industry's distinct environment. Cannabis bankers must not only grasp the intricacies and comprehend the regulatory challenges and operational hurdles encountered by their clients. Attending industry gatherings, becoming members of cannabis trade groups, and actively engaging in discussions can be ways for bankers to integrate themselves into the cannabis community and showcase their dedication to the field.

Collaborations with cannabis businesses can be enhanced by offering value beyond banking services. This might involve providing materials on financial compliance, organizing workshops on business and professional growth, or backing research projects that promote the advancement of the cannabis sector. Through endeavors such as these, banks can exhibit their commitment to supporting their client's success, thereby strengthening these critical trust-based relationships.[14]

Banks can form partnerships with firms, consultants, and other service providers in the cannabis industry to create a support system for their clients. These collaborations can enhance the range of services offered, including assisting cannabis businesses in managing not only their banking requirements but also the legal and operational aspects of the industry.

It is crucial to recognize that networking within this industry demands transparency and adherence to regulations. Trust plays an important role, which can be established through compliance with rules, maintaining client confidentiality, and operating ethically. Building trust takes time and it requires each interaction or transaction to reinforce the bank's reputation as a reliable partner.[15]

Digital networking platforms are also tools for relationship building. By utilizing media, online forums, and virtual conferences, banks can broaden their connections with cannabis businesses on a larger scale. However, it is important that these digital initiatives complement, rather than replace, the depth of relationships formed through face-to-face interactions and personal meetings.[16]

Establishing networks and partnerships in the cannabis banking field involves outreach efforts combined with in-depth knowledge, value creation alignment, and ongoing compliant engagement practices. By engaging in these strategies, cannabis bankers can establish themselves as partners for CRBs as they delve into this growing industry together.

Collaborations with Industry Associations

Networking and establishing partnerships are essential for bankers looking to succeed in an industry that values relationships and collaborations. Creating connections with cannabis businesses goes beyond the banker-client relationship; it also involves grasping the challenges these companies encounter. For bankers this could involve offering tailored guidance, providing resources for compliance, and devising specialized banking solutions tailored to the cannabis sector. Engaging with business owners through industry events, discussions, and personal consultations fosters an understanding and trust setting the groundwork for professional bonds.

Working together with industry associations is key because these associations often represent the voice of the industry by offering advocacy, education, and networking opportunities. By participating in these groups, cannabis bankers can stay informed about industry trends, regulatory shifts, and best practices. Organizations like the National Cannabis Industry Association (NCIA) and the ACB provide platforms for interaction and dialogue that are invaluable for bankers looking to establish themselves as players in the cannabis market.

These collaborative endeavors empower cannabis bankers to assist the businesses they work with, and also to contribute to shaping the future of the industry. By collaborating with industry organizations, bankers can actively engage in conversations that could impact policies and regulations showcasing their best business practices and expertise in supporting the development and stability of the cannabis industry. Building connections and alliances strengthens the bank's value offering and sets it apart in the competitive arena of cannabis banking.[17]

Engaging with Regulatory Bodies

Engaging with authorities is crucial for bankers in the cannabis industry. Establishing a relationship with these organizations goes beyond just adhering to rules; it involves advocating for the industry and staying informed about changing regulations. For banks serving cannabis companies, maintaining communication with both state and federal regulators is key to staying up to date on the latest updates and interpretations of regulations, enabling them to adjust banking practices accordingly and provide top-notch guidance to their clients.

There are ways to engage in this process, such as participating in workshops, attending public hearings, and offering feedback on proposed rule changes. These proactive steps allow banks to voice concerns and push for regulations that consider the practicalities of cannabis banking and potentially influencing policy decisions in a way that supports financial services for the sector.

Actively engaging in dialogues with regulatory bodies helps cannabis bankers anticipate changes, proactively prepare for compliance requirements, and shape their bank's long-term strategies. When cannabis bankers interact with authorities, they can demonstrate their dedication to following laws and ethical standards. This helps ensure that their offerings follow regulations and that their customers are kept informed. By working in this manner, a connection can be established between the sector and the regulators promoting a feeling of shared comprehension and admiration that benefits everyone involved.

Regulations that govern bank marketing[18]:

- Regulation DD (Truth in Saving Act) requires banks to provide accurate information about the terms and conditions of deposit accounts.
- Regulation Z (Truth in Lending Act) mandates that advertisements for credit products must clearly disclose terms such as the annual percentage rate (APR) and other costs associated with the credit.
- Regulation P (Privacy of Consumer Financial Information) governs how banks handle nonpublic personal information about consumers.

EDUCATIONAL MARKETING

Educational marketing proves to be a useful tool for cannabis bankers, allowing them to offer value to potential clients while showcasing their industry expertise. Hosting workshops and webinars serves as a method to engage an audience and exhibit a bank's deep understanding of the intricate issues faced by cannabis businesses. These educational platforms enable banks to delve into topics such as compliance, financial planning, industry best practices, and emerging market trends.

By offering these learning opportunities, cannabis bankers can bridge the information divide in this changing sector. Workshops and webinars establish communication channels with the market, enabling banks to address pressing questions and concerns from cannabis business owners. Additionally, these platforms provide a space for bankers to highlight their services and industry acumen in a sales setting, fostering trust and credibility among participants. These educational sessions serve as a means of gaining insights into the needs and obstacles within the industry. Interactive workshops and webinars that encourage participation can unveil perspectives from clients aiding banks in refining their services and customizing their approach to better align with market demands.[19]

Utilizing marketing via workshops and webinars proves to be a strategy that can greatly enhance the value proposition of a cannabis bank. This approach showcases a dedication to fostering industry advancement and establishes the bank as a leading authority all while nurturing ties with the community.

Publishing Informative Guides and Whitepapers

Marketing in the education sector using guides and whitepapers is an approach for cannabis bankers looking to establish their expertise in the marketplace. These resources offer insights on topics ranging from compliance challenges to market trends within the cannabis industry. By offering industry content, banks can help cannabis businesses make well-informed decisions, paving the way for long-lasting banking relationships.

Developing and sharing whitepapers and guides requires research and a deep understanding of industry requirements. For example, a whitepaper focusing on how banking regulations affect cannabis enterprises not only showcases the bank's proficiency but also serves as a go-to resource for businesses seeking clarity on regulatory issues. Similarly, a guide outlining practices for cannabis companies can assist clients (and attract potential clients) in enhancing their operations while positioning the bank as an indispensable partner in their growth. These materials can help clarify the complexities of cannabis banking by presenting information in an easily understandable manner. Distributing these guides and whitepapers through channels such as the bank's website, email newsletters, or at industry events can expand reach, delivering value to both current and prospective clients.[20]

Ultimately, creating tools, guides, and whitepapers is crucial for banking marketing. These materials highlight the bank's knowledge and commitment to the cannabis sector, offering information to customers and solidifying the bank's position as a trusted authority in the field.

EVENT MARKETING AND SPONSORSHIPS

Participating in events and sponsoring them are strategies for bankers to enhance their brand visibility, gain trust, and cultivate connections in the cannabis sector. By engaging with cannabis businesses at trade shows, conferences, and expos, banks can showcase their dedication to the industry's development and success. These gatherings offer chances for networking, enabling banks to liaise with customers, collaborators, and key figures in the industry.

Event marketing and sponsorship strategies for cannabis bankers can include:

- Trade shows and conferences
- Event marketing and sponsorships
- Hosting exclusive roundtable discussions

Trade Shows and Conferences

Trade shows and conferences offer an opportunity for cannabis bankers to expand their presence in the industry. These events serve as a platform for networking, exchanging knowledge, and showcasing services to a targeted audience of cannabis business owners, industry influencers, and potential partners. For bankers, participating in events allows them to engage directly with clients, stay informed about industry trends and challenges, and establish themselves as experts.

When banks sponsor trade shows and conferences, they benefit from increased brand visibility. Sponsorship packages often include speaking opportunities, branded items in event bags, or the chance to host sessions. These interactions are crucial for demonstrating the bank's dedication to the industry and sharing expertise on topics like compliance, financial best practices, lending, and investment opportunities in the cannabis market. Additionally, sponsorships can cause media coverage since these events are typically featured in industry publications. Participating in these events goes beyond having a booth or logo on display. It involves thought leadership elements such as leading panel discussions, joining roundtable conversations, and hosting workshops.[21]

Attending these gatherings often sparks discussions that can lead to building connections that might evolve into business prospects. For professionals in cannabis banking, this could involve collaborating on offerings tailored specifically to the sector or providing guidance on navigating the intricate realm of cannabis banking laws.

It's crucial to approach these occasions with a plan in place. Before participating, those in banking should establish goals, whether it's increasing brand recognition, generating leads, or showcasing expertise. Throughout the event, collecting contacts and promptly following up can enhance the return on investment. Evaluating outcomes against objectives post event can offer insights for future event strategies and involvement.

Engaging in event marketing and sponsorships at industry trade shows and conferences goes beyond presence within the cannabis sector. It entails engaging in discussions, grasping market needs, and presenting solutions that address the challenges encountered by cannabis enterprises. For professionals in cannabis banking, these events present an opportunity to showcase their worth in a field where their services are greatly needed.

Event Marketing and Sponsorships

Sponsoring industry events plays a role for bankers aiming to boost their presence and reputation in the cannabis sector. By supporting events, banks demonstrate their dedication to the industry, which can enhance their brand image as a leading financial service provider for cannabis businesses. Associating a bank's name and logo with industry gatherings signifies an investment in the sector's future and a commitment to its development.

In addition, sponsoring these events offers a chance to connect directly with stakeholders, including business owners, investors, regulatory authorities, and other important figures in the cannabis field. These interactions not only help build connections but also reinforce existing ones, providing valuable insights into industry needs and trends. Banks can use these opportunities to highlight their products and services tailored specifically for cannabis businesses, showcasing an understanding of the industry's regulatory framework and operational requirements.

Event sponsorship opens doors to networking possibilities such as VIP dinners or special sessions with industry leaders. These settings encourage in-depth discussions that could lead to partnerships, collaborative projects, or new client relationships. Sponsoring events gives banks the opportunity to create interactive experiences that leave a lasting impression on attendees. Whether it's through a booth setup, an educational presentation, or interactive workshops, providing experiences can greatly improve brand recognition and showcase the bank as a friendly and knowledgeable presence in the cannabis banking sector.[22]

By selecting industry events to sponsor that align with their objectives, cannabis bankers can effectively focus their marketing initiatives to boost their brand reputation while establishing a strong leadership position in the cannabis industry. These targeted sponsorships represent an investment in the bank's future in the cannabis market and demonstrate its dedication to the industry's prosperity.

Hosting Exclusive Roundtable Discussions

Organizing talks serves as a powerful strategy for cannabis bankers looking to boost event marketing and sponsorship efforts. These intimate gatherings offer a platform for industry experts and key stakeholders to gather and discuss the challenges within the cannabis banking sector. For bankers, hosting discussions allows them to showcase their role as facilitators of dialogues, fostering a collaborative space where peers can openly share insights on challenges, strategies, and innovations.

The topics covered in these discussions may include areas such as compliance, risk management, and the creation of innovative financial products customized for the cannabis sector. By selecting guests representing diverse backgrounds – including business owners, policymakers, and legal professionals – cannabis bankers can use these events to gain a comprehensive perspective on the industry. Furthermore, the knowledge acquired through these roundtables can shape the development of banking services that cater specifically to the needs of cannabis enterprises, solidifying the bank's reputation as a partner in their success.[23]

Ultimately, through hosting talks, cannabis bankers not only contribute to industry advancement but also bolster their status as dedicated allies with deep expertise in supporting cannabis businesses. These gatherings can offer content for marketing endeavors, while reinforcing the bank's position as a leading authority, in this specialized field.

COMPLIANCE-CENTRIC MARKETING

For professionals in the cannabis banking sector, focusing on compliance-driven marketing is crucial due to the regulations governing the industry. By promoting their services within boundaries, banks can mitigate the risks associated with offering solutions related to a federally controlled substance, despite variations in state laws. It is imperative for banks to strategically market their services by highlighting aspects that follow all jurisdictions, such as their expertise in compliance risk management and their understanding of the banking requirements of the cannabis industry.

Marketing within Legal Boundaries

Each piece of marketing collateral must undergo scrutiny to ensure it remains within boundaries and does not inadvertently endorse or facilitate illegal activities. The language of promotional content should underscore the bank's commitment to adherence to regulations, robust due diligence processes, and support for cannabis enterprises in aligning with state and federal laws. This approach aims to position the bank as a partner for CRBs seeking compliance amidst an intense regulatory environment.

Compliance-focused marketing involves staying vigilant toward evolving regulations since the legal framework surrounding the cannabis sector is dynamic. Banks must remain informed and adaptable, ready to overhaul their marketing approaches under new legislation and policies. Taking a stance protects the bank from potential legal issues and also reassures clients that the bank is a knowledgeable and dependable partner that can assist them through the complex regulatory requirements. Sharing content can be highly effective in this field. By offering workshops, online seminars, and informational guides on compliance and best practices, banks can showcase their value to clients without violating advertising regulations. This approach also positions the bank as a voice in cannabis banking, establishing trust with both prospective and existing clients.

Essentially for those in banking, the marketing focus should emphasize not just promoting cannabis itself but highlighting the importance of assisting businesses in navigating the industry. By giving priority to compliance and education in their marketing approaches, banks can expand their presence in the cannabis sector while upholding adherence to standards.

Educating Clients on Regulatory Compliance

Marketing efforts must prioritize educating clients on regulatory compliance. A compliance-centric approach to marketing emphasizes the bank's expertise and commitment to legal adherence, and positions the bank as an educational leader. Providing clients with the knowledge they need to build trust and position the bank as an indispensable resource is always a great strategy.

Cannabis bankers can utilize various platforms to disseminate this knowledge. Content marketing strategies could include the publication of articles, blog posts, and whitepapers that cover recent regulatory updates, interpret complex compliance issues, and offer best practices and solutions for cannabis business operations within the legal framework. By translating the often dense and legalese-ridden language of regulations into actionable insights for cannabis business owners, banks can reinforce their role as a critical ally in the industry.

Beyond written content, webinars and interactive online forums can be an effective way to engage with clients and discuss regulatory issues in real time. These sessions offer the added benefit of allowing clients to ask questions and interact with the bank's compliance experts, creating a dynamic learning environment that can adapt to the attendees' immediate concerns.

These educational efforts should also be personalized where possible. Tailoring compliance resources to the specific needs of different segments within the cannabis industry – from growers to retailers to ancillary service providers – ensures that the information is relevant and immediately applicable. Personalization demonstrates the bank's understanding of the diverse ecosystem within the cannabis industry and its nuanced regulatory demands.

In essence, compliance-centric marketing strategies that focus on educating clients not only mitigate risk but also foster client loyalty. By prioritizing education in their marketing efforts, cannabis bankers can cultivate a more informed client base, which in turn, contributes to a more compliant and robust cannabis industry overall.

Transparent and Ethical Marketing Practices

Focusing on compliance in marketing is not a preference but a vital requirement for cannabis bankers. By embracing ethical marketing strategies, banks demonstrate their dedication to honesty and establish a solid foundation of trust with their clients. Each marketing message and promotional material must adhere to industry regulations to avoid any confusion or misrepresentation of the services provided or the legal framework governing the sector.

Transparency in marketing involves discussing the bank's role, capabilities, and limitations when serving cannabis businesses. It entails communication about compliance complexities and the measures taken by the bank to ensure adherence to all laws. Ethical marketing transcends avoidance of falsehoods; it entails empowering clients with accurate and comprehensive information for making informed decisions.

Integrating transparency and ethical principles across all marketing efforts enables bankers to establish a trustworthy brand within the industry. This trust is crucial for attracting clients and also fostering enduring relationships in a field where credibility is a key to prosperity.

ANALYZING AND ADAPTING TO MARKET TRENDS

To stay updated on developments, cannabis bankers can adopt a strategy that includes maintaining ties with professionals in the industry, subscribing to legal publications, and participating in conferences focused on cannabis law to gain early insights into potential regulatory shifts. Additionally, leveraging legal analysis tools that track legislation and regulations can provide real-time updates on any changes that could impact banking operations.

Keeping Updated on Legal Changes

As regulations continue to evolve, it's important for cannabis bankers to be agile in adjusting their services and advice for clients. This could involve updating compliance protocols and providing clients with current guidance on operating within the bounds of the law. Proactively adapting to changes not only safeguards both the bank and its clients, but also showcases a commitment to being a leader in cannabis banking.

Essentially, keeping up with changing regulations and being able to adapt is not simply a choice for cannabis bankers – it is crucial for transparency and compliance. It involves adopting an approach to gathering information, having a business model, and taking a proactive approach to engaging with the market. Those banks that can handle this effectively will be in a position to lead in the expanding cannabis industry, known for its growth potential and regulatory intricacies.

Utilizing Data for Market Insights

For professionals working in the cannabis banking sector, keeping up with the fast pace of changes in the industry requires more than just a grasp of financial concepts. It also requires understanding of market shifts and customer behaviors. Utilizing data to analyze and respond to market trends is essential for staying competitive and ensuring growth in the cannabis field. Making decisions based on data empowers bankers to anticipate market movements, comprehend consumer preferences, and recognize both risks and opportunities.

To leverage data for market insights, the initial step involves gathering information from various sources such as sales figures, customer profiles, regulatory updates, and broader economic cues. Sophisticated analytical tools can then process this data to unveil patterns and trends that might not be readily apparent. For instance, a sudden surge in demand for a cannabis strain or product category could signal changing consumer tastes. It's important for cannabis bankers to stay vigilant about these developments to adjust their strategies and guidance accordingly.

Predictive analytics can be a game changer for bankers. By creating models based on data and trends, bankers can predict market behaviors. This predictive ability is especially valuable in an industry like cannabis, where legalities and market conditions are constantly evolving. Insights based on predictions help financial institutions prepare effectively for changes, enabling them to offer stability and assistance to their clients during times of change.

The use of data analytics aids in tailoring products and services to suit the requirements of cannabis businesses. Whether it's creating loan options for peak buying periods (like before major holidays) or implementing flexible pricing structures for financial services, data empowers banks to be more agile and responsive.

It's essential for cannabis bankers to regularly enhance their data management and analysis capabilities. This involves investing in technologies and providing training to staff members to stay abreast of developments in data science and analytics. As the cannabis industry evolves, being able to interpret and act on market insights will set leading institutions apart from the rest. By integrating data analysis into their decision-making, cannabis bankers can manage the intricacies of the field while offering clients forward-looking advice rooted in reliable data.

Agility in Marketing Strategy

It's necessary for cannabis bankers to keep up with market trends to effectively support their clients and work through regulatory challenges. With more states legalizing cannabis for both medical and recreational use, market dynamics can shift rapidly, impacting consumer behaviors and product pricing. This calls for a marketing approach that can swiftly respond to opportunities and changes.

Forming partnerships and collaborations can be a way to boost market flexibility. By partnering with technology providers, cannabis bankers can utilize tools like blockchain for payments or CRM systems to gain insights into consumer behaviors and preferences. These partnerships not only enhance efficiencies but also elevate the customer experience, simplifying business management for clients.

For cannabis bankers, the ability to analyze and adapt to market trends goes beyond staying competitive; it's about being a trusted advisor to their clients guiding them through the intricacies of the cannabis market confidently. Flexibility in marketing strategies supported by data analysis, regulatory knowledge, and strategic alliances is vital in achieving this goal, ensuring that bankers can promptly and effectively respond to any shifts in the market.

CONCLUSION

In conclusion, a comprehensive discussion on marketing strategies for cannabis bankers is important to encapsulate the key points that drive successful marketing in this unique sector. The cannabis industry presents a labyrinth of regulatory frameworks, consumer trends, and competitive pressures that demand a nuanced and dynamic approach to marketing.

Recap of Key Marketing Strategies

Firstly, a robust understanding of the regulatory environment cannot be overstated. Cannabis bankers must be versed in the legalities that govern the industry – not just at the federal level, but down to the nuances of state and local jurisdictions. Bankers must be able to forecast the impacts of regulatory changes on their clients' businesses and adjust their marketing narratives to match.

Secondly, staying data-driven is key. The use of analytics to drive marketing decisions enables cannabis bankers to be more proactive and less reactive. By understanding consumer behaviors, product trends, and market fluctuations through data, bankers can tailor their services to the most pressing needs of the market. This may involve targeted product financing solutions, advisory services, or investment strategies that resonate with the current market demands.

Personalization and segmentation form the bedrock of effective marketing in the cannabis industry. Given the diversity of cannabis consumers and businesses, a one-size-fits-all approach is ineffectual. Cannabis bankers should focus on creating personalized experiences and tailored financial products that cater to different segments, whether they are medical dispensaries, recreational retailers, cultivators, or ancillary service providers.

Additionally, agility is essential. The cannabis market is not static; it is shaped by a variety of external factors, including social attitudes, technological advancements, and economic conditions. An agile marketing strategy – one that is flexible and responsive – allows cannabis bankers to pivot as needed and to capitalize on emerging opportunities. It could be leveraging social media and digital platforms for brand building, or developing new financing packages that support sustainable business practices in cannabis cultivation.

Cannabis bankers should integrate these strategic pillars into their marketing playbook:

- Regulatory fluency at both the federal and state level
- Data-driven decision-making
- Personalized marketing
- Strategic agility

By taking this approach, individuals can effectively maneuver through the intricacies of the industry while also delivering benefits to their clients. This will help foster robust connections in a market that is set for expansion and transformation.

The Future of Marketing in Cannabis Banking

As the cannabis industry continues to grow and integrate with mainstream businesses, the role of bankers is expected to evolve in the field of marketing. The future of marketing in banking will involve keeping up with industry advancements and predicting and influencing its direction through innovative strategies.

Looking ahead, technology will play a vital role in shaping marketing for banking. By incorporating AI and machine learning, bankers can gain insights into customer preferences allowing for services on a whole new level. The use of platforms and fintech solutions is expected to increase, offering ways to engage with clients and enhance their banking experience. Marketing approaches are likely to become more data driven, focusing heavily on cybersecurity and data protection due to the nature of personal information involved.

Sustainability and social responsibility are projected to play a role in marketing narratives. With consumers and businesses placing emphasis on ethical concerns, cannabis bankers will need to promote their services in a manner that aligns with these values. This may involve highlighting eco-friendly financing options for cultivation practices or supporting community projects aimed at areas impacted by previous cannabis regulations.

The future of marketing in the cannabis banking sector looks dynamic and full of potential. It necessitates a mix of embracing technology, practicing marketing, and possessing knowledge. Those in banking who can adapt, embrace technology, and prioritize responsibility will lead the industry by utilizing these qualities to stand out in a competitive and ever-changing market.

Final Thoughts and Call to Action

As we reflect on the state of cannabis banking, one prevailing theme emerges: evolution. The industry has progressed significantly, with cannabis bankers playing a leading role in its growth and development. Looking ahead, these professionals are met with a variety of opportunities and complexities. To succeed, they must adapt to the present while also looking ahead to shape the future of cannabis finance.

Cannabis bankers hold a responsibility in fostering trust, acting as intermediaries between the cannabis sector and the financial realm, so they must continuously earn their client's trust by showcasing expertise in an industry that still grapples with approval. This trust is established through transparency, dependability, and a thorough grasp of regulatory frameworks. It is also reinforced by staying informed about market trends and technological progress, assuring clients that their financial well-being is managed with foresight and sophistication.

Marketing approaches should mirror the industry's values, emphasizing education, compliance, and empowerment. Bankers should aim to simplify the intricacies of cannabis banking for their clients, guiding them through a landscape that can often seem confusing. This educational method also acts as a call to action for customers portraying the cannabis banker as a trusted advisor and partner in seizing the opportunities presented by compliance and innovation.

The ultimate directive for bankers is to strengthen their reputation as pioneers in marketing. With the expansion of the cannabis market, bankers should utilize all resources, from marketing to community involvement, to establish their presence in this industry. They must push for advancement, whether through changes or technological advancements, positioning themselves not just as service providers, but also as influential thinkers and catalysts for change within the sector.

In essence, the role of cannabis bankers goes beyond banking norms. They stand at the forefront of an emerging industry with the ability to shape its trajectory. By adopting a thoughtful marketing approach aligned with the nature of their field, they will drive growth for their clients' enterprises and set a path for overall sector development. As abstract ideas transition into actions, cannabis bankers should step up and shape tomorrow with foresight, dedication, and an unwavering commitment to innovation.

NOTES

1. CannabizTeam. "Marketing in the Cannabis Industry Guide." Last modified September 2023. Accessed May 29, 2024. https://cannabizteam.com/2023/09/marketing-in-the-cannabis-industry-guide.
2. Ibid.
3. Ibid.
4. Flowhub. "Cannabis Marketing Strategies." Accessed June 12, 2024. https://flowhub.com/learn/cannabis-marketing-strategies.
5. Ibid. at 1.
6. Ibid.
7. Galactic Fed. "The Role of Corporate Social Responsibility in Marketing." Accessed June 15, 2024. https://www.galacticfed.com/blog/the-role-of-corporate-social-responsibility-in-marketing#:~:text=Therefore%2C%20CSR%20in%20marketing%20means,to%20social%20and%20environmental%20causes.
8. Ibid. at 4.
9. Ibid.
10. Ibid.
11. Ibid.
12. Ibid. at 1.
13. Ibid.
14. Ibid.
15. Ibid. at 4.
16. Ibid.
17. The Cannabis Marketing Association. "Cultivating Digital Growth: SEO and Content Marketing for Cannabis Brands." Accessed May 14, 2024. https://thecannabismarketingassociation.com/cultivating-digital-growth-seo-and-content-marketing-for-cannabis-brands.
18. Consumer Financial Protection Bureau. Accessed May 15, 2024. https://www.consumerfinance.gov.
19. Ibid. at 4.
20. Ibid. at 1.
21. Ibid. at 4.
22. Ibid.
23. Ibid.

CHAPTER NINE

Competition

INTRODUCTION

Let us discuss a topic that holds increasing significance within the field of cannabis banking – competition. Think back to the days when the cannabis industry began gaining momentum in the early to mid-2010s. At that time, conventional banks were notably and understandably cautious about engaging with anything related to cannabis. This created a void that credit unions, community banks, and private lenders swiftly moved into to establish cannabis-related businesses (CRBs) within the banking system. These pioneers embraced the associated risks, created compliant cannabis programs, and played a role in establishing norms for delivering financial services tailored to cannabis enterprises. However, as the industry demonstrates its resilience and profitability over time, and with rescheduling and other regulatory changes coming, an increasing number of institutions are now turning their focus toward this new industry.

Increasing Interest in Cannabis Banking

Presently, we are witnessing an increase in interest from financial institutions, including some larger, more established banks, cautiously venturing into this arena. Their motivation in part comes from recognizing the opportunities presented by the growing cannabis market, which is forecasted to reach figures in the billions in terms of revenue within just a few years.[1] With new players entering the scene, competition is on the rise in the cannabis banking industry. However, this uptick also sparks a wave of creativity and better services as financial institutions strive to stand out.

An emerging feature of this evolving landscape is the participation of fintech companies. These innovative firms bring ideas and solutions to the table, such as blockchain-based payments and cutting-edge compliance tools. Their ability to swiftly adapt without being weighed down by traditional banking structures allows them to cater effectively to the needs of cannabis enterprises.

As competition intensifies, differentiation becomes crucial. For bankers, this includes identifying and highlighting offerings that set you apart from the rest. Whether it's customer service, tailored financial products, or rigorous compliance measures, we must showcase critical strengths and continually evolve alongside industry trends. The key lies in remaining flexible, embracing new technologies and methodologies, and consistently prioritizing the requirements of cannabis businesses in the approach. In essence, although competition in banking cannabis is increasing, it presents an opportunity for growth rather than a setback.

Impact of Regulatory Changes on Competition

Changes in regulations within the cannabis banking sector influence competition in several ways. On one side, with regulations on the horizon possibly becoming more favorable, like the possible passing of the SAFER Banking Act, it is expected that traditional financial institutions will join the market. This entry of players could lead to competition by lowering fees, enhancing service quality, and increasing access to capital for cannabis businesses.

Market Share and Growth Trends

The cannabis banking industry has seen changes in market share and growth patterns due to shifting regulations, increased acceptance of cannabis, and the entry of financial institutions. While initially dominated by pioneering credit unions and community banks, the sector is now witnessing the emergence of larger traditional banks, fintech companies, and private lenders. The evolving dynamics among these players are reshaping the industry and driving growth in the industry.

Originally, the cannabis banking sector had a handful of institutions willing to bear the associated risks and offered them critical services. Credit unions and community banks led the way by leaning into their customer-centered approaches to offer financial services to cannabis enterprises. By servicing this niche market when larger banks were hesitant, these institutions gained market share by delivering tailored banking solutions and cultivating client connections. Their early involvement played a role in supporting the fledgling cannabis industry's access to banking services and therefore its overall growth.

Private lenders like venture capitalists and specialized lending firms have also emerged as players in this space, bridging the financing and lending gaps left by banks. These lenders, such as FundCanna, are more open to taking on risks and offering financing solutions customized for cannabis businesses. Their support has been crucial in fueling the growth of the cannabis industry across the seed-to-sale players. As the industry matures, private lenders are expected to continue playing a growing role, adding diversity to the current situation.

Cannabis banking is changing significantly as a variety of institutions will enter the market and impact market share and growth patterns. While credit unions and community banks have traditionally held sway, they will be facing competition from larger banks, fintech firms offering banking solutions, and private lenders providing flexible financing options. As regulations evolve and the cannabis industry expands, the competitive environment in banking is expected to become more intense, presenting both challenges and opportunities for all parties involved.[2]

COMPETITIVE STRATEGIES OF TRADITIONAL BANKS

An essential initial step for traditional financial institutions is to set up a cannabis compliance framework. This includes putting in place anti-money laundering (AML) programs, conducting thorough client due diligence, and ensuring continuous adherence to laws like the Bank Secrecy Act (BSA) and other relevant regulations. By showcasing a dedication to compliance, financial institutions can reduce legal risks and foster trust with both regulators and clients.

Approaches to Entering the Cannabis Market

Another effective tactic is starting small and expanding gradually, sometimes called a "crawl, walk, run" strategy. Financial institutions can begin by providing services – such as deposit accounts and basic payment processing – to cannabis businesses before venturing into more intricate and riskier financial offerings like loans and credit lines. This gradual approach enables banks to develop expertise and refine processes steadily while minimizing exposure to risks. Starting with a small-scale approach allows companies to assess market demand and adapt their strategies accordingly.

Research conducted by the Association for Cannabis Banking and RiskScout in 2023 of banking professionals involved in cannabis banking shows that smaller financial institutions have an optimistic view of the future of CRB banking. For institutions with under $5 billion in assets, 59% of respondents felt the industry would be "Somewhat" or "Much" better over the next three years. This is comparatively higher than the 40% of professionals who felt similarly optimistic at institutions with more than $5 billion in assets. This optimism is critical for helping banks decide on taking on additional risk associated with providing loans and lines of credit to CRBs.

Forming partnerships and collaborations can greatly assist an institution that wishes to enter into the cannabis market. By teaming up with established entities in the cannabis sector or fintech firms specializing in compliance solutions, banks can make use of existing knowledge and infrastructure. These partnerships offer access to expertise and technology, reduce the learning curve, increase scale, and enhance services for clients. Working together also helps spread out the risk making it more manageable for financial institutions.

Engaging with regulators and industry stakeholders is crucial for institutions stepping into the cannabis market. Proactive involvement helps banks stay updated on changes that could impact their operations. Through participation in industry discussions and maintaining communication, financial institutions can advocate for clearer regulations that are more supportive and transparent for their cannabis clients.

Financial institutions should look into these factors when considering banking cannabis:

- Creating a compliance framework
- Starting modestly before expanding
- Forming strategic partnerships
- Investing in technology
- Collaborating with regulators
- Promoting transparency and education in financial institutions

As this industry progresses further, these methodologies will be pivotal for maintaining a competitive edge and attaining success in cannabis banking.

Competitive Advantages and Disadvantages of Traditional Banks

Traditional banks have advantages when they step into the cannabis banking industry mostly due to their established infrastructure, ample resources, and wide range of financial services. These banks typically have compliance frameworks and advanced risk management systems in place, allowing them to navigate the complex regulations of the cannabis sector more effectively. Their thorough processes for AML compliance, customer verification, and transaction monitoring serve as a solid foundation for handling the increased risks associated with cannabis banking.

Traditional banks can use their network of branches and ATMs to offer easily accessible banking services to cannabis companies. With both branch locations and advanced digital banking platforms, they can provide an integrated banking experience. Additionally, these banks have the capability to provide products and services like business loans, credit lines, payment processing, and cash management solutions. This diverse range of services positions them as one potential hub for cannabis businesses looking for financial support.

Despite these advantages, there are challenges that come with traditional banks entering the cannabis market. Traditional banks, those operating nationally, might be more cautious when it comes to risk appetite. The legal uncertainty could discourage banks from embracing the cannabis industry, limiting their ability to compete with flexible and agile financial institutions like community banks, credit unions, and fintech companies.

Traditional banks often have established relationships with a clientele that includes risk-averse stakeholders. Getting involved with the cannabis industry could affect these relationships as some clients might see the association with cannabis as controversial or ethically questionable. To address this risk, traditional banks need to manage their image carefully and communicate transparently while showcasing their commitment to compliance and ethical standards.

Additionally, traditional banks may encounter pushback and operational hurdles when venturing into the cannabis market. Their current systems and processes tailored for traditional industries may need significant modifications to cater to the specific requirements of CRBs. This entails updating compliance procedures, educating staff on industry regulations, and investing in technologies capable of handling the large volume of cash transactions that are typical in the cannabis industry. Making these changes could end up being expensive and time consuming, which might slow down the bank's ability to compete effectively in the cannabis market.

Even though traditional banks have advantages when it comes to resources, infrastructure, and services, they also deal with challenges like legal risks, reputation issues, and operational obstacles. By capitalizing on their strengths and addressing their weaknesses, traditional banks can establish themselves as successful collaborators in the expanding and changing cannabis sector.

THE RISE OF FINTECH COMPANIES

The cannabis industry has faced challenges related to regulations and finances leading to the creation of solutions tailored specifically for cannabis businesses. Fintech companies and traditional financial institutions are driving these advancements to address the obstacles cannabis entrepreneurs face.

Innovative Solutions Tailored for Cannabis Businesses

Apart from technology, fintech firms are creating tools for compliance to assist cannabis businesses in navigating complex regulatory environments. These tools utilize algorithms and artificial intelligence (AI) to automate compliance checks, monitor transactions for activities, and ensure adherence to state as well as federal regulations. By incorporating these compliance solutions, cannabis enterprises can significantly lessen the workload and risks linked with compliance procedures. Not only does this help ensure that businesses comply with regulations, but it also enables them to focus more on their main operations and strategies for growth.[3]

Traditional banks, cautious about entering this sector due to risk uncertainties, are now collaborating with fintech companies to offer hybrid solutions. These partnerships combine the compliance knowledge of fintech firms with the capabilities, customer base, and service structures of banks. Tailored services like checking and savings accounts, merchant processing, and lending products are being developed to cater to the needs of cannabis enterprises. For example, some banks provide cash management solutions that include vaulting and transportation services, which mitigates the security risks associated with handling and transporting large amounts of cash.

Digital lending platforms have transformed access to capital for cannabis businesses. These platforms streamline the loan application process offering faster access to funds compared to banking methods. They often utilize credit evaluation models that consider the financial profiles of cannabis enterprises, which may not align directly with conventional lending standards. By doing this, they create avenues for funding start-ups and small to mid-sized companies in the cannabis industry, thereby supporting their growth and expansion.

Competitive Advantages of Fintech Firms

Fintech companies have become contenders in the cannabis banking sector, using their expertise and innovative approaches to tackle the unique challenges that cannabis businesses face. Their competitive edge comes from their flexibility, advanced technology skills, and customer-focused solutions, positioning them well to meet the changing demands of the cannabis industry. Fintech companies can use data-driven insights to offer loan options, improve pricing strategies, and forecast financial requirements for cannabis clients resulting in a more tailored and efficient banking experience.

Focusing on customer needs is also a strength of fintech firms. They prioritize user experiences by designing platforms to use intuitive interfaces and seamless digital interactions. This emphasis on design ensures that cannabis businesses can access and manage their services effortlessly without requiring extensive training or assistance. Additionally, fintech companies typically deliver customer service through various communication channels, providing timely help and support. This high level of engagement builds relationships and loyalty among clients seeking to stand out in a competitive market.

Another advantage of fintech firms is their ability to operate across jurisdictions in the cannabis industry with flexibility. Many fintech companies have experience dealing with environments allowing them to implement compliance solutions adaptable to different state laws and regulations. This adaptability enables them to effectively serve cannabis businesses in multiple regions ensuring a consistent banking experience regardless of location.[4]

In summary, fintech companies:

- Possess strengths that equip them to address the needs of the cannabis banking sector
- Adapt quickly to creating technology-based solutions
- Have expertise in analyzing data and data-driven decision-making
- Focus on customer needs and have the ability to adjust swiftly to regulations

With the expansion and advancement of the cannabis sector, fintech companies are expected to play a prominent role in offering tailored financial services essential for growth and inclusion in the wider financial services industry.

Competition

COMPETITIVE CHALLENGES AND OPPORTUNITIES

Venturing into the cannabis banking sector poses challenges for new players mainly due to the intricate regulatory and legal landscape, substantial compliance expenses, and perceived potential damage to reputation linked with the cannabis industry. These obstacles set barriers to entry that may discourage prospective entrants and demand considerable resources and strategic foresight to surmount.

The federal cannabis ban creates a regulatory minefield for financial institutions, exposing them to potential federal prosecution and complicating compliance efforts. New entrants must navigate through a web of state rules and federal directives like the BSA and AML requirements. Ensuring adherence to these regulations calls for controls and thorough due diligence processes, which can be both time consuming and expensive to put in place.

The financial strain of meeting compliance standards presents another obstacle. Establishing a cannabis banking operation requires investments in technology, legal know-how, and continuous staff training. Financial institutions must implement monitoring systems to monitor transactions, identify suspicious activities, and ensure all operations comply with regulatory norms. Meeting compliance requirements often comes with ongoing costs, which can be challenging for smaller financial institutions or newcomers with limited funds.

Barriers to Entry for New Competitors

Entering the cannabis banking sector poses potential risks for new players. Dealing with the industry might be seen as controversial due to varying views on cannabis. Financial institutions risk distancing stakeholders or clients who may not support their involvement with cannabis companies. Managing perception and communication effectively is crucial for entrants to navigate this perceived reputational risk. Being transparent about compliance efforts and showcasing the advantages of serving the cannabis sector can help reduce these risks. However, establishing and upholding an image of compliance, flexibility, and reliability in this field demands dedication, expertise, and strategic planning.

Additionally, established competitors in the cannabis banking industry have already fostered ties with cannabis businesses and acquired the necessary specialized knowledge. New entrants face challenges competing against these established players who understand the industry's specific requirements and obstacles. To gain market share, offering top-notch service is essential but can be tough without substantial investments in innovation, compliance, and customer relations management.

Breaking into the cannabis banking sector poses challenges for competitors due to a variety of factors. The intricate regulations, compliance requirements, potential damage to reputation, and fierce competition from existing players all contribute to the obstacles that newcomers must surmount. Overcoming these barriers demands resources, careful planning, and a balanced dedication to both following regulations and fostering innovation.

Strategies for Existing Players to Maintain a Competitive Edge

For institutions already involved in cannabis banking, staying competitive means leveraging innovation, following regulations, and putting customers first. With the market getting increasingly crowded and rules changing, existing players need to keep adapting to stay on top.

An important strategy is focusing on customer experience and managing relationships. Building connections with cannabis businesses goes beyond just offering banking services. Financial institutions should provide personalized solutions that meet the needs of cannabis clients – such as tailored loan products, flexible payment options, and dedicated account management services. Offering top-notch customer service and keeping communication open can help establish trust and loyalty. Organizing workshops and online seminars about financial management and regulatory compliance can show a strong dedication to supporting the progress and prosperity of cannabis businesses and the industry at large.

Advocating for cannabis banking regulations is crucial for staying ahead in the industry. Involvement in industry discussions, engaging with policymakers, and pushing for regulatory changes can help financial institutions adapt to evolving laws while influencing policies that benefit the sector. Building a reputation as a leading player in banking can be achieved through proactive engagement with regulators and industry peers.

By implementing these approaches, traditional financial organizations can effectively address the obstacles presented by the cannabis industry, maintain an edge over emerging players, and uphold their commitment to serving their cannabis clientele. Adapting to the changing landscape of the industry will require a dedication to creativity, regulatory adherence, and prioritizing customer needs for prosperity in banking.

Future Trends in Competition within the Cannabis Banking Sector

The cannabis banking industry is on the brink of changes in the upcoming years driven by shifting regulations, technological progress, and the maturation of the market. It's crucial for institutions to grasp these developments to stay competitive and seize opportunities in this fast-growing sector. Traditional banks, previously cautious due to risk uncertainties, might enter the market more boldly, intensifying competition. The entry of institutions could bring more resources and a wider array of services to cannabis companies, potentially lowering costs, and enhancing service quality.[5]

Globally, the cannabis industry is set for expansion as more countries move toward legalization. Banks and fintech companies that can establish a footprint will tap into the increasing demand for cannabis banking solutions. However, achieving this will necessitate an understanding of regulatory frameworks across different regions and the agility to adapt swiftly.

Competition in the cannabis banking sector's future will be influenced by legalization possibilities, technological advancements, strategic partnerships, and global reach. To succeed in this market, financial institutions that can predict and adjust to these developments will have a strong advantage. By being flexible, embracing technology, and nurturing partnerships, banks and fintech firms can secure their leading positions in this changing, exciting, and fast-paced sector.

NOTES

1. Bloomberg News. "Marijuana Banking Is Moving Forward Despite Federal Uncertainty." *Bloomberg*, January 18, 2022. Accessed May 15, 2024. https://www.bloomberg.com/news/newsletters/2022-01-18/marijuana-banking-is-moving-forward-despite-federal-uncertainty.
2. Green Market Report. "Unlocking Growth: Navigating the Evolving Landscape of Cannabis Lending." Accessed May 23, 2024. https://www.greenmarketreport.com/unlocking-growth-navigating-the-evolving-landscape-of-cannabis-lending.
3. SH Financial. "Financial Technology Solutions in Cannabis Banking: Do They Really Work?" Accessed July 23, 2024. https://shfinancial.org/financial-technology-solutions-in-cannabis-banking-do-they-really-work.
4. Ibid.
5. Ibid, at 2.

CHAPTER TEN

Indigenous Tribes – Challenges, Opportunities, and Financial Access

REGULATORY LANDSCAPE FOR TRIBAL NATIONS

The ongoing legalization of cannabis has opened new economic opportunities, especially for indigenous tribes. Due to their status with the US Government, indigenous tribes have the authority to both regulate and participate in the cannabis industry. However, this journey is complicated by challenges and regulatory obstacles. Despite these difficulties, the potential economic advantages are substantial. Cannabis enterprises can generate income, produce employment opportunities, and support community services such as healthcare and education. Nevertheless, tribes must maneuver through a system of state regulations that often clash with each other, creating a precarious legal situation.

Legal Challenges

One of the biggest hurdles for tribes, much like we see in states around the country, is the categorization of cannabis as a Schedule I substance under the Controlled Substances Act (CSA). This designation places cannabis in the same category as heroin and LSD, labeling it as having a potential for abuse and no recognized medical benefits. While the potential for rescheduling opened up in

2024, this current federal stance still conflicts with the increasing number of states that have legalized cannabis for recreational purposes. While the Rohrabacher–Farr amendment (also known as the Rohrabacher–Blumenauer amendment and introduced by US Representative Maurice Hinchey in 2001) prohibits the Justice Department from spending funds to interfere with the implementation of state medical cannabis laws, it does not fully shield tribes engaged in cannabis businesses.[1]

Guidance from the Wilkinson Memo

The guidance outlined in the 2014 Wilkinson Memo offered some direction to tribes suggesting that the Department of Justice (DOJ) would generally not prioritize enforcement against tribes that follow state laws. However, it's important to note that this memo does not carry the weight of law and could be revoked by any administration. Tribes must adhere to the Indian Gaming Regulatory Act (IGRA), which regulates gaming activities on territories. While the IGRA does not *explicitly* address cannabis, certain provisions could be interpreted as applying to cannabis businesses situated on trust lands. Sadly, this adds another layer of ambiguity for tribes to manage carefully.[2]

FINANCIAL ACCESS AND BANKING CHALLENGES

Limited Access to Banking Services

Similar to other non-tribal businesses, tribes must also face the challenges of limited access to traditional banking services. These federal restrictions have led banks to hesitate in offering services to cannabis-related businesses (CRBs), leaving tribes reliant on cash-only transactions, often lacking access to financial technologies and workarounds available to non-tribal companies. Unfortunately, relying heavily on cash transactions not only brings security and safety concerns, but also makes financial management and regulatory compliance more challenging.

Security and Management Issues

Mary Jane Oatman, Executive Director of the indigenous Cannabis Industry Association, highlights the challenges and opportunities for tribes: "Tribes very much maintain those relationships through trade of commodities, and cannabis has just been one of those during that prohibition era that has stayed within the veins of commerce."[3] This highlights the importance of understanding the context of trade and the economic opportunities that cannabis presents for indigenous groups.

The current situation for tribes in the cannabis industry is filled with uncertainty and it also carries a sense of anticipation. Despite these challenges, the growing acceptance of cannabis, combined with the increasing number of states legalizing it, offers tribes a chance to participate in this expanding market. Successful tribal cannabis ventures can serve as role models for tribes that are newly entering the industry.

Josiah Chissoe, from The Monarch Enterprise, reflects on the frustrations and hopes shared by leaders. "It seems the average American thinks that tribes on reservations can do whatever they want because of the unrestrictive laws and gaming and tobacco sales . . . without knowing how dependent on federal funding and protection under strict guidelines [they are]."[4] These tribes heavily rely on funding and must adhere to strict regulations for their protection. This sentiment sheds light on the challenges faced by sovereignty and emphasizes the importance of garnering support and understanding from both the public and policymakers.

This chapter will delve deeper into the legal hurdles, potential risks, opportunities, and the current landscape confronting indigenous tribes in the cannabis industry. Additionally, we will explore real-life examples and offer strategies to address financial barriers that impede the progress of tribal cannabis enterprises.

LEGAL CHALLENGES

Tribes looking to join the cannabis industry must confront complex regulatory requirements. While the federal government still classifies cannabis as a Schedule I drug under the CSA, the Rohrabacher–Farr amendment prevents the DOJ from interfering with state medical cannabis programs, creating a legal gray area for tribes that must comply with both federal and state laws.

Tribes must follow the IGRA governing gaming on territories. Although IGRA does not specifically address cannabis, certain provisions might come into play if cannabis businesses operate on trust lands.[5] This intersection of regulations poses significant challenges and risks for tribal communities seeking to set up and run cannabis enterprises. The overlap of these regulatory frameworks can lead to legal ambiguities and operational difficulties for tribal cannabis businesses.

TRIBAL CANNABIS OPERATIONS

Tribal sovereignty brings a layer of complexity to the growing cannabis industry. Unlike non-tribal entities, tribal lands are not entirely subject to state laws, requiring navigation through a patchwork of federal, state, and tribal regulations. This legal status offers both advantages and challenges for tribes entering the cannabis market.

NuWu Cannabis Marketplace

One noted example is the NuWu Cannabis Marketplace, by the Las Vegas Paiute Tribe. Being one of Nevada's dispensaries, NuWu benefits from its tribal status by avoiding certain state taxes and enabling competitive pricing. However, the tribe encounters uncertainties due to conflicting regulations. This situation emphasizes the fine line tribes must walk between their rights and compliance with legal frameworks.

"This is a moment. It marks the instance of a nation within the continental United States participating in the cannabis industry" stated Benny Tso, a former War Chief of the Las Vegas Paiute Tribe at NuWu's grand opening in 2017.[6] This statement underscores the groundbreaking nature of tribal involvement in cannabis, as well as the unique legal and cultural considerations that come with it. The NuWu Cannabis Marketplace in Las Vegas is among the largest marijuana retail stores in the world.

The intricate blend of sovereignty and cannabis regulations forms an uneven and complex situation. While tribes such as the Las Vegas Paiute Tribe showcase success potential, they also grapple with hurdles. The lack of federal guidance adds another layer of complexity, underscoring the importance for tribes to thoroughly evaluate risks and rewards before venturing into the cannabis market.

ECONOMIC AND SOCIAL IMPACTS

The emerging cannabis industry presents an opportunity for indigenous tribes to strengthen independence and preserve their cultural heritage. By utilizing their status and deep ties to the land, tribes are paving a path toward prosperity while also addressing past injustices and systemic disparities.

A prime illustration of this is the Oglala Sioux Tribe in South Dakota. Faced with poverty and limited economic prospects, the tribe embraced cannabis as a solution. The earnings from their cannabis ventures have played a role in funding community initiatives, enhancing infrastructure, and delivering services to tribal members. This success story underscores the impact of cannabis on communities grappling with economic challenges.

"The cannabis industry has been a game-changer for our tribe," stated an Oglala Sioux Tribe representative to GreenState, "It has provided us with the resources to address critical needs and invest in our future." This sentiment is echoed by numerous other tribes who have embraced cannabis as a means of economic empowerment.[7]

Another compelling case can be seen with the Shinnecock Nation in New York. Their cannabis project, Little Beach Harvest, goes beyond business; it's an endeavor that reflects the tribe's profound connection to the plant. Chenae Bullock, Managing Director of Little Beach Harvest, eloquently captures this sentiment, "What we are doing with this sacred plant is going to heal not only the Shinnecock community but people around the world."[8]

The holistic approach taken by tribes toward cultivating and sharing cannabis mirrors a trend. Many see cannabis as more than a product; it holds special value with healing and spiritual properties. By integrating wisdom, history, and customs into their cannabis activities, tribes are reclaiming their roots and fostering a sense of pride and solidarity within their communities.

As an example of reinvesting back into the community, the Stillaguamish Tribe charges a tribal tax on cannabis sales that is at least 100% of the state tax. "The biggest upside is the fact that the state cannot collect excise taxes from us for cannabis sales. We are required to charge a Tribal Tax which is 'at least 100%' of the state's tax on cannabis products, but the entirety of that tax goes back to the Tribe, allowing us to re-invest in our communities directly," the Stillaguamish Board explained.[9]

Despite these obstacles the future appears promising for engagement with tribes. With growing backing for legalization and an increasing acknowledgment of rights, tribes are well-equipped to take on prominent roles within the cannabis sector. Their distinct outlook and dedication to communal tribal practices serve as an example for the entire industry and it is important to acknowledge and appreciate the contributions made by indigenous tribes.

CURRENT ENVIRONMENT AND BANKING CHALLENGES

As of 2024, there were 57 tribally owned cannabis dispensaries – both medical and adult-use – operating across nine states in the United States. This is a 25% increase from January 2023, highlighting rapid growth and economic potential of tribal cannabis businesses. While many of these stores are located on tribal lands, some operate on non-tribal land as well. This significant growth underscores the increasing participation of Native American tribes in the cannabis industry. The number of tribes operating these businesses has also risen, with 47 different tribes now involved, an increase of approximately 30% since January 2023.[10]

As mentioned earlier, this rapid growth highlights the seriousness of limited availability of banking services and newer financial technologies for indigenous tribes entering the growing cannabis industry, and is even more dire for tribes than for their non-indigenous counterparts. Even though cannabis is legal in some states, the federal ban still poses a challenge, making it difficult for tribes to fully engage in this profitable, growing market.

Excluding cannabis businesses from the system also has broader economic consequences. A 2021 report by the Minority Cannabis Business Association (MCBA) highlights that the lack of banking access "prevents tribes from creating jobs, generating tax revenue, and investing in their communities."[11] This untapped revenue could play a role in addressing social issues, like poverty, healthcare, and education within tribal areas.

A policy paper by the National Indian Gaming Association (NIGA) states that "The current banking situation for cannabis businesses is not only unfair, it's dangerous." The reliance on cash transactions not only increases the risk of crime but also makes it difficult for tribes to track and report their financial activity, potentially leading to compliance issues with regulatory authorities.[12]

The absence of regulations, like the SAFER Banking Act, further complicates this situation. The current legislation aims to protect banks engaged in cannabis businesses. The delay in approval by Congress has left tribes in a state of uncertainty and financial exposure. Only a handful of state-chartered banks and credit unions are open to providing services to tribal enterprises, leaving limited options for financial services.

The repercussions of the lack of banking access are also noticeable in the inefficiencies it introduces into operations. For instance, tribal businesses often resort to expensive methods for managing payroll and financial transactions. This not only raises expenses, but also redirects resources from essential areas like community growth and social services.

The absence of banking access for tribal cannabis ventures is an issue with widespread implications. It obstructs the advancement of communities while perpetuating systemic inequalities. Overcoming these obstacles is key to unleashing the opportunities of tribal cannabis enterprises and promoting lasting growth within tribal societies.

CASE STUDY 1 **SHINNECOCK NATION**[13]

The Shinnecock Nation in New York is making strides in the cannabis industry by establishing an operation that includes a dispensary, wellness center, and cultivation facilities. This pioneering effort showcases how Native American tribes can participate in, and reap the benefits of, the growing cannabis market.

At the core of the Shinnecock Nation's endeavor is their partnership with TILT Holdings, a company specializing in providing cannabis business solutions for integrated operations. Through this collaboration, the Shinnecock Nation has built a vertically integrated cannabis business by leveraging TILT Holdings' expertise in cultivation, manufacturing, and retail to expand their capabilities and market presence.

Beyond being a business endeavor, the Shinnecock Nation's entrance into cannabis represents their sovereignty and economic self-determination. This venture into the industry opens up opportunities for their community, and asserts their rights and independence. This step holds significance considering the challenges Native American tribes have faced in achieving economic self-sufficiency.

The wellness center linked to the Shinnecock Nation's cannabis business aims to provide services that support mental and spiritual well-being. This is in line with the goal of using cannabis for healing and wellness, echoing its medicinal use in indigenous cultures. Furthermore, the cultivation facilities ensure that the cannabis products maintain high quality standards, blending industry norms with modern cultivation methods.

The holistic approach taken by the Shinnecock Nation toward their enterprise serves as a blueprint for tribes contemplating entry into the field. Through partnerships and a focus on integration, tribes can establish sustainable business models that honor their heritage while fostering economic growth.

The collaboration between the Shinnecock Nation and TILT Holdings in the cannabis sector exemplifies a blend of principles with modern business expertise. It showcases how the cannabis industry has potential not just for progress, but also for promoting healing within Native American communities.

CASE STUDY 2   **OGLALA SIOUX TRIBE**[14]

The cannabis business owned by the Oglala Sioux Tribe on the Pine Ridge Reservation serves as an example of ownership guaranteeing that all profits and tax revenues directly support the tribe. This strategy plays a role in promoting growth and alleviating poverty within the community.

The cannabis enterprise on the Pine Ridge Reservation marks a stride toward self-reliance for the Oglala Sioux Tribe. By maintaining ownership of the venture, the tribe ensures that all financial benefits remain within the community, offering resources for social initiatives, infrastructure enhancements, and other communal advantages. This approach sets it apart from cannabis ventures that may involve investors who share in the profits.

Trent Hancock, a member of the Oglala Sioux community, highlights the distinctive and empowering aspect of this business model: "The Oglala Sioux Tribe was the first to pass a 'required small business ordinance.' All owners have to be tribal members, no outside investors were allowed."[15] This regulation guarantees that all economic gains from the cannabis industry are specifically allocated to members, nurturing a sense of belonging and pride within the community.

This ordinance ensures that all economic benefits from the cannabis sector are exclusively reserved for members cultivating a feeling of ownership and communal pride. The profits generated from cannabis sales are used to support a variety of community projects and services, including healthcare, education, and housing, directly enhancing the well-being of its members. Additionally, the cannabis sector offers a range of job opportunities within the tribe from farming roles to management and technical positions. This diverse approach aids in skill development and community capacity, solidifying the tribe's base.

The Oglala Sioux Tribe's strategy for cannabis business sets an example for Native American tribes by showcasing how tribal sovereignty and resources can be harnessed to establish sustainable and self-sufficient economic models. This endeavor emphasizes the significance of maintaining control over endeavors to ensure that the community reaps the benefits.

The Oglala Sioux Tribe's cannabis business on the Pine Ridge Reservation exemplifies the power of full tribal ownership in driving economic development and reducing poverty. Trent Hancock's statement underscores the tribe's commitment to self-determination and community empowerment. By keeping external investors out and focusing on internal growth, the Oglala Sioux Tribe is setting a precedent for economic resilience and community-centric development.

CONCLUSION

As highlighted in this chapter, while there are many similarities between indigenous tribes and other non-tribal CRBs, tribes face very different and unique challenges, and unique opportunities associated with setting up tribal businesses. These include:

- Regulations and Restrictions: Due to tribal laws intersecting with federal, state, and local restrictions, tribes confront a myriad of additional hurdles associated with operating legal cannabis operations on reservations. It is imperative that indigenous nations fully understand how these regulations and laws impact their own CRBs, and consult with appropriate legal counsel and experienced consultants to navigate these complicated waters.
- Economic Impacts: Even more than other non-indigenous communities that experience upticks in economic benefits associated with new CRBs opening up, tribal nations have experienced more pronounced and significant benefits from cannabis sales. With indigenous tribes continuing to lag the rest of the nation in job growth, revenues, and community improvements, the opportunities that arise from cannabis revenue can mean significant improvements and economic autonomy over capital projects, self-determination, and new job growth.
- Banking Challenges: Much like their non-tribal counterparts, launching and sustaining CRBs requires access to financial products and services, payment channels, insurance, and other resources necessary to operate these indigenous businesses. While most non-tribal CRBs have been able to develop various workarounds and fintech solutions to aid them in transacting business activity without relying solely upon cash, indigenous businesses often lack these resources, creating additional economic and security concerns for tribal businesses.

As the nation awaits Washington D.C. and politicians to sort out the myriad of laws, guidelines, and regulations governing the cannabis industry in the US, indigenous tribes face an even longer and more circuitous route to legalization. Lawmakers must realize how imperative it is that they do not overlook tribal concerns and challenges, as these revenue streams can mean significant growth and opportunities for people who struggle every day to just meet the needs for basic standard of living.

NOTES

1. Schroeder, Michael "the Aging Ent." "Medical Cannabis Protection: Rohrabacher-Farr Amendment." *CannaCon*. Accessed June 8, 2024. https://cannacon.org/medical-cannabis-protection-rohrabacher-farr-amendment.
2. U.S. Department of Justice. "Policy Statement Regarding Marijuana Issues in Indian Country." Memorandum from Monty Wilkinson, Director of the Executive Office for United States Attorneys. October 28, 2014.
3. "Indigenous Cannabis Industry Association: An Interview with Mary Jane Oatman." *Cannabis Business Times*. Accessed April 19, 2024. https://www.cannabisbusinesstimes.com/news/indigenous-cannabis-industry-association-mary-jane-oatman-interview.
4. StratCann. "How Cannabis Is Taking Shape for Native Americans and First Nations Tribes." Accessed June 2, 2024. https://stratcann.com/insight/how-cannabis-is-taking-shape-for-native-americans-and-first-nations-tribes-2.
5. National Indian Gaming Commission. "Frequently Asked Questions regarding IGRA and Cannabis." Accessed June 8, 2024. www.nigc.gov.
6. Tso, Benny. As quoted in "Native American Tribe Opens Marijuana Dispensary in Las Vegas." Accessed May 26, 2024. https://nvmarijuana.com/4153/nevada-marijuana-news/native-american-tribe-opens-marijuana-dispensary-in-las-vegas.
7. "Native American Cannabis Business." *GreenState*. Accessed June 30, 2024. https://www.greenstate.com/news/native-american-cannabis-business.
8. "Chenae Bullock: Bringing Ancestral Wisdom to Modern Cannabis." Veriheal. Accessed July 23, 2024. https://www.veriheal.com/blog/chenae-bullock-bringing-ancestral-wisdom-to-modern-cannabis.
9. Downs, David. "Native American Cannabis Business." *GreenState*. Accessed June 23, 2024. https://www.greenstate.com/news/native-american-cannabis-business.
10. "High Times MJ Biz Data Shows Growing Number of Native American Tribal Cannabis Business Owners." Cannabis Law Report. Accessed July 8, 2024. https://cannabislaw.report/high-times-mj-biz-data-shows-growing-number-of-native-american-tribal-cannabis-business-owners.
11. Minority Cannabis Business Association. "MCBA Social Equity Report." Accessed July 2, 2024. https://minoritycannabis.org/1739-2.
12. Ibid. at 5.
13. Levenson, Max Savage. "Native Tribes Leading New York Legal Cannabis." Leafly. Accessed July 23, 2024. https://www.leafly.com/news/industry/native-tribes-leading-new-york-legal-cannabis.
14. Downs, David. "Native American Cannabis Business." *GreenState*. Accessed July 23, 2024. https://www.greenstate.com/news/native-american-cannabis-business.
15. Ibid.

CHAPTER ELEVEN

Cannabis Insurance and Its Impact on Bankers

 INSURANCE OVERVIEW

The cannabis industry, which used to be on the outskirts of legality and societal acceptance, has experienced growth and integration into mainstream society in recent years. This expanding sector includes activities such as cultivation, production, distribution, and retailing. Despite its steady growth and expansion, the cannabis industry faces challenges due to its intricate regulatory landscape and the enduring stigma surrounding cannabis consumption.

Obtaining Insurance Is a Major Obstacle for CRBs
A major obstacle for cannabis companies is obtaining insurance coverage. Unlike traditional industries, these businesses operate within a legal gray area where state laws often conflict with federal regulations. This discrepancy makes it difficult to secure insurance as many insurers are wary of entering a market that is perceived as high risk. As a result, cannabis businesses often struggle with coverage and face steep premiums for limited insurance options available to them.

Cannabis insurance is a field that focuses on addressing the risks that come with the cannabis industry. It includes types of policies such as liability, product liability, property insurance, and crop insurance that are customized to meet the specific needs of cannabis businesses. These policies are meant to provide protection against risks like theft, property damage, and regulatory compliance issues. As the cannabis market evolves so does the landscape of cannabis insurance, highlighting the importance of understanding this sector for all parties involved.[1]

The Importance of Understanding Cannabis Insurance

For bankers, having a grasp of cannabis insurance is essential for several reasons. Firstly, having proper insurance coverage serves as an indicator of a company's stability and its ability to manage risks effectively. When assessing clients for loans or financial services, bankers need to evaluate their insurance policies to ensure they offer protection against potential losses and liabilities. This thorough examination safeguards the bank's investments and promotes a more stable and long-lasting financial partnership.

The complexities of insuring cannabis have an impact on how banks follow banking regulations. Banks that serve the cannabis sector must maneuver through a maze of state and federal laws including the Bank Secrecy Act (BSA) and regulations on anti-money laundering (AML). By ensuring that their cannabis clients have insurance coverage, banks can meet compliance requirements reducing financial risks.[2] Understanding the specifics of cannabis insurance empowers bankers to better assist their clients while following guidelines.

The significance of cannabis insurance goes beyond compliance and risk management. It also shapes how the cannabis industry is perceived and its legitimacy. With more insurers entering the market offering coverage, the industry gains credibility and stability. This can attract services and investments driving further growth and normalization of cannabis businesses.[3] Bankers can play a role in this process by advocating for their clients to have access to insurance products.

Insurance Innovations in the Industry

The cannabis insurance sector is rapidly evolving, introducing products and services to meet unaddressed needs. Innovations, like crop insurance tailored to cannabis strains and coverage for cyber threats targeting cannabis businesses, showcase the nature of this industry.[4] It is crucial for bankers to stay updated on these advancements to offer advice and assistance to their clients ensuring they are well protected against emerging risks.

The convergence of cannabis insurance and banking is an area requiring attention and expertise. By grasping the challenges of the cannabis industry and the nuances of cannabis insurance, bankers can effectively assess and support their clients. This understanding boosts the stability and growth of cannabis businesses and contributes to the overall development and acceptance of the industry within the broader financial landscape. With the expanding cannabis market, informed and proactive bankers will play a role in navigating its intricacies and unlocking its potential.

UNDERSTANDING CANNABIS INSURANCE

Insurance for cannabis-related businesses is a sector within the insurance industry that caters to the specific needs and risks of businesses involved in cannabis. This kind of insurance is crucial for managing the risks that come with operating in the cannabis industry, such as cultivation, manufacturing, distribution, and retail. Given the complexities of the cannabis sector, having the right insurance coverage is essential for running a successful business. Cannabis insurance helps companies handle losses and liabilities while promoting stability and growth in this growing market.

Cannabis insurance covers a variety of policies designed to address the risks faced by cannabis businesses. These policies include:

- Liability insurance for injury and property damage claims
- Product liability insurance to guard against claims related to cannabis product use
- Property insurance for physical assets like buildings and equipment
- Crop insurance to protect cannabis plants from risks like fire, theft, and natural disasters

Each type of insurance plays a role in protecting cannabis businesses from financial challenges. Having insurance coverage is crucial for any cannabis business as it protects against risks like customer injuries on the premises or damage from business operations. This insurance is especially vital in the cannabis industry, where accidents and injuries can be prevalent due to the nature of the products and work environment. For example, dispensaries with a lot of visitors or cultivation facilities with industrial equipment may face risks, making general liability insurance essential for protection.[5]

Types of Insurance for CRBs

Cannabis insurance includes product liability coverage which is crucial for safeguarding businesses from claims concerning the quality and safety of their products. With regulations and the risk of challenges arising from adverse reactions or faults in cannabis goods, this insurance plays a vital role. For instance, should a consumer suffer health issues after using a cannabis item, product liability insurance can handle expenses and any compensation payouts. This safeguard is indispensable for securing the stability of enterprises and securing their future sustainability.[6]

Property insurance is crucial for cannabis companies to safeguard their assets. This encompasses protecting buildings, equipment, inventory, and other tangible resources. Cultivation and manufacturing sites typically require investments in specialized equipment and infrastructure. Property insurance serves to reduce the losses resulting from fire, theft, vandalism, or natural calamities. Such insurance coverage enables businesses to swiftly bounce back and recommence operations following an incident, thereby reducing downtime and financial repercussions.[7]

Crop insurance is made for cannabis farmers to safeguard their plants from risks. Like any crop, cannabis can be harmed by things like lack of water, pests, and diseases. Crop insurance gives money to cover losses caused by these risks, which helps farmers deal with the unpredictability of farming. This insurance is crucial for marijuana growers because they could lose a lot of money if they do not have protection.[8]

Navigating the world of insurance for cannabis businesses can be quite challenging due to the absence of uniformity and the changing regulatory landscape. It is crucial for these businesses to assess their insurance requirements diligently and collaborate with brokers and insurers to obtain coverage. This entails recognizing the risks linked to their activities, staying aware of updates, and guaranteeing that their insurance plans are thorough and current. By taking these steps, cannabis enterprises can effectively mitigate risks and safeguard their interests.

 REGULATORY LANDSCAPE

The world of cannabis insurance is intricate and always evolving, posing challenges and opportunities for both insurers and cannabis companies. While cannabis is labeled as a Schedule I substance at the federal level, making it legally complex, many states have legalized its recreational use, leading to a diverse range of state regulations with varying demands and enforcement measures.

Overview of Federal and State Regulations Affecting Cannabis Insurance

Federal rules significantly impact the cannabis insurance sector. Due to the federal ban on cannabis, insurance providers are hesitant to cover cannabis businesses due to legal concerns. This ban also complicates matters related to commerce across state lines and banking, which restricts the availability of insurance products tailored for the cannabis industry. Nonetheless, federal entities like FinCEN have issued guidance to institutions on offering services to cannabis businesses while complying with laws.[9]

State regulations also play a role in shaping the landscape of cannabis insurance. States that have legalized cannabis have set up their structures with specific requirements for insurance coverage in place for cannabis businesses. In states like California and Colorado, cannabis companies are required to have insurance coverage, including liability and product liability insurance, to acquire and retain their licenses. These regulations are unique to each state and aim to guarantee that cannabis businesses have insurance protection against risks and legal responsibilities.

Compliance Requirements for Insurers and Cannabis Businesses

Operating in the cannabis market, insurance companies face complex compliance rules. They need to adhere to both state laws and make sure their policies align with the requirements of each jurisdiction. This often involves checks on clients to ensure they follow state regulations, manage risks effectively, and meet insurance standards. Noncompliance can have financial consequences for insurers.

For cannabis businesses, following insurance regulations is crucial. They must have the coverage to operate legally in their states, meeting minimum requirements like liability, product liability, and property insurance, set by regulators. It's essential for these businesses to keep their policies updated to reflect any regulatory changes.

Regulatory changes significantly impact cannabis insurance policies and premiums. Shifts at the state level can change the risk landscape for these businesses, influencing their insurance needs and costs. Changes in state regulations, such as those that raise licensing criteria or enforce safety protocols, may cause insurance costs to go up as insurers adapt their pricing to account for the risks. On the other hand, regulatory modifications that offer increased clarity and stability to cannabis enterprises could lead to reduced premiums and better insurance conditions for this industry.

Impact of Regulatory Changes on Insurance Policies and Premiums

In recent times the cannabis insurance market has seen some regulatory changes. The passing of the Farm Bill in 2018, which made hemp and its products legal, has greatly impacted how insurance works in this sector. This law has led to insurance options for businesses, showing a potential blueprint for how national legalization of cannabis could shake up the wider cannabis insurance market.

Additionally, certain states are taking measures to boost transparency and accountability in the cannabis industry. For example, California's Bureau of Cannabis Control now requires cannabis businesses to reveal their insurance policies during the licensing process. These rules aim to make sure that these businesses have insurance coverage and give regulators oversight.[10]

The changing regulatory environment is also driving insurance innovation. As the industry grows and regulations solidify, insurers are offering products tailored to meet cannabis companies' needs. These offerings include coverage for risks like crop failure, cyber threats, and product recalls. By addressing needs in the industry, these innovations are improving risk management solutions for businesses.[11]

However, despite these developments there are still hurdles ahead. The absence of legalization remains a barrier hindering the availability of insurance products and services for cannabis companies. The varying regulations across states creates a sometimes perplexing situation for insurers and businesses alike.

The regulatory framework for cannabis insurance is characterized by intricacy and evolution. For insurers and cannabis enterprises, staying aware of updates and adhering to standards are crucial for navigating this dynamic sector. With potential changes in regulations on the horizon, the cannabis insurance sector is poised for expansion and innovation, offering new opportunities for both insurers and businesses.

 THE ROLE OF INSURANCE IN RISK MANAGEMENT

Insurance plays a role in helping cannabis businesses manage risks by providing protection against various potential losses and liabilities. With the growth and changes in the cannabis sector, companies encounter a range of risks, including product recalls, regulatory issues, property damage, and theft. By obtaining the right insurance coverage, cannabis firms can reduce these risks ensuring their sustainability and financial well-being.

How Insurance Helps Mitigate Risks for Cannabis Businesses

The significance of insurance in mitigating risks for cannabis businesses lies in its ability to offer support for losses. For instance, general liability insurance can cover expenses linked to harm or property damage claims while product liability insurance guards against claims concerning the safety and effectiveness of cannabis products. These insurance policies are crucial for protecting a business's stability during legal battles or other significant liabilities.

Furthermore, insurance aids companies in adhering to standards – an aspect of risk management within the cannabis field. Many states require that cannabis businesses have types of insurance as a prerequisite for their permits. Ensuring that businesses have sufficient insurance coverage is crucial for them to follow state regulations. This helps them avoid fines, penalties, and the risk of being shut down. Compliance reduces risks and also boosts the reputation and credibility of the cannabis industry in general.

Importance of Comprehensive Risk Management Strategies

It is imperative that cannabis companies have risk management plans to effectively manage the unpredictable nature of the industry. These plans include recognizing risks, evaluating how likely they are to occur and their potential effects, and putting in place actions to reduce them. Insurance plays a role in these plans by offering a safety cushion that enables businesses to bounce back from incidents and maintain their operations. Inadequate insurance coverage could spell disaster for a cannabis business as a single substantial loss might lead to ruin or closure.

Examples of Effective Risk Management Practices in the Cannabis Industry

Effective risk management within the cannabis industry goes beyond getting insurance. It involves taking steps like implementing internal controls such as regular safety checks, employee training programs, and strict quality assurance processes. For example, cultivation sites might invest in high-tech security systems to prevent theft, while dispensaries could follow inventory management practices to reduce losses and stay compliant with state regulations. These actions help decrease the chances of incidents that may lead to insurance claims, ultimately reducing risk exposure.

Another effective risk management strategy in the cannabis sector is using technology to boost efficiency and minimize risks. Many cannabis companies are now using seed-to-sale tracking systems that monitor every stage of a cannabis product's life cycle from cultivation to sale. These systems help businesses follow regulations and offer valuable insights to identify and address potential issues proactively. By leveraging technology, cannabis companies can enhance their risk management efforts and strengthen their resilience.

Insurance also plays a role in supporting business continuity planning, a part of risk management. Business continuity planning involves creating procedures and strategies to ensure a business can keep running during disruptions. Business interruption insurance can offer assistance to cover lost revenue and operational costs in case a business has to temporarily shut down due to a covered incident such as a fire or natural disaster. This kind of insurance is essential for supporting cannabis businesses in staying stable and recovering swiftly from disruptions.

Apart from the insurance options, there are insurance products emerging to tackle the unique risks faced by the cannabis sector. For instance, crop insurance customized for cannabis growers provides coverage for losses caused by weather conditions, pests, and other farming risks. Similarly, cyber liability insurance shields against data breaches and cyberattacks, which are on the rise as cannabis companies embrace technology tools and platforms. These specialized insurances bridge gaps in coverage and offer comprehensive risk management solutions tailored for the cannabis industry.[12]

Effective risk management strategies in the cannabis field often involve working with insurance brokers and risk management experts. These professionals assist companies in identifying their risk factors, assessing their insurance requirements, and devising customized risk management strategies. By collaborating with professionals, cannabis businesses can ensure they have coverage and plans in place to minimize risks and safeguard their operations.

Insurance plays a role in the risk management framework for cannabis enterprises offering safeguards against diverse risks. Implementing risk management strategies, paired with insurance coverage and proactive initiatives, is essential for securing the long-term prosperity and stability of cannabis ventures. Through adoption of risk management techniques, utilization of technology advancements, and nurturing a risk management culture, cannabis businesses can mitigate potential setbacks, meet regulatory obligations, and strengthen their operational durability in an ever-evolving industry.

INSURANCE CONSIDERATIONS FOR BANKERS

It is important for bankers involved in the cannabis sector to understand the intricacies of cannabis insurance. Insurance not only helps reduce risks for cannabis companies, but also influences the banking dynamic significantly. Due to the nature of the cannabis industry and its intricate regulatory landscape, having insurance coverage offers a sense of security that can enhance the appeal of cannabis clients to banking institutions by ensuring that cannabis businesses have insurance to mitigate their risk levels. This helps establish stronger, more lucrative partnerships.

How Cannabis Insurance Affects the Banking Relationship

Insuring cannabis has an impact on the banking connection in several ways. It acts as a way to manage risks that can safeguard both the bank and the cannabis company from harm. For instance, if there is a claim of product liability or property damage, having insurance can avoid financial setbacks for the cannabis business, ultimately lowering the chances of loan defaults or other financial issues for the bank. This security makes banks more comfortable in offering loans, lines of credit, and other financial assistance to cannabis customers.

Assessing the Adequacy of a Cannabis Client's Insurance Coverage

Evaluating the insurance coverage of a business in the cannabis industry is crucial for banks to maintain a banking relationship. This evaluation includes examining the types and amounts of insurance coverage, ensuring that the policies are current, and confirming that the coverage meets industry norms and regulatory standards. By conducting insurance reviews, banks can gain an understanding of their cannabis clients' risk profiles and make well-informed decisions regarding offering credit and other financial services.

Ensuring Compliance with Banking Regulations through Proper Insurance

Proper insurance plays an important role in helping banks in the cannabis industry follow banking regulations. To provide services to cannabis businesses, banks must follow state laws like the BSA and AML regulations. Having the right insurance coverage is essential for banks to show that their cannabis clients are managing risks effectively and operating legally. For example, having liability insurance is vital for a cannabis business's compliance program, which in turn supports the bank's efforts to comply with regulations.

The influence of cannabis insurance on lending decisions and assessing credit risks is significant. Insurance coverage can impact whether a bank approves or denies a loan application from a cannabis business. Banks often require borrowers to have specific types of insurance, such as liability and property insurance as part of the loan conditions. This ensures that borrowers have protection in place, reducing the chances of loan defaults and enhancing the creditworthiness of the cannabis business overall. Having insurance coverage can have an impact on how a bank views the risk profile of a cannabis business, potentially aiding the business in obtaining more favorable loan terms.

Impact on Lending Practices and Credit Risk Assessment

Banks must consider the dangers of providing loans to cannabis businesses without insurance coverage. Insufficient insurance could expose the bank to increased risks, like loan defaults and legal obligations. By mandating that cannabis clients hold insurance policies, banks can shield themselves from these risks and ensure they are lending to businesses capable of managing potential financial challenges.

Insurance considerations are also vital in monitoring customer relationships. Banks must regularly update their clients' insurance plans to guarantee they meet requirements and follow regulations. Through oversight of their clients' insurance protection, banks can proactively mitigate risks and thereby address any emerging issues promptly.

Apart from safeguarding the bank's interests, ensuring that cannabis clients have sufficient insurance coverage can be advantageous for the clients themselves. Robust insurance coverage can bolster the stability and resilience of cannabis enterprises making them dependable partners for banks. This could foster lasting banking relationships founded on trust and assurance.

Moreover, banks have the opportunity to educate their clients about the significance of insurance and assist them in navigating the insurance market. By offering advice on selecting insurance policies and linking clients with insurance providers, banks can strengthen their client connections and contribute to the enduring success of cannabis enterprises. This collaborative strategy fosters partnerships and cultivates a positive image for the bank within the cannabis sector.

To sum up, considering insurance matters is a component of the banking association with cannabis enterprises. By ensuring that cannabis clients possess fitting insurance coverage, banks can mitigate risks, adhere to mandates, and make well-informed lending judgments. Extensive insurance protection safeguards not only the concerns of both the bank and the cannabis enterprise, but also elevates the general dependability and credibility of the cannabis industry. As the cannabis industry progresses, the role of insurance in risk management and banking relationships will remain crucial for both banks and their cannabis clientele.

CHALLENGES FACED BY BANKERS

Banking professionals involved in the cannabis sector encounter hurdles due to the intricate nature and uncertainties associated with cannabis insurance. A key challenge lies in verifying and comprehending the insurance plans maintained by enterprises. Unlike sectors with established insurance standards, the cannabis industry is relatively young and lacks consistent practices in insurance. This absence of uniformity presents difficulties for bankers in evaluating the sufficiency and legitimacy of the insurance protection held by their cannabis clientele.

Difficulties in Verifying and Understanding Cannabis Insurance Policies

The complexities of insuring cannabis businesses often require bankers to have knowledge that goes beyond financial expertise. Unique risks faced by these businesses such as crop failure, regulatory compliance issues, and product liability concerns call for insurance products tailored to the needs of the cannabis industry. It's crucial for bankers to grasp the details of these policies from terms and conditions to exclusions, to accurately assess the risk profiles of their clients. However, obtaining this level of understanding can be challenging due to the changing landscape of the cannabis insurance market.

The absence of insurance practices within the cannabis industry adds another layer of intricacy. Insurance providers serving cannabis companies may vary in experience and expertise, resulting in differences in policy offerings and coverage terms. This variability makes it challenging for bankers to compare policies and determine if their clients are adequately covered. The lack of industry standards also means that banks must dedicate time and resources to ensure their cannabis customers have adequate and sufficient insurance protection.

Overcoming Stigma and Misconceptions about Cannabis Insurance

One of the obstacles to overcome is changing perceptions and misunderstandings linked to cannabis insurance. Despite the increasing acceptance and legalization of cannabis, there is still a prevailing stigma that can affect how individuals in the banking sector view it. Some bankers might hesitate to engage with cannabis-related businesses due to concerns about their reputation or misconceptions about the legality and legitimacy of operations. This stigma can cause reluctance to offer services to cannabis clients, including examining their insurance coverage.

The Importance of Developing Expertise in Insurance

To tackle these obstacles, banks need to cultivate knowledge and strong internal procedures for managing clients in the cannabis sector. This involves training employees to grasp the risks and insurance requirements of the cannabis industry, establishing criteria for assessing insurance plans, and staying informed about regulatory changes. By acquiring this expertise, banks can better evaluate their cannabis clients' risk profiles and offer suitable financial services.

Promoting communication and collaboration with insurance providers can assist banks in overcoming challenges related to verifying and understanding cannabis insurance policies. By collaborating with reputable insurers specializing in cannabis, banks can gain insights into available coverage options and ensure adequate protection for their clients. This cooperative approach can also help standardize practices and enhance transparency within the cannabis insurance market.

Bankers encounter obstacles when dealing with clients in the cannabis industry, especially when it comes to verifying and comprehending insurance policies related to cannabis. Addressing the absence of procedures, overcoming prejudices, and managing legal ambiguities pose substantial challenges that demand expertise and proactive approaches. Through promoting learning, encouraging cooperation, and adopting a collaborative mindset, financial institutions can enhance their support for the cannabis sector and contribute positively to its ongoing development and acceptance.

CONCLUSION

Recap of Key Points Discussed in the Chapter

In this chapter we have explored the significance of insurance in the cannabis industry, emphasizing its role in managing risks and influencing banking relationships. We started by outlining the range of insurance options to cannabis companies such as liability, product liability, property insurance, and crop insurance. These policies are fundamental for addressing the risks that come with operating in the cannabis sector, providing a financial safety net that ensures business stability and continuity.

We also delved into the regulatory environment, examining how both federal and state regulations impact cannabis insurance. The legal complexities at the federal level, combined with varying state regulations, create a landscape for insurers and cannabis-related businesses alike. Compliance with these regulations is essential not only for shielding businesses from consequences but also for boosting their credibility and standing within the industry. For bankers, understanding these intricacies is critical for evaluating risk with their clients' insurance coverage and ensuring compliance with banking laws.

Comprehensive insurance coverage assists cannabis businesses in mitigating losses, maintaining adherence, and bolstering overall operational resilience. Risk management is crucial for the success of cannabis businesses and this includes having adequate insurance coverage and taking steps such as safety audits and embracing technology.

We also discussed the importance of insurance considerations for bankers, stressing the need for evaluation of cannabis clients' insurance policies. Making sure that clients have coverage is about safeguarding the bank's financial interests and complying with regulations. The type of insurance a client has can impact lending decisions, affect credit risk evaluations, and enhance banking relationships with cannabis businesses.

Bankers face challenges when dealing with the cannabis industry, such as verifying and understanding cannabis insurance policies, navigating through practices, and overcoming negative perceptions. To tackle these challenges effectively, banks need to build knowledge, collaborate with trusted insurers, and take an approach to managing relationships with cannabis clients. Overcoming these hurdles can lead to sustainable partnerships between banks and cannabis enterprises.

Encouragement for Bankers to Engage Proactively with Cannabis Businesses and Insurers

In summary, insurance plays a role in managing risks for cannabis businesses, supporting their stability both operationally and financially. Bankers need to grasp the nuances of cannabis insurance to manage risks effectively, maintain compliance, and build banking relationships with clients. By staying updated, taking a stance, and addressing the challenges of the cannabis sector, banks can contribute to its growth and integration into the wider financial framework. Collaboration among banks, insurers, and cannabis businesses will be crucial in navigating the complexities of this evolving industry and realizing its potential.

NOTES

1. Sarah M. Davis, "Compliance and Cannabis banking: Navigating regulatory challenges," *Journal of Financial Regulation and Compliance*, 30, 2, 2022, 134–156.
2. Ibid.
3. John R. Maloney, "The impact of insurance on the legitimacy of the Cannabis industry," *Journal of Business Ethics*, 168, 2, 2021, 201–218.
4. "Understanding the Issues Around Insuring Cannabis-Related Businesses." CRC Group. Accessed July 23, 2024. https://www.crcgroup.com/Tools-Intel/post/understanding-the-issues-around-insuring-cannabis-related-businesses.
5. Anne E. Kleffner, "Insurance for Cannabis Businesses: Risk and regulatory perspectives," *Risk Management and Insurance Review*, 23, 1, 2020, 89–112.
6. Ibid.
7. Ibid.
8. Ibid.
9. Financial Crimes Enforcement Network. "Guidance." Accessed June 23, 2024. https://www.fincen.gov/resources/statutes-regulations/guidance.
10. "License Types." California Cannabis Portal. Accessed June 20, 2024. https://cannabis.ca.gov/applicants/license-types.
11. Ibid. at 4.
12. Emily H. Gray, "Navigating the green rush: Challenges in Cannabis insurance," *Journal of Insurance Issues*, 44, 2, 2021, 123–145.

CHAPTER TWELVE

Innovations and Future Trends

 INTRODUCTION

While cannabis remains illegal at the federal level, banks are left with a decision to make. Do they want to take on the extra work that comes with Know Your Customer (KYC) compliance, and the red tape to work with and support cannabis-related businesses (CRBs) in their community? For some, that risk is a bridge too far. It makes more sense to wait until cannabis becomes legal, or at least until protections are put in place for banks via the SAFER Banking Act. For those who do venture into the CRB space, it requires a modicum of creativity to navigate the murky waters. But the good news is that this space is changing and evolving every day, making it slightly easier for cannabis businesses to be financially viable and to grow into the market. One of the ways in which they do this is by looking toward technology, software, and emerging trends within the banking and cannabis industries to find workarounds to barriers and help streamline the processes needed to reduce risks. This chapter will highlight a variety of ways that banks and CRBs can use fintech solutions to enhance their businesses.

CRB TECHNOLOGY OPTIONS

Cannabis businesses are currently facing a myriad of challenges in this volatile market. However, there are also technological innovations on the rise to help CRBs streamline their day-to-day operations and provide solutions to some of the more challenging aspects of running a cannabis business. While not all of the options listed here will be applicable for banks, having insight to opportunities within the cannabis industry can help set up your bank or financial institution as a helpful ally to your CRB customers.

 ## INTERNET OF THINGS (IOT)

The Internet of Things (IoT) refers to a collection of physical devices, all connected through internet capabilities, that can exchange real-time information via sensors and software. Many times, the IoT can refer to smart devices within one's home – such as appliances, thermostats, doorbells, cars, etc. These types of devices can interact either with each other or with a central device, such as a smartphone, via Bluetooth or a Wi-Fi connection. However, the idea of the IoT can also span into business services and should not be overlooked by cannabis companies or cannabis bankers.

IoT devices can be used in dispensaries and other CRBs to help keep track of inventory and assets – having access to a central hub of connected devices allows owners or managers to keep a close eye over the many various aspects of their business. Companies can also use these devices to connect with accounting or other banking systems to improve their financial transparency. CRBs will have to use some creativity in finding a combination of devices that will work best for them, but anything that can help automate and document business transactions is a win-win for everyone involved.

 ## CLOUD COMPUTING

Cloud-based banking and storage solutions can offer a multitude of benefits for CRBs. The first is that the Cloud is a cost-effective storage system for most businesses. By using solutions such as Dropbox, Google Drive, Microsoft OneDrive, or any similar data storage companies, CRBs can eliminate the need for technology hardware to be installed on-site, along with the need to hire a dedicated IT team. It also provides a level of security so that any data being collected – whether it's customer information or accounting books – can remain safe and secure. Finally, cloud computing offers scalability with platforms that are able to grow and expand with the business.

OPEN BANKING APIs

Open Banking APIs (Application Programming Interfaces) are applications that allow the secure sharing of customer data to third-party apps, with the explicit consent of the customer. For everyday banking, APIs pose benefits both to the customers and the bank. First, they enable customers to have greater control over who has access to their personal information, which in turn creates more trust between the customer and the bank since APIs rely on transparency and consent. They can also tailor products and services to customers based on spending habits and preferences and can offer a more holistic view of a customer's financial health. For companies in the cannabis industry, APIs offer many of the same benefits as other fintech solutions. APIs offer transparency and traceability for transactions, creating a clear audit trail and streamlining the bank's Enhanced Due Diligence (EDD). They also offer secure digital payment options, reducing the reliance on cash and automating payment systems for CRBs such as tax calculations. Finally, APIs can be used to empower the customer. Cannabis business owners can use open banking APIs to connect with fintech companies they could partner with for specialized financial services, or to manage their finances more efficiently with options such as real-time account monitoring and automated bill payments.

CRYPTOCURRENCIES AND BLOCKCHAIN

One of the most notable challenges for CRBs is the inability for them to use mainstream debit or credit cards. MasterCard is one of the most prominent card companies that has publicly condemned the use of cannabis purchases to be charged through their payment rails.[1] Subsequently, most of these CRBs turn to cash or cashless ATMs for transactions. However, Visa has also warned against the misuse of cashless ATMs at dispensaries, since this would be non-compliant under their operating agreement.[2] While this has not completely stopped cannabis companies from using the cashless ATM workaround, they could be subject to penalties or fines should they be caught. So, as we talk about risk vs. reward for businesses in the cannabis industry, it is not solely banks and financial institutions that take on some form of risk. This is because cash-reliant operations create a plethora of additional challenges, from sales tracking to security concerns – both onsite and for transportation. CRBs have therefore started looking toward cryptocurrencies and blockchain as additional payment methods. But what exactly is blockchain? Blockchain is a technological system that creates a virtual and transparent ledger for transactions, allowing companies to view these records, but they cannot adjust the data.

This type of option is attractive for several reasons. The first benefit of blockchain is that it is a secure system. Blockchain is encompassed by a network of systems, meaning that it is not housed in one central location. This makes it highly resistant to fraud and tampering – a substantial benefit when the cannabis industry is often viewed as a front for money laundering. Another plus is that it is a transparent system. Anyone with network access can view the transaction history. For relationships such as those between a CRB and their bank, this is a crucial aspect to building a professional and trusting relationship. A third benefit to cryptocurrencies is that it reduces the overhead cost for CRBs. The reliance on cash for cannabis businesses presents a handful of additional challenges, the first being the issue of security. With large amounts of cash needed for sales, it becomes crucial for any CRB to invest in security, typically in the forms of cameras and surveillance systems, and security guards who work on-site. There is also an increased need for secure transportation for CRBs to move cash to the bank regularly. Just these few extra requirements ensure that cannabis businesses are spending a fair amount of both their time and money just to ensure their business can operate safely and smoothly. These additional costs could be minimized with the addition of a digital payment method. Finally, blockchain is efficient and immutable. It records all transactions, reducing the manpower needed for manual documentation. Once a sale is recorded, it cannot be altered or deleted. In this sense, a business's history is kept permanently and in full.

At the end of the day, CRBs just want to run their business like everyone else. Banks just want to secure their business by doing their due diligence with customers. However, the legal restrictions combined with the social stigma of cannabis have driven a wedge between these two industries. Any payment solution that can help with sales transparency, such as blockchain, is beneficial for all parties.

However, cryptocurrencies aren't necessarily a one-size-fits-all solution. The reality of the situation currently is that the average consumer is not prepared for paying via cryptocurrency. In the US this has not yet taken off as a daily payment method. Until such a time when it becomes more widely adopted,

CRBs will still have to rely on the more traditional cash handling system. Additionally, blockchain technologies are still new and create potential issues for scalability as we look toward a future where cannabis could become legal at the national level. It is uncertain how they would be able to handle larger volumes of sales. The final hurdle for using cryptocurrencies as a payment solution comes at the regulatory level. According to articles by MJ Biz Daily, bills like SAFE or SAFER are in a precarious position – there has not been enough support historically for these bills to pass on their own, so they get lumped in with other bills.[3,4] The SAFE Banking Act of 2022 was added in with a budget defense spending bill but was ultimately unsuccessful. There is now talk of the SAFER Banking Act being added to a cryptocurrency bill to try and get it pushed through. While this, in theory, could offer much needed clarity for CRBs and financial institutions on payment regulations, it is more likely that these bill combinations are a simple tactic to leech onto a larger bill that will almost certainly be passed, and not an actual attempt at reforming an industry that needs guidance and support.

ARTIFICIAL INTELLIGENCE

The emergence of Artificial Intelligence (AI) is making waves in the banking industry when it comes to streamlining processes like KYC, anti-money laundering (AML) checks, and risk assessments. Here are some ways in which it's improving branch functions:

- Speeding Things Up and Cutting Costs: AI can automate the analysis and verification of documents, slashing the time and manual effort needed for KYC checks and account maintenance. It can streamline data entry and analysis for financial reporting and compliance, saving time and resources. This means staff can focus on more important or complex tasks that require human judgment, and customers are still able to open their accounts in a timely manner.
- Spotting Fishy Activity: AI can sift through massive amounts of data in minimal time to detect suspicious patterns and fraud. It can pick out things like mismatches between a customer's history and profile, or unusual details in documents that might otherwise go unnoticed. AI also helps banks pinpoint high-risk customers that may need closer scrutiny, while streamlining processes for low-risk ones by crunching customer data and transaction history.

- Getting It Right: AI keeps learning and honing its ability to spot questionable activity, cutting down on false alarms and making sure banks focus on the important cases. The longer that AI programs are on the market, the more tailored and accurate they become.
- Risk Assessment: AI can sift through loads of data on a customer, including financial history, credit scores, and even social media information, giving a more complete view of a borrower's risk. This leads to a more accurate assessment compared to old-school methods. It can also streamline the workflows for loan and claims processing, which enhances overall operational efficiency.
- Keeping It Current: AI keeps updating risk scores based on new information, giving a real-time view of a borrower's risk. This lets banks adjust loan terms or interest rates as needed. AI also keeps an eye on transactions as they happen, flagging anything suspicious based on set rules or by learning to recognize unusual customer behavior. This can stop fraudulent transactions before they even start.
- Looking Ahead: AI spots patterns and trends that could mean there's a possibility for future risks, letting banks manage them ahead of time. For example, AI might predict a borrower is likely to default on a loan based on their spending habits or economic forecasts.
- Uncovering Complex Fraud: AI spots hidden connections between transactions and people that human analysts might miss. This is a big help in uncovering crafty money laundering schemes.
- Keeping Up with the Bad Guys: Fraudsters are always coming up with new tricks. Machine learning, a type of AI, helps fraud detection systems keep learning and adapting to new threats, constantly getting better over time.
- Efficiency: AI-powered chatbots or virtual assistants are available 24/7 and can handle routine customer service questions or requests, freeing up bankers to tackle more complex issues. AI can also help banks meet regulatory requirements more efficiently by verifying documents and doing data analysis to ensure that the bank is meeting all necessary regulations.
- Personalized Recommendations: By analyzing customer data, AI can help increase engagement and revenue for banks by recommending personalized financial products and services.

Overall, AI brings big benefits to banks for KYC and AML compliance by improving efficiency, cutting costs, and managing risks. But remember, AI is just a tool, and its performance depends on the quality of the data it's trained on. Banks need to make sure their AI systems are transparent, reliable, and follow all rules and regulations, particularly with respect to banking cannabis customers. If it is set up correctly, AI can mean better financial health for both the bank and its customers.

The benefits that AI can bring to banks are numerous and limited only by the creativity of the bank and their tech partners. Many banks are turning to AI to cut down on the time-intensive tasks, thus freeing up their employees to tackle the projects that are more complex or that need human expertise. In using AI for repetitive tasks, you can reduce labor costs, minimize errors, and improve accuracy. For customer-related tasks, AI can personalize service and be available 24/7 for routine questions, leading to improved customer satisfaction.

It is important to remember that successful AI implementation requires careful planning and investment in data quality and infrastructure. If a financial institution wishes to start using AI to streamline tasks for their employees, they should be diligent in their research and ensure that they are working with the proper tech experts who can help them implement a successful AI program.

MISCELLANEOUS SOLUTIONS

Although blockchain and cryptocurrencies can be enticing options, they may not help CRBs with their immediate payment struggles. Since regular payment networks do not usually work for cannabis transactions, fintech is designing helpful payment processing alternatives that would work at dispensaries, like closed-loop systems or prepaid cards. These options follow the compliance rules more closely than cashless ATMs while still allowing cannabis businesses and their customers to go cashless. While most plastic cards, such as Visa and MasterCard, operate on an open system and can therefore be used at virtually any store, they will not work with cannabis businesses due to the federal red tape surrounding cannabis. Closed-loop systems would offer greater payment flexibility for the consumer – they would be able to load an amount of money onto a digital wallet or prepaid card that can then only be used within the stipulations of the system provider. Most times this would mean the prepaid amount can only be used at a specific location, or at a certain brand's store locations, if there are multiple. This type of payment system is already in place for many businesses, such as public transportation cards. For example, a Chicago

Ventra card is preloaded with funds, which can then be used on buses and trains within the city. Closed-loop payment processors for dispensaries would work much the same way.

The biggest benefit to these payment options is that they tend to be more convenient for the user. Consumers can reload the card as needed and not have to worry about taking cash in advance. Businesses can also tie rewards programs to prepaid card systems, enticing the customers to keep coming back. This also offers a level of security for customers as the card would have a limited amount of funds and can only be used at certain locations. This reduces the potential for fraud that could come from the open-loop systems.

Banking as a Service (BaaS) is another option that has been an innovation started by fintech companies as an alternate solution for traditional banking. BaaS allows third-party companies to offer traditional banking services without having to be a bank. This is obviously an enticing option for CRBs, as they cannot typically access the same banking services that businesses in any other industry can. By teaming up with BaaS platforms, banks can offer accounts and services that work for cannabis businesses without handling the cash directly. These platforms handle the setup and know-how, allowing banks to indirectly serve the cannabis industry.

Conclusion

It's worth noting that the cannabis industry is still changing, and the laws and regulations can differ greatly by state. Banks should choose fintech partners who know the ins and outs of cannabis laws to properly navigate this tricky legal landscape. However, there are numerous benefits banks can reap from using fintech solutions for cannabis clients that should not be overlooked or ignored. Banks can expand their reach to more CRBs and increase their revenue streams. The good news is that with fintech solutions helping out, taking on more cannabis customers does not necessarily have to come with more risk. There are a multitude of tech solutions available to cannabis companies that steer them away from cash transactions, lessening risks of money laundering, while ensuring they remain compliant to the rules and regulations put in place by their state. In combination with tracking technology such as blockchain, the cannabis seed-to-sale supply chain becomes much more transparent, leading to more trust and better relationships between the cannabis and banking industries. Finally, fintech solutions help to boost efficiency, automating workflows and saving time and resources for banks and cannabis businesses alike.

INTERNATIONAL CANNABIS BANKING TRENDS

The cannabis industry is finding its footing across the globe, with markets emerging in countries such as Canada, Germany, Luxembourg, Uruguay, South Africa, and Mexico, just to name a few. And the scope of these industries runs the gamut – from Georgia, where a 2018 law allows citizens the freedom to consume marijuana but still bans any production, sale, or distribution of the drug, to Uruguay, which became the first country to fully legalize marijuana in 2013 for any citizen 18+.[5,6]

With more and more countries joining in, we are seeing some inspiring new cannabis banking solutions emerging. By studying what's happening in these other canna-friendly countries, we can glean insights and ideas on solutions we can implement here in the US.

Government Involvement

When Uruguay legalized cannabis, they created an industry that was heavily regulated and under almost full control of the government. They opened The IRCCA (The Institute for the Regulation and Control of Cannabis) to be the overseer for the cultivation, distribution, and sale of cannabis within the country. Additionally, any citizen interested in purchasing cannabis must first register with the IRCCA.[7] This helps reduce risk for the banks and creates a more secure financial environment. One of the biggest concerns for banks in the US currently is the amount of risk they take on with CRB customers. By creating a dedicated government entity to act as a stable backing and provide resources and training, more banks would likely be interested in getting involved.

Integration with Fintech Solutions

Just like in the US, fintech is playing a major role in cannabis banking worldwide. Even though Canada legalized recreational cannabis in 2018, many of their banks are still hesitant to do business in the cannabis market. This is because many banks have international customers and with the federal status of cannabis in the US, banks are concerned that if they open their doors fully to cannabis, they could face money laundering issues. Until the US legalizes cannabis federally, Canadian banks will likely not take that leap to fully service CRBs. Therefore, Canada is one such country that has seen the rise of blockchain systems to track seed-to-sale, and has also implemented third-party BaaS platforms working to connect CRBs with banking solutions.[8]

Regulatory Sandbox Programs

Countries like Israel are taking things to the next level by implementing "sandbox programs." These programs enable banks and fintech companies to test innovative cannabis industry solutions in a controlled environment. This is a great way to encourage new ideas while being proactive in managing potential risks. One of the ways in which they are doing this is by lessening restrictions in medical arenas: specialist doctors will have more freedom to administer medical cannabis at their professional discretion, the stipulation that medical cannabis can only be used as a last resort has been overturned, and they are transferring patients from a "license" system to a "prescription" model.[9] All of these changes, which were implemented in early 2024, will allow cannabis to be used and studied in controlled, medical environments, with the potential to substantially progress research on cannabis for medical use.

Cannabis Clubs and Coffee Shops

While the idea of opening cannabis-specific clubs or coffee shops – as is seen in Spain and the Netherlands respectively – does not necessarily offer insight to cannabis banking solutions, it does present an interesting way that some countries have circumnavigated the illegal status of cannabis. Spain and the Netherlands are two countries that have embraced the legal gray area. Spain has found outlets in opening up cannabis clubs, where non-profit social clubs offer memberships, and members can then use the cannabis grown by the club for personal use.[10] In the Netherlands, cannabis is categorized as a "soft drug" meaning that it is not as harmful to one's health, and therefore, it is able to be sold in small amounts from Dutch coffee shops, as long as the business adheres to a list of rules.[11] The main difference between these two countries comes with the reaction from the legal authorities. In the Netherlands, strict rules govern the way in which coffee shops operate, but as long as they do not break the rules, the government continues to allow them to operate. In Spain, cannabis clubs have been under threat of closure for the past couple of years since the country still has fairly strict cannabis laws on the books.

Many countries are joining the cannabis movement, though the ways in which they are getting involved vary greatly from country to country. Much of this can be boiled down to the government's willingness to allow it. Some countries are going all-in on a cannabis market, some are hesitant but taking small steps in the direction toward legalization, some are focused solely on the medical aspect, and some remain steadfastly anti-cannabis. Regardless, the international cannabis banking landscape is a goldmine of ideas for the United States. By learning from these trends and adopting successful models, we can build a stronger, safer financial system for the legal cannabis industry.

POTENTIAL FEDERAL LEGALIZATION EFFORTS

The future of cannabis legislation in the US is still up in the air. Trends in public support, as well as legal actions already underway, lead us to project that recreational cannabis could very well be legalized in the near future. While there has not been much movement on federal bills that target full cannabis legalization, there are a couple of bills to keep your eyes on. One is the SAFER Banking Act. The most important aspect of this bill is that it aims to protect banks from any legal repercussions they may face when dealing with CRBs.[12] If this passes and is signed into law, it would remove a huge concern for banks that are hesitant to take on cannabis customers. The other movement happening federally is the rescheduling of cannabis from a Schedule I drug to a Schedule III drug (as per DEA categorization). This potential rescheduling has split pro-legalization fans on how they view this move. For some, this is an opportunity to remove even more hurdles within the industry, making cannabis more accessible and paving the way to full federal legalization. However, others view it as a step that could potentially create more hurdles. This is because Schedule III drugs are controlled by healthcare and pharmacies and almost always need a prescription to access them. A rescheduling would not legalize cannabis, and while it may prove to be a step in that direction, it also brings the possibility of reframing the burgeoning industry to give more regulation and control of cannabis over to the pharmaceutical companies. "So, unlike Schedule I drugs, these drugs [Schedule III] are considered to have moderate to low potential for physical or psychological dependence. They are known to have some benefits. And they also are subject to some federal regulatory requirements and are to be used for medical purposes only. . . there's still not going to be any federal legality insofar as recreational use is concerned," notes Chris Van Dyck, a partner at Cogent Law Group, as he spoke on a webinar on the topic of rescheduling. On the other hand, rescheduling might open up opportunities for financial institutions. Chris continues, "but one big change with Schedule III is that section 283 from the IRS 280 E tax code will go away. That's the provision in the tax code which disallows CRBs from deducting business expenses from their bottom line. And because of that, I think that these folks are going to be much more attractive potential borrowers for financial institutions."[13] Another potential benefit for financial institutions would come in the form of public perception – more acceptance of cannabis use, even if just for medical purposes, will help cut down on the reputational risk they may face while servicing CRBs currently. However, Chris also notes that banks and FIs need to be steadfast about their due diligence and suspicious activity report (SAR) filings to combat this. Without adhering to strict compliance guidelines, banks not only risk legal action, they also risk their reputation, as noncompliance can become public information; thus, customers are less likely to do business with the bank in the future.

The only way for cannabis to reach full legalization within the US would come from a complete descheduling. While this is not being discussed in any real, meaningful way at the present time, it does not mean that this option is off the table completely. We have seen it happen within the industry already – the 2018 Farm Bill descheduled hemp, which had been federally illegal since the creation of the Controlled Substances Act in 1970.[14] Most policies rely on public support and new scientific data, if applicable. If states continue to expand into the legal cannabis market, one can reasonably assume that federal legalization might be in the cards eventually.

PREDICTIONS FOR THE FUTURE OF CANNABIS BANKING

The US cannabis industry is poised to experience significant growth in the next few years, thanks to factors like increased legalization and nation wide acceptance among the people. Based on current trends, this is a possible glimpse into what the industry's future might look like:

Near-future

- Continued Growth: According to market research, the industry is expected to keep growing steadily. In 2023, cannabis tax revenue topped $4.18 billion nation wide, which is up from $3.8 billion that was earned in 2022.[15,16] This upward trend has been fairly steady since 2014, when the first legal markets were opened. According to statistics from the Marijuana Policy Project, the only deviation was 2022, which was only

slightly down from the $3.9 billion earned in 2021. However, this small dip could probably be attributed to the COVID-19 pandemic, which saw an uptick in cannabis sales. It is likely that these sales trends will carry on in the subsequent years.
- Expansion of Legal Markets: We can anticipate more states jumping on the bandwagon and legalizing recreational cannabis. This will not only broaden the customer base but also drive sales growth.
- Increased Competition: As the market expands, we can expect competition among producers and retailers to heat up. This could lead to lower prices for customers and a wider range of products for consumers to choose from.
- With an expanding market, we can also assume more banks and financial institutions will open their doors to cannabis customers. As of 2024, only about 300 banks nationwide are taking on CRBs, and most of them are local banks and credit unions. We can expect this number to keep climbing with more and more dispensaries opening and seeking banking services.

Mid-future

- Federal Legalization Potential: While it's not a sure thing, there is a significant chance that cannabis will be rescheduled, with the potential to be completely descheduled eventually. If, or when, that happens, it could be a game-changer for the industry. Traditional banking would become fully accessible for cannabis businesses, potentially fueling even more growth in the industry.
- Innovation and Product Development: Get ready for a wave of new cannabis products hitting the market! We're talking about edibles, topicals, beverages, and more, all tailored to cater to different consumer preferences. And that's not all – advancements in cultivation and processing techniques are also being honed and refined, so we may see new growth tools and technologies hitting the market as well. With the expansion and availability of products, both for consumers and suppliers, competition among banks will also heat up. Banks will have to find new and creative ways to attract CRB customers they once turned away.
- Focus on Medical Applications: Research into the medical benefits of cannabis is expected to gain momentum. This could lead to the development of new cannabis-based medicines and greater adoption among patients.

Long-term

- Mainstream Acceptance: The social stigma surrounding cannabis use is likely to continue fading away. This will cause broader acceptance within society and could even influence efforts toward federal legalization. Much like with the alcohol, tobacco, and gambling industries, some social pushback is to be expected, and will certainly continue even after cannabis is fully legalized. However, the consistent growth trends we have seen since 2012 when Colorado and Washington legalized recreational cannabis have led us to believe that cannabis is here to stay.
- Maturation of the Industry: Over the next decade, the cannabis industry could grow into a mature market, complete with well-established brands and regulations. We might even see some big corporations entering the space.
- Global Market Integration: The US cannabis industry has the potential to become a major player on the international stage. We could see exports and participation in a global cannabis market.

Keep in mind that these are projections, and the actual path of the industry could be greatly altered by unforeseen factors like political changes, economic fluctuations, or major scientific discoveries related to cannabis. Federal legalization still poses a significant hurdle for the cannabis industry at large, and it is unclear when or how it will happen.

Overall, it's safe to say that the US cannabis industry is well-positioned for substantial growth in the next decade. With the potential to become a mainstream and well-regulated market, the future looks bright!

NOTES

1. Matza, Max. "Mastercard Demands US Cannabis Shops Stop Accepting Debit Cards." Www.bbc.com, July 26, 2023, http://www.bbc.com/news/world-us-canada-66320970. Accessed April 25, 2024.
2. Adlin, Ben. "Visa Warns against Misuse of "Cashless ATMs" Used by Cannabis Retailers to Skirt Restrictions." Marijuana Moment, December 10, 2021, http://www.marijuanamoment.net/visa-warns-against-misuse-of-cashless-atms-used-by-cannabis-retailers-to-skirt-restrictions. Accessed March 13, 2024.
3. Roberts, Chris. "SAFE Banking's Failure: Who's to Blame, and What's next for Marijuana Industry?" MJ Biz Daily, December 22, 2022, mjbizdaily.com/why-safe-banking-failed-and-what-are-next-steps-for-marijuana-industry/. Accessed June 29, 2024.

4. "Congress Could Include Cannabis Banking in FAA, Crypto Bills." *MJ Biz Daily*, April, 24 2024, mjbizdaily.com/congress-could-include-cannabis-banking-in-faa-crypto-bills/. Accessed June 29, 2024.
5. Walsh, John, and Geoff Ramsey. Uruguay's Drug Policy: Major Innovations, Major Challenges. 2015.
6. Wayne, Shawn. "Smoking Marijuana Legalized in Georgia." *Georgia Today*, July 30, 2018, web.archive.org/web/20180808160506/georgiatoday.ge/news/11592/Smoking-Marijuana-Legalized-in-Georgia. Accessed June 29, 2024.
7. "Organización." IRCCA, ircca.gub.uy/organizacion/.
8. David. "Cannabis Banking in Canada: An Ongoing Challenge for Retailers." TechPOS, June 20, 2023, techpos.ca/articles/cannabis-banking-in-canada/. Accessed June 29, 2024.
9. Lamers, Matt. "Israel's New Rules Might Spur Growth in Medical Cannabis Industry." *MJ Biz Daily*, June 29, 2024, mjbizdaily.com/new-rules-might-spur-growth-in-israel-medical-cannabis-industry/. Accessed June 29, 2024.
10. Sabaghi, Dario. "Barcelona City Council Threatens to Shut down Cannabis Social Clubs." *Forbes*, January 4, 2024, http://www.forbes.com/sites/dariosabaghi/2024/01/04/barcelona-city-council-threatens-to-shut-down-cannabis-social-clubs. Accessed June 29, 2024.
11. Government of the Netherlands. "Toleration Policy Regarding Soft Drugs and Coffee Shops." *Government.nl*, 2013, http://www.government.nl/topics/drugs/toleration-policy-regarding-soft-drugs-and-coffee-shops.
12. "S.2860 – 118th Congress (2023–2024): SAFER Banking Act." *Congress.gov*, Library of Congress, December 6, 2023, https://www.congress.gov/bill/118th-congress/senate-bill/2860.
13. Van Dyck, Chris. "Rescheduling Explained: What Banks and Credit Unions Need to Know NOW." Webinar from The Association for Cannabis Banking, Placitas, NM, May 15, 2024.
14. "H.R.2 – 115th Congress (2017–2018): An act to provide for the reform and continuation of agricultural and other programs of the Department of Agriculture through fiscal year 2023, and for other purposes." *Congress.gov*, Library of Congress, December 20, 2018, https://www.congress.gov/bill/115th-congress/house-bill/2.
15. Marijuana Policy Project. "Cannabis Tax Revenue in States That Regulate Cannabis for Adult Use." *MPP*, April 5, 2022, http://www.mpp.org/issues/legalization/cannabis-tax-revenue-states-regulate-cannabis-adult-use.
16. Krishna, Mrinalini. "The Economic Benefits of Legalizing Marijuana." *Investopedia*, November 16, 2022, http://www.investopedia.com/articles/insights/110916/economic-benefits-legalizing-weed.asp#:~:text=In%202021%2C%20the%20states%20that.

About the Authors

Erin O'Donnell

Erin O'Donnell is a leader and an advocate in the intersection of finance and cannabis, serving as the Co-Founder and Chair of the Board of Directors of the Association for Cannabis Banking. Her work focuses on product innovation and education, driven by her passion for lifelong education inspired by her father, a high school English teacher and her mother, who at age 91, still reads voraciously and has a growing library of books in her home in Allentown, Pennsylvania.

As a visionary in banking education, Erin launched the industry's first cannabis banking certification, the Cannabis Banking Professional (CBP), during her time as the Co-Founder of BankersHub, an online portal for banking education. She is recognized as an influential voice at industry conferences, sharing her expertise on the vital role of cannabis banking in financial services.

Erin's background also includes collaboration with notable geophysicist and global warming expert, Dr. Gordon MacDonald at the University of California's Institute on Global Conflict and Cooperation, where she helped manage conferences that convened government officials, scientists, and academics. She was also the director of publications for the inaugural UCSD student-founded *"Journal of Environment and Development"* in 1992, which is still in publication today.

As a dedicated Cannabis Banking Professional (CBP) and a fervent supporter of the advancement of women in business, Erin spearheads the Association for Cannabis Banking's scholarship program. Erin also holds certifications as a Digital Event Strategist (DES) and a Certified Meeting Manager (CMM). She earned her B.S. in Business Administration from Bloomsburg University in Pennsylvania, underpinning her career that bridges the worlds of finance, events technology, and emerging industries.

Meridith Beird

Meridith Beird is a virtual event manager, certified Digital Event Specialist (DES), and a Co-Founder of the Association for Cannabis Banking. She has a dual BA in French and Anthropology and received her MS degree in Developmental Linguistics from the University of Edinburgh. She has more than 10 years of experience in the virtual education sector, working the technical side of creating bank training webinars.

Meridith later found an interest in cannabis after working as the manager of an acupuncture and massage therapy clinic in Chicago, where she learned about the medical benefits of cannabis. She advocates for the federal legalization of cannabis and works to promote scholarships for education at the ACB for women and minorities, who have historically been unfairly persecuted for cannabis possession and use.

Michael Beird

Michael Beird is a seasoned banking executive, change consultant, and entrepreneur with more than four decades of experience in the financial services industry. Having lost his father to a heart attack when he was just eight, Michael spent his early years engrossed in books of all kinds when children his age were outside playing. After moving from Chicago to Palm Springs, California, at age 14, his curiosity of the world around him led him to become an American Field Service (AFS) exchange student to West Germany for his senior year of high school.

In the years that followed, Michael had the opportunity to become expert in almost all aspects of retail banking, quickly rising up through the ranks of leadership at Bank of America and Shawmut Bank Boston. This hands-on banking experience enabled him to transition easily into international management consulting, leading large-scale engagements across four continents to optimize operations, workforce management, customer experience, and regulatory compliance.

As Practice Director at J.D. Power & Associates, Michael spearheaded award-winning research initiatives for top financial institutions, collaborating closely with the Consumer Financial Protection Bureau (CFPB) on critical data analysis. His entrepreneurial spirit led him to co-found and successfully sell two SaaS platforms, BankerStuff and BankersHub, demonstrating his business acumen and ability to identify emerging market opportunities.

Recognized as a thought leader in the banking industry, Michael is a sought-after speaker and author on topics ranging from cannabis banking to financial technology. He is a Co-Founder of the Association for Cannabis

Banking and is passionate about educating professionals on the complexities of banking in this burgeoning industry.

His expertise has also been sought in legal proceedings, where he has served as an expert witness for major banks. Michael has been retained for his insights and testimony dealing with regulatory banking disputes, payments challenges, and other matters requiring expert knowledge and understanding of financial services.

Beyond his professional achievements, Michael is an avid runner, having completed four marathons. He holds a BA in Social Psychology from the University of California Irvine, and an MBA in Finance and Accounting from Cornell University. He has been married to Daria Beird for more than 42 years and they have two daughters: Meridith, linguist, project manager, and co-author of this book; and Allyssa, elementary school teacher and regular athlete on NBC's American Ninja Warrior.

Index

Note: Page references in *italics* refer to figures and tables.

ACB *see* Association for Cannabis Banking
access to capital, 128–9 *see also* cannabis lending
ACH (Automated Clearing House) transactions, 117–19, 122
agility, 55, 156–7
AI (Artificial Intelligence), 199–201
alert generation and escalation, 98
anti-money laundering (AML) programs, 35–7
   Artificial Intelligence for, 199–201
   and cannabis insurance, 182
   and lending, 133–4
   risk assessment in, 100–2
Artificial Intelligence (AI), 199–201
Association for Cannabis Banking (ACB), 138, 141, 147
ATMs, 113 *see also* cashless ATMs
ATM transactions, 120
audits, 92–4
   of alerts in transaction monitoring systems, 98
   of bank's due diligence procedures, 92
   of customer compliance, 96–7
   federal regulations for, 93
   of internal controls, 94
   of policy and procedure compliance, 94–6
   of risk assessments, 91
   of SARs, 99–100
   as sound recordkeeping practice, 106
   state or local regulations for, 46, 93–4
   of transaction monitoring, 99
Automated Clearing House (ACH) transactions, 117–19, 122
auxiliary (Tier 3) CRBs, 8, 9

BaaS (Banking as a Service), 202
banking, 13–24
   for cannabis-related businesses, 24–9 (*see also* cannabis banking)

Cole Memo's impact on, 49
high-risk, 102–3
history of, 13–17
oversight of, 19
role of, 17–21
traditional (*see* traditional banks)
types of banks and financial institutions, 21–4, *23*
use of term in this text, xvi
Banking as a Service (BaaS), 202
Bank of England, 14
Bank of North America (BNA), 14–15
banks
   lending by, 130, 131
   types of, 21–4 (*see also individual types*)
Bank Secrecy Act (BSA), 32, 34–5
   and cannabis insurance, 182
   and lending, 133
   and reporting, 104
bill payments, 123
BioTrackTHC, 66
blockchain, 116, 197–9
BNA (Bank of North America), 14–15
boards of directorsm, risk exposure and, 89–91
brand identity, 141–2
brand messaging, 140–1, *141*
brand positioning, 139–40
breeding, 69–70
BSA *see* Bank Secrecy Act
Bullock, Chenae, 175
business continuity planning, 188
business to business payments, 122–3
   Automated Clearing House transactions, 122
   bill payments, 123
   checks, 123
   wire transfers, 122–3

215

Index

business to consumer payments, 118–21
  buy now pay later, 121
  cashless ATMs, 120
  checks, 119–20
  consumer-to-merchant, 120–1
  credit cards, 118–10
  crypto, 121
  debit cards, 119
  digital payments, 120
buy now pay later, 121

Cannabichromene (CBC), 5
cannabidiols (CBD), 5, 69 *see also* CBD products
Cannabigerol (CBG), 5
cannabinoids, 5, 69
Cannabinol (CBN), 5
cannabis, 1–6
  components of, 4–6, 5
  under Controlled Substance Act, 3–4
  defined, 4
  genetics and breeding of, 69–70
  health benefits of, 4
  history of, 1–2
  legal, xi, xii, xv (*see also* legalization of cannabis)
  medical (*see* medical cannabis)
  public perception of, 206
  public support for legalization of, 3–4
  recreational (*see* recreational cannabis)
  regulation history for hemp and marijuana, 2–3
  as Schedule I drug, 31, 34, 52–3, 171, 205
  as Schedule III drug, 52, 53, 205–6
  seed selection, 68–9
  seed-to-sale life cycle for, 66–70, 67
  strains of, 69
  views on, xi
  see also hemp; marijuana
Cannabis Administration and Opportunity Act (CAOA), 53
cannabis banking, xii, 24–9
  Cole Memo's role in practices of, 50–1
  competition in, 161–70
  complexity of, xv
  compliance in, 51–2
  future outlook for, 52–5, 164, 203–5
  guidelines for, 46–7
  impact of cannabis insurance on, 181–94
  implications of Schedule I status for, 34
  increasing interest in, 161–2
  for indigenous tribes, 172–3, 175–8
  influence of Federal Reserve on, 44
  international, 203–5
  lending in, 125–35
  marketing strategies for, 137–60

  market share and growth trends in, 162–3
  oversight of, 19–20 (*see also* regulation[s])
  payments in, 111–24
  predictions for future of, 54, 206–8
  retail banking products and services in, 24–6
  risk management in, 89–108
  services in, 20–1
  strategies for, 54
  treasury services in, 26, 28
  see also specific topics
cannabis clubs or coffee shops, 204–5
cannabis industry, xv, 6–10
  current market valuations in, 63
  dispelling misconceptions around, 138
  economic impact of, 6–7
  effective risk management policies in, 187–9 (*see also* risk management)
  future growth estimates for, 63
  future trends and innovations for, 195–208
  indigenous tribes in, 171–9
  industrial hemp and CBD in, 65–6
  insurance innovations in, 182–3
  limitations of financial services for, 25–6
  market size and growth projections for, 60–3, 61
  maturation of, 208
  medical marijuana sector in, 3–4, 64, 64–5 (*see also* medical cannabis)
  oversight of, 19–20
  PATRIOT Act impact on, 39–40
  predicted growth in, 206–7
  recreational marijuana sector in, 2, 65 (*see also* recreational cannabis)
  state laws governing, 44–6
  stigma surrounding, 51–2
  Tier 1 (direct) CRBs, 7–9
  Tier 2 (indirect) CRBs, 8, 9
  Tier 3 (auxiliary) CRBs, 8, 9
cannabis lending, 125–35
  complexities of, 125–6
  impact of insurance on, 190–1
  importance of, 128–9
  interest rates and fees in, 132–3
  legalization and growth of market for, 126–8, 127
  loan products in, 131–2
  regulatory considerations with, 133–4
  rise of, 126
  risks associated with, 19
  types of lenders, 130–1
  types of loans, 126
"Cannabis Payments Guidelines" (Emerging Markets Coalition), 118
cannabis-related businesses (CRBs), 59–60
  auxiliary (Tier 3), 8, 9
  banking guidelines for, 46–7

banking solutions for, 24–9
banks' acceptance of deposits from, 18–19
cultivation and growing techniques in, 70–4
current legal environment for, xii
current market valuations of, 63
customer base of, 138–9
direct (Tier 1), 7–9
distribution and supply chain management for, 79–82
extraction by, 75–6
future technologies for, 196
hemp-centered, 32–3
indirect (Tier 2), 8, 9
innovative fintech company solutions for, 166–7
insurance for, 181–94
lending to, 125–35
manufacturing and product development by, 77–9
PATRIOT Act impact on, 38–40
payment processing in, 111–24
processing methods in, 74–5
quality control and testing standards for, 76
retail and dispensing, 82–5
risk levels of, 100
seed-to-sale life cycle in, 66–70, 67
state regulations for, 45–6
understanding of, xii, xiii
CannaFirst Financial, 141
CAOA (Cannabis Administration and Opportunity Act), 53
card payments, 113–14, 117–19, 201
cash flow management, 129
cash handling systems, 199
cashless ATMs, 113, 114, 120
cash management, 26, 28, 100
cash payments, 112–13
CBC (Cannabichromene), 5
CBD (cannabidiols), 5, 69
CBD products
under Farm Bill of 2018, 33
market for, 65–6
predicted expansion and availability of, 207
state and federal regulation of, 5
see also product development
CBG (Cannabigerol), 5
CBN (Cannabinol), 5
CDD (Customer Due Diligence), 40, 94–7
change
adapting to, 169
proactive anticipation of, 56
regulatory, 155, 162, 185–6 (see also specific laws)
check payments
business to business, 123
business to consumer, 119–20
Chissoe, Josiah, 173

CIP (Customer Identification Program), 35
closed loop payment systems, 112–13, 201–2
cloud computing, 196–7
clubs, cannabis-specific, 204–5
coffee shops, 204–5
Cole, James M., 3, 47
Cole Memo, 3, 47–51, 97
collaborations
former, when entering cannabis market, 164
with industry associations, 146–7
with insurance providers, 192
of traditional banks and fintech companies, 166
commercial banks, 21, 22, 23 see also banking
communication strategies, 140–1, 141, 192
community banks
in early days of cannabis banking, 161
lending by, 130, 131
as sector leaders, 163
see also banking
Compassionate Use Act, 3
competition, 161–70
and barriers to market entry, 168–9
challenges and opportunities with, 168–70
future trends in, 170
impact of regulatory changes on, 162
and maintaining competitive edge, 169
predicted increase in, 207
and rise of fintech companies, 162, 166–7
traditional bank's competitive strategies, 163–6
competitive advantages
of existing players, 169
of fintech companies, 162, 167
of traditional banks, 165–6
compliance
AML compliance officer, 36
brand positioning for, 139–40
in cannabis banking, 51–2
with cannabis insurance, 185–6
creating framework for, 55
in distribution, 81–2
educating clients on, 153–4
as essential, 206
Fed's and FDIC's role in, 43–4
financial strain of, 168
as heart of audits, 92
integration of transaction monitoring with, 99
and legacy of Cole Memo, 50–1
with PATRIOT Act, 40–2
planning for, 108, 133–4
in product development, 77–8
in retail and dispensing, 84
role of insurance in, 190
when starting CRBs, 129

218 ■ Index

compliance assessments, 106 *see also* audits
compliance-centric marketing, 152–4
   educating clients on compliance, 153–4
   legal boundaries for, 152–3
   transparent and ethical practices in, 154
concentrates, creating, 77
conferences, 150–1
consumer-to-merchant payments, 120–1
content marketing
   for educating clients on compliance, 153
   role of, 140
   for thought leadership 143–4
continuous learning, 47
Controlled Substances Act of 1970 (CSA), 3–5, 31–2, 206
corporate social responsibility (CSR), 141–2
CRBs *see* cannabis-related businesses
credit card payments, 118–10
credit risk assessment, 190–1
credit unions, 21, 22, 23
   in early days of cannabis banking, 161
   lending by, 130, 131
   NCUA oversight of, 20
   as sector leaders, 163
   see also banking
crop insurance, 183, 184, 188
cryptocurrencies
   benefits with, 198
   for CRB payments, 113, 116, 118, 121
   future trends with, 197–9
   hurdles for using, 198–9
CSA *see* Controlled Substances Act of 1970
CSR (corporate social responsibility), 141–2
CTRs *see* Currency Transaction Reports
cultivation and growing techniques, 66, 68–74
   harvesting and curing processes, 73–4
   indoor vs. outdoor cultivation, 71–2
   quality control for, 76
   safety measures in, 78
   sustainable and organic practices, 72–3
   tribes' holistic approach to, 175
curing processes, 73–4
Currency Transaction Reports (CTRs), 35, 37, 104
customer base of CRBs, 138–9
Customer Due Diligence (CDD), 40, 94–7
customer experience, 83–4, 169
   with fintech companies, 167
Customer Identification Program (CIP), 35
cyber liability insurance, 188

data, 155–6
data analytics, 156
data management, 156
data privacy, 145

DEA (Drug Enforcement Administration), 4, 115
debit card payments, 113–14, 119
decision hurdles, 106, *107*, 108
delta-9 tetrahydrocannabinols (THC), 5, 69
Department of Justice (DOJ), 20, 172
deposits, 18–19, 21
differentiation, 162
digital lending platforms, 166–7
digital marketing techniques, 142–5
   cautious use of, 140
   content marketing for thought leadership, 143–4
   leveraging social media responsibility, 144–6
   website and SEO best practices, 142–3
digital networking platforms, 146
digital payments, 120
direct (Tier 1) CRBs, 7–9
dispensaries
   and cash transactions, 112
   fintech solutions for, 196
   insurance for, 183
   inventory management for, 187
   tribally-owned, 174–6
   see also retail and dispensing
distribution and supply chain management, 79–82
   ensuring compliance in distribution, 81–2
   logistics and transportation, 79–81
   supply chain overview, 79
documentation, 81–2 *see also* reporting and recordkeeping
DOJ (Department of Justice), 20, 172
Drug Enforcement Administration (DEA), 4, 115
due diligence procedures
   Customer, 37, 40, 94–7
   Enhanced, 37, 40–1, 96–7, 115
   and legacy of Cole Memo, 50–1
   for packaging and labeling, 79
   in risk management, 92

economy
   impacts of cannabis industry on, 6–7, 174–5
   for indigenous tribes, 174–5
   putting CRB dollars back into, 18–19
   role of banking and financial services in, 17
EDD *see* Enhanced Due Diligence
edibles, creating, 77
educational marketing, 148–9
Electronic Payment Network (EPN), 122
Emerging Markets Coalition, 118
employee training, 85
Enhanced Due Diligence (EDD), 37, 40–1, 96–7, 115

Index

entering the market
   approaches to, 163–4
   barriers to, 168–9
   state rules and federal directive when, 168
   traditional banks' advantages and disadvantages in, 165–6
EPN (Electronic Payment Network), 122
equipment financing, 131–2
ethical marketing practices, 154
event marketing, 149–52
   hosting roundtable discussions, 152
   and sponsorships, 151
   trade shows and conferences, 150–1
expansion capital, 129
expenses
   in launching CRBs, 128–9
   loan fees, 132–3
extraction, 75–6

Farm Bill of 2014, 5
Farm Bill of 2018, 5–6, 32–3, 186, 206
FDA (Food and Drug Administration), 33
Federal Deposit Insurance Corporation (FDIC), 17, 43–4
federal legalization efforts, 205–6
federal policy
   attention to potential changes in, 52–4
   Cole Memo's impact on, 48
   Sessions Memo's impact on, 49, 50
federal regulations/laws
   for banking, xiii
   for cannabis insurance, 185
   for CBD products, 5
   compliance audits for, 93
   conflict between state laws and, 115
   for hemp and marijuana, 2–4
   and marijuana odor on cash deposits, xii
   for medical or recreational marijuana, 3
   and payment processing, 115–16
   staying informed about changes in, 32
   see also individual laws
Federal Reserve Act of 1913, 16–17
Federal Reserve Bank, 43
Federal Reserve System (the Fed), 16–19, 43–4, 122
fees, in lending, 132–3
filing *see* reporting and filing
Financial Crimes Enforcement Network (FinCEN), 19, 32, 34, 35
financial services
   for cannabis businesses, xii–xiii, 24–9
   for high risk businesses, xii
   indigenous tribes' access to, 172–3
   ripple effect from lack of, 52

role of, 17–21
types of banks and financial institutions, 23, 24–9
see also banking
FinCEN *see* Financial Crimes Enforcement Network
fintech
   integration of, 203
   trends in, 195–202
fintech companies, 166–7
   competitive advantages of, 162, 167
   innovative CRB solutions from, 166–7
   see also banking
First Bank of the United States, 15
Food and Drug Administration (FDA), 33
fraud prevention, 28, 200
Free Banking Era, 15–16
funding for cannabis-related businesses, 62
future outlook
   for cannabis banking, 52–5, 164, 206–8
   for cannabis industry, 170
   for cannabis lending, 126
   for competition in banking sector, 170
   for industry growth, 63
   for marketing in cannabis banking, 158–9
   predictions about, 206–8
future trends and innovations, 195–208
   Artificial Intelligence, 199–201
   cannabis banking predictions, 206–8
   cloud computing, 196–7
   for CRB technologies, 196
   cryptocurrencies and blockchain, 197–9
   federal legalization efforts, 205–6
   in international cannabis banking, 203–5
   Internet of Things, 196
   Open Banking APIs, 197
   payment processing options, 201–2

genetics, 68–70
growing techniques *see* cultivation and growing techniques
guides, publishing, 149

Hamilton, Alexander, 15
Hancock, Trent, 178
harvesting processes, 73–4
health benefits of marijuana, 4
hemp
   defined, 32
   under Farm Bill of 2018, 32–3
   first law for, 1–2
   history of regulation of, 2–3
   legal distinction of marijuana from, 32–3
   market for, 65–6

hemp (*continued*)
  in medical treatments, 4
  regulation of, 5–6
  as species of cannabis, 4
  THC in, 5
hemp-based CBD, 5
high-risk banking, 102–3
high-risk businesses, financial controls for, xii
high-risk industries, risk assessment in, 102–3
high-risk payments
  merchant services for, 116–17
  processing of, 113–14
history
  of banking, 13–17
  of cannabis, 1–2
  of regulation of hemp and marijuana, 2–3
hybrid strains, 69

Indian Gaming Regulatory Act (IGRA), 172, 173
indica strains, 69
indigenous tribes, 171–9
  banking challenges for, 175–8
  cannabis operations for, 174
  current environment for, 175–8
  economic and social impacts of industry on, 174–5
  financial access and banking challenges for, 172–3
  legal challenges for, 171–3
  regulatory landscape for, 171–2
  and Wilkinson Memo, 172
indirect (Tier 2) CRBs, 8, 9
indoor cultivation, 71–2
industrial hemp market, 65–6
industry associations, collaborations with, 146–7
information sources
  on laws and regulations, 55
  websites, xvi
informative guides, publishing, 149
initial bank meetings with CRBs, 26, 27
insurance, 181–94
  assessing adequacy of, 189
  bankers' considerations concerning, 189–93
  complexities of, 182
  compliance role of, 190
  developing expertise in, 192–3
  FDIC, 43–4
  innovations in, 182–3
  obtaining, 181–2
  overview of, 183
  regulatory landscape for, 184–6
  risk management role of, 186–9
  stigma and misconceptions about, 192
  types of, 183, 184
  verifying and understanding, 191–2

interest rates, 132–3
internal controls, 94
international cannabis banking, 203–5
Internet of Things (IoT), 196
inventory management, 83, 187
inventory tracking systems, 85
investment banks, 22, 23
IoT (Internet of Things), 196

Jackson, Andrew, 15

Kemmerling, Steven, 7
Know Your Customer (KYC), 37–43
  Artificial Intelligence for, 199–201
  in high-risk banking, 103
  in lending, 133–4
  in risk management, 94–5

labeling requirements, 78–9
Las Vegas Paiute Tribe, 174
law enforcement, Cole Memo's impact on, 49
leadership executives, 90–1
Leary v. United States, 3
legal challenges, for indigenous tribes, 171–3
legal changes, 50, 155
legalization of cannabis, 39
  Cole Memo guidance on, 47–51
  as contentious subject, 52
  economic impact of, 6–7
  facts about, 61–2
  government oversight of, 203
  and growth of cannabis sector, 160
  and insurance coverage, 185
  and market growth, 126–8, 127
  potential federal efforts for, 205–7
  pressure on federal legislators for, 53
  public support for, 3, 10
  by states, federal prohibition and, 39–40
legalization of hemp products, 6, 32–3
legalization of marijuana, 4, 7, 60
legal marketing boundaries, 152–3
legislation
  websites for information on, xvi
  see also regulation(s); *specific laws*
lenders, types of, 130–1
lending, 21 *see also* cannabis lending
liability insurance, 183, 187
licensing, 45, 46, 82
lines of credit, 131
loans
  challenge in securing, 125
  types of, 126, 131–2
  see also cannabis lending
local regulations/rules
  compliance audits for, 93–4
  for distribution, 81

Index

location for cannabis stores, 82
logistics challenges, 79–81
loyalty programs, 84

management
  cash, 26, 28, 100
  cash flow, 129
  data, 156
  distribution and supply chain, 79–82
  inventory, 83, 187
  risk (*see* risk management)
  tribal issues with, 172–3
manufacturing, 77–9
Marihuana Tax Act of 1969, 3
marijuana
  health benefits of, 4
  hemp legally separated from, 32–3
  history of regulation of, 2–3
  medical, 3–4, 64, 64–5 (*see also* medical cannabis)
  public support for legalization of, 3–4 (*see also* legalization of marijuana)
  recreational, 2 (*see also* recreational cannabis)
  as Schedule I drug, 4
  as Schedule III drug, 115
  social stigma of, 2
  as species of cannabis, 4
  THC in, 5
Marijuana Enforcement Tracking Reporting & Compliance (METRC), 45, 66
Marijuana Opportunity Reinvestment and Expungement Act (MORE Act), 53
marijuana-related jobs, 7
Marijuana Tax Act of 1937, 5
market(s)
  analyzing and adapting to trends in, 155–7
  cannabis legalization and growth of, 126–8, *127*
  entry approaches to, 163–4
  global, 208
  growth in, 163
  for industrial hemp and CBD, 65–6
  for medical marijuana, *64*, 64–5
  predicted expansion of, 207
  for recreational marijuana, 65
  size and growth projections for, 60–3, *61*
  understanding your, 138–9
marketing, 137–60
  analyzing and adapting to trends in, 155–7
  brand positioning in, 139–40
  compliance-centric, 152–4
  and corporate social responsibility, 141–2
  digital techniques for, 142–5
  educational, 148–9
  event marketing and sponsorships in, 149–52
  future of, 158–9
  importance of, 137–8
  messaging and communication strategies for, 140–1, *141*
  networking and partnerships in, 145–8
  regulations governing, 148
  and understanding of markets, 138–9
market valuations, 63
medical cannabis
  Cole Memo guidance for, 47–51
  predicted focus on, 207
  "sandbox programs" for, 204
  state laws governing, 44–6, 53
medical marijuana
  market for, *64*, 64–5
  state programs for, 3–4
Medici Bank, 14
merchant services, 116–17
messaging, 140–1, *141*
METRC (Marijuana Enforcement Tracking Reporting & Compliance), 45, 66
Minority Cannabis Business Association (MCBA), 176
money creation, 18, 19
money laundering
  anti-money laundering programs, 35–7 (*see also* anti-money laundering (AML) programs)
  risk of, 31–2, 96–7, 100
monitoring
  Fed's and FDIC's role in, 43–4
  ongoing, 93, 96
  state regulation of, 45
  technologies for, 51
  transaction, 36, 38, 97–9
MORE Act (Marijuana Opportunity Reinvestment and Expungement Act), 53

NACHA (National ACH Association) Operating Rules, 122
National Banking Act of 1863, 16
National Cannabis Industry Association (NCIA), 147
National Credit Union Administration (NCUA), 20
National Indian Gaming Association (NIGA), 176
NCIA (National Cannabis Industry Association), 147
NCUA (National Credit Union Administration), 20

222 ■ Index

networking, 145–8
  engaging with regulatory bodies, 147–8
  industry association collaborations, 146–7
NIGA (National Indian Gaming Association), 176
NuWu Cannabis Marketplace, 174

Oatman, Mary Jane, 172
Office of the Comptroller of the Currency (OCC), 19–20
Oglala Sioux Tribe, 174–5, 178
Open Banking APIs, 197
operations
  across jurisdictions, 167
  state regulation of, 46
  transaction processing difficulties in, 51–2
  for tribal nations, 174
organic practices, 72–3
outdoor cultivation, 71–2

packaging, 78–9
partnerships
  with authorities, 47
  to boost market flexibility, 156
  establishing and nurturing, 145–8
  former, when entering cannabis market, 164
  with payment processors, 114
  of traditional banks and fintech companies, 166
PATRIOT Act, 37–42, 103
payments, 21, 111–24
  business to business, 122–3
  business to consumer, 118–21
  heavy reliance on cash for, 112–13
  high-risk, 113–14
  impact of federal regulations on, 115–16
  merchant service providers, 116–17
  methods of and risk considerations with, 117–18
  processing, xii, 113–14, 201–2
Peterson, David L., xiii
Point of Banking systems, 114, 120
Point-of-Sale (POS) systems, 83–4, 114
policies, compliance with, 94–6
political landscape, 53
POS (Point-of-Sale) systems, 83–4, 114
predictive analytics, 156
privacy, data, 145
private lenders, 130, 131, 161, 163
procedures, compliance with, 94–6
processing cannabis, 74–5
product development
  creating edibles, topicals, and concentrates, 77
  packaging and labeling requirements, 78–9
  safety and compliance in, 77–8

product liability insurance, 183, 184, 187
product safety, state regulation of, 45
property insurance, 183, 184

quality control (QC), 76

Real-Time Payments, 123
recordkeeping *see* reporting and recordkeeping
recreational cannabis
  Cole Memo guidance for, 47–51
  market for, 65
  state laws governing, 44–6, 53
  state taxation of, 6–7
recreational marijuana, 2
regulation(s), 31–51
  advocating for, 169
  anti-money laundering programs, 35–7
  banking guidelines for CRBs, 46–7
  for bank marketing, 148
  of banks and credit unions, 22
  Bank Secrecy Act, 34–5
  of cannabis insurance, 184–6
  of cannabis lending, 133–4
  and cannabis' Schedule I drug classification, 34
  of CBD vs. of THC, 5
  Cole Memo guidance, 47–51
  compliance with (*see* compliance)
  Controlled Substances Act, 31–2
  of CRBs, 85
  of hemp and marijuana, 2–3
  keeping up with changes in, 155
  Know Your Customer, 37–43
  need for, 50
  and networking, 146
  oversight bodies, 19–20
  PATRIOT Act, 37–42
  reporting requirements, 104–5
  role of Federal Reserve and FDIC in, 43–4
  "sandbox programs," 204
  state variations in, 44–6
  for tribal nations, 171–3
  2018 Farm Bill, 32–3
  websites for information on, xvi
  see also federal regulations/laws; local regulations/rules; state regulations/laws; *specific laws*
regulatory bodies
  engaging with, 47, 147–8, 164
  overview of, 19–20
  see also individual bodies
Repanich, Tony, 133
reporting
  Currency Transaction Reports, 35, 37
  state regulation of, 45, 46
  Suspicious Activity Reports, 35, 37

Index

reporting and filing, 99–101
   risk assessment in AML, 100–2
   suspicious activity reports, 99–100
reporting and recordkeeping, 104–6
   audit and compliance assessment records, 106
   audits and compliance assessments, 106
   best recordkeeping practices, 105
   CRBs' requirements for, 85
   in distribution, 81–2
   recordkeeping best practices, 105
   regulatory reporting requirements, 104–5
retail and dispensing, 82–5
   customer experience and point-of-sale systems, 83–4
   regulatory requirements, 85
   security and compliance in, 84
   setting up retail operation, 82–3
retail banking products and services, 24–6
risk assessments
   AI in, 200
   in AML, 100–2
   credit risk, 190–1
   customer, 96–7
   in high-risk industries, 102–3
   with payments, 118
   process of, 91
risk management, 89–108, *107*
   at board of directors level, 89–91
   compliance with policies and procedures, 94–6
   comprehensive strategies for, 187
   customer due diligence and enhanced due diligence, 96–7
   due diligence procedures, 92
   effective, 187–9
   establishing risk policies and procedures, 91
   government involvement in, 203
   in high-risk industries, 102–3
   insurance role in, 186–9
   internal controls and audits, 92–4
   and legacy of Cole Memo, 50–1
   ongoing monitoring for, 96
   with payments, 113, 117–18
   reporting and filing, 99–101
   reporting and recordkeeping, 104–6
   risk assessment process, 91
   transaction monitoring, 97–9
   see also insurance
risk policies and procedures, 91
risk tolerance, 89
Rohrabacher–Farr amendment, 172
roundtable discussions, 152

SAFE Banking Act of 2022, 199
SAFER Banking Act, 32, 34, 53, 199, 205

safety
   in product development, 77–8
   during transportation, 80
"sandbox programs," 204
SARs *see* Suspicious Activity Reports
sativa strains, 69
Schedule I drug(s), 4, 31, 34, 52–3, 171, 205
Schedule III drug(s), 52, 53, 115, 205–6
Second Bank of the United States, 15
security
   with blockchain, 198
   with cloud computing, 196–7
   for cultivation sites, 187
   in retail and dispensing, 84, 85
   tribal issues with, 172–3
seed selection, 68–9
seed-to-sale life cycle, 66–70, *67*
seed-to-sale tracking systems, 188
SEO best practices, 142, 143
Sessions, Jeff, 48, 50
Sessions Memo, 49, 50
Shield Compliance, 133
"The Shield Compliance Cannabis Lending Guide," 134
Shinnecock Nation, 175, 177
skill development, 47
social impacts of industry, 174–5
social media marketing, 140, 144–6
sponsorships, 149–51
staffing cannabis businesses, 82
stakeholders, 164, 165
state-chartered banks, 16
state regulations/laws, xiii
   for cannabis industry, 44–6
   for cannabis insurance, 185
   for CBD products, 5
   Cole Memo on, 47–51
   compliance audits for, 93–4
   conflict between federal laws and, 115
   for distribution, 81
   for indigenous tribes, 172
   interaction between CSA and, 32
   of licensing, 82
   logistics issues related to, 80
   for medical or recreational marijuana, 3–4
   for recreational and medical cannabis, 45
   for reporting, 105
states
   risk vs. reward of cannabis legalization for, 6
   taxation of recreational cannabis by, 6–7
stigma
   around cannabis industry, 51–2
   around cannabis insurance, 192
   around marijuana, 2
   predicted fading away of, 208
Stillaguamish Tribe, 175

strains of cannabis, 69
supply chain, 79 *see also* distribution and supply chain management
surveillance systems, 84
Suspicious Activity Reports (SARs), 32, 34–7, 99–100, 104
sustainable practices, 72–3

target market, 138
taxation
　of recreational cannabis, 6–7
　state regulation of, 45, 46
　on tribal cannabis sales, 175
technologies
　embracing advancements in, 57
　future, 195–202
　to improve compliance processes, 51
　in payment sector, 113
　for record management, 105
　for risk management, 188
term loans, 131
terpenes, strains' levels of, 69
testing standards, 76
THC (delta-9 tetrahydrocannabinols), 5, 69
thought leadership, content marketing for, 143–4
Tier 1 (direct) CRBs, 7–9
Tier 2 (indirect) CRBs, 8, 9
Tier 3 (auxiliary) CRBs, 8, 9
TILT Holdings, 177
topicals, creating, 77
tracking systems, 81
trade shows, 150–1
traditional banks
　and cannabis lending, 125
　competitive advantages and disadvantages of, 165–6
　competitive strategies of, 163–6
　in early days of cannabis banking, 151
　fintech company collaborations with, 166
transaction monitoring, 97–9
　alert generation and escalation, 98
　in AML programs, 36
　integration with compliance processes, 99
　KYC requirements for, 38
　rules and scenarios for, 98
　systems for, 97–8
transactions, in CRBs, 112–15
　cash, 112–13
　with cashless ATMs, 114
　debit-card, 113–14
　see also payments
transparent practices
　insurance-related, 186
　in marketing, 154
　in networking, 146
　state regulation of, 46
transportation challenges, 79–81
treasury services, 26, 28
trends
　analyzing and adapting to, 155–7
　anticipating (*see* future trends and innovations)
　in competition, 170
　in market share and growth, 162–3
tribal nations *see* indigenous tribes
trust
　brand positioning for, 139–40
　content marketing for building, 143–4
　establishing, 146
Tso, Benny, 174

unbanked customers, 25, 42, 43
underbanked customers, 25, 42, 43
United States Department of Agriculture (USDA), 33

Van Dyck, Chris, 205–6
Visa, on cashless ATMs, 113, 114, 120

website, 142–3
whitepapers, publishing, 149
Wilkinson Memo, 172
wire transfers, 122–3